The Middle Atlantic
League, 1925–1952

ALSO BY WILLIAM E. AKIN

West Virginia Baseball: A History, 1865–2000 (McFarland, 2006)

The Middle Atlantic League, 1925–1952

A Baseball History

WILLIAM E. AKIN

McFarland & Company, Inc., Publishers
Jefferson, North Carolina

LIBRARY OF CONGRESS CATALOGUING-IN-PUBLICATION DATA

Akin, William E.
　The Middle Atlantic League, 1925–1952 : a baseball history / William E. Akin.
　　p. cm.
　Includes bibliographical references and index.

　ISBN 978-0-7864-9766-9 (softcover : acid free paper) ∞
　ISBN 978-1-4766-1934-7 (ebook)

　1. Middle Atlantic League (Baseball league)—History.
I. Title.
GV875.M475.A45　2015
796.357'640974—dc23　　　　　　　　　　2015025313

BRITISH LIBRARY CATALOGUING DATA ARE AVAILABLE

© 2015 William E. Akin. All rights reserved

No part of this book may be reproduced or transmitted in any form or by any means, electronic or mechanical, including photocopying or recording, or by any information storage and retrieval system, without permission in writing from the publisher.

Front cover: Dayton Ducks manager Howard "Ducky" Holmes (Wright State University Library).

Printed in the United States of America

McFarland & Company, Inc., Publishers
　Box 611, Jefferson, North Carolina 28640
　　www.mcfarlandpub.com

To Lynn Suzanne Akin

Table of Contents

Acknowledgments ix

Introduction 1

1. Ghosts, Cokers, Black Diamonds, Milltown Yanks and Stogies: Survival Years, 1925–1929 5
2. Expanding in the Depression Years: The "Mad-Atlantic League," 1930–1933 43
3. A Minor League with Its Own Minor League: Pennsylvania State Association, 1934–1942 83
4. "Happy Days Are Here Again": Glory Years, 1934–1939 108
5. "We intend to keep things going": War Years, 1940–1945 147
6. "The muddle gets muddier": Postwar Years, 1946–1952 172

Chapter Notes 201
Bibliography 210
Index 213

Acknowledgments

My passion for minor league baseball began more than sixty years ago when in my tenth summer, my uncle, Dr. Ernest Williams, took me to see the Opelika Owls of the Alabama-Georgia League. I still recall the Owls' stars—Bubba Ball, Luke Gunnells, Wheeler Flemming and Bill Kallaher. When I close my eyes I can see clearly the skinned infield, the dim lights, the overgrown outfield grass and the tingling feeling I experienced when we pulled into the parking lot and the Pepperell Park lights came into view. The following spring I attended Opening Day at Griffith Stadium in Washington but that experience failed to match the excitement of a night at Pepperell Park.

This book grew out of my peculiar affection for minor leagues born in that most delightful summer. A decade ago, while working on *West Virginia Baseball: A History, 1865–2000*, I discovered the Middle Atlantic League because Clarksburg, Fairmont, Wheeling, Parkersburg, Charleston, Huntington and Beckley, all West Virginia towns, had teams in that league at one time or another. The Mid-Atlantic was the most powerful league of the lower minors at one time. Its cities, stretching from Lockport, New York, to Dayton, Ohio, constituted the industrial heartland of America in the heyday of heavy industry, the second quarter of the twentieth century.

Since *West Virginia Baseball* the Internet has made doing research much more accessible. Nevertheless, libraries and their staff remain necessary institutions to researchers. Wherever I went I found library staffs anxious to help. I am particularly thankful to Charlie Jamison and his staff at Myrin Library of Ursinus College, the Lewes (Delaware) Public Library, Monessen (Pennsylvania) Public Library, Akron-Summit County Public Library, the Wright State University Library and Salem International University Library. The National Baseball Hall of Fame and its Giamatti Research Center are indispensable to baseball researchers. I especially thank Pat Kelly of the Hall of Fame for her help. Several people read portions of the manuscript or pointed me in fruitful directions, especially John Wiseman, Dave Sherman and Jon Volkmer. Special thanks to Michele Duncan for drafting the maps.

My family remain tolerant of my baseball obsession, looking upon it with a certain benign good humor. For that I thank daughter Lynn Akin, the Brauers (Adana, Sydney and Chloe) and the Coverts (Binker, Jacqui, Brenden and Griffen). As always I have been blessed to share life with my wife, Elizabeth Teter Akin.

Introduction

Historians hardly noticed minor leagues until the revival of the minors began with the popularity of the blockbuster movie *Bull Durham* (1988). The exception to that generalization was Robert Obojski's seminal *Bush League* (1975). Neil Sullivan's *The Minors* (1991) and David Pietrusza's *Minor Miracles* (1995) touched off serious interest in minor league history. In the years that followed, historians examined the high minor leagues, but relatively little has been written about the low minors. Dennis Snelling's *The Greatest Minor League: A History of the Pacific Coast League, 1903–1957* (2012) set the standard for histories of the high minors. Among the few noteworthy histories of the low minors are Charlie Bevis's *The New England League: A Baseball History, 1885–1949* (2007), Barry Swanton's *The ManDak League: Haven for Former Negro League Ball Players, 1950–1957* (2006), Jim Sumner's *Separating the Men from the Boys: The First Half Century of the Carolina League* (1994), and Lucan Mann's *Class A: Baseball in the Middle of Everywhere* (2013).

This study details the history of a Class C baseball league, the Middle Atlantic League, which operated during the second quarter of the twentieth century in small and mid-sized industrial cities in America's industrial heartland, centered in western Pennsylvania and Ohio. The Mid-Atlantic was special. Obojski termed it "the toughest Class C circuit in the history of Organized Baseball." At its peak in the pre–World War II years, the population of its cities dwarfed that of others in the low minors. It churned out future major leaguers at a prodigious rate, sending far more alumni to the major leagues than any other circuit in the low minors.

During the course of its twenty-two years of operation, its member cities varied in size from tiny Scottdale, Pennsylvania (under 10,000), to Akron, Ohio (over 243,000). Regardless of their size, league cities all reached their peak of industrial production, prosperity, population and influence while members of the Mid-Atlantic. The mills and factories of these cities, and the mountains surrounding them, produced America's steel, iron, coal, glass, and chemicals that made America the world's great industrial country. Without a doubt they were dirty, gritty places with throngs of recent immigrants doing most of the dirty work.

The Middle Atlantic League came into being as an outgrowth of an informal semi-professional circuit that existed in Pittsburgh's hinterland. In the first few years, the league was in some ways a throwback to an older culture where communities rallied around something as innocent and traditional as baseball. Merchants closed down on Opening Day to allow everyone to attend the game. Fans knew the player, who either came from town or from nearby communities, and who played on the local nine year after year. Team owners, of course, dealt with a complex of legal and economic issues including legal strictures against Sunday baseball and the sale of alcohol, inadequate financing, the effects of coal mine strikes, and the fickleness of fans. The overriding challenge for men who operated teams was just to stay above the water line. Not all could meet the challenge. Fortunately, the league found a leader, Elmer Daily, who served as the league president for all but its first year and who worked tirelessly to keep the league afloat.

It seems counterintuitive, but the Mid-Atlantic flourished in the years of the Great Depression. Three developments accounted for the relative prosperity of the league in the 1930s. First, the introduction of night baseball has been said to have saved professional baseball at all levels in these years. Night baseball, which came to the MAL in 1930, did not just strengthen attendance, it changed the face of the fan base by giving greater opportunity for working class men and their families to see the national game. Second, becoming part of the farm system of a major league team provided a modicum of financial stability to local franchises. Affiliation with major league teams also meant that teams no longer had to find their players locally. As the big league clubs stocked MAL clubs, they contributed an infusion of outstanding young players to the league. Third, the Middle Atlantic used these lean years to break out of its original geographic footprint by expanding into new territory. That expansion included experimenting unsuccessfully with a twelve-team circuit. Expansion into Ohio's industrial centers of Akron, Canton, Dayton, Portsmouth, Springfield, Youngtown and Zanesville gave the league vitality to make it through the lean years.

During the Depression the Middle Atlantic became so confident of its future that it even experimented with having its own minor league. In the early 1930s, the MAL created what Elmer Daily visualized as a feeder league in small western Pennsylvania cities that the league had recently abandoned. The Class D Pennsylvania State Association shared major league affiliates with MAL partners, allowing the parent club to coordinate their Class C and Class D affiliates and player development. In the end the Penn State circuit failed to function as the MAL initially hoped, but it provided baseball for small, western Pennsylvania cities until after Pearl Harbor.

Following World War II, key Ohio cities turned in their franchises for a variety of reasons, forcing the Middle Atlantic League to retreat to its original footprint in western Pennsylvania. After the initial enthusiasm that followed America's victory, the shifting cultural and economic patterns of postwar America began to batter both the Mid-Atlantic and its member cities. America experienced seismic cultural and economic shifts during the Truman years. King Coal was being replaced by oil and clean natural gas as the energy that drove the industrial machine. Much of that industry was moving south and west to warmth and away from unions. At the same time, the national media, especially television, identified baseball as major league baseball and all other forms of the game as "bush league" ball. Why would people listen or watch, much less pay to see, a lesser product when the air waves offered the real deal? The real crisis for the league, and ultimately the entire minor league structure, came from a complex of cultural changes. This "perfect storm," a complex of cultural shifts associated with television, the baby boom, the move to suburbs and changes in family values, turned society inward and away from community. Few baseball leagues could be expected to stand against such forces. The Middle Atlantic League had stood for a quarter of a century, but it could not last into the Eisenhower years.

1

Ghosts, Cokers, Black Diamonds, Milltown Yanks and Stogies
Survival Years, 1925–1929

In the first quarter of the twentieth century, baseball was not just the National Game; it was the only game, at least the only game that mattered to most American boys. In autumn boys might play football, and in deepest winter a few found gyms where they played basketball, but those activities were mere diversions until baseball arrived in early spring. As the weather warmed, boys of all ages joined in pick-up games whenever they could. In small towns and on farms there was no shortage of vacant lots or pastures for playing ball. Boys might play barefooted and in overalls, but always on fields without fences, backstops or real bases. City kids in knickers played in the streets; fire hydrants and manhole covers served as bases. Deep in the mountainside coal camps of Pennsylvania and West Virginia, whatever flat land could be found became a ball field. Across America, boys congregated on sandlots, pastures and streets to play whatever variant of the game they chose.

The creativeness of American boys allowed games to go on regardless of the number of people available to play. Even if only two showed up, they could have a game of catch. One of the richest and most evocative mythologies embedded in baseball has developed about the father-son bonding inherent in boys playing catch with their fathers. The emotional pull of that simple event is displayed in the final scene of numerous movies. Few grown men can watch the final scene of the movie *Field of Dreams* without their eyes swelling up when Ray Kinsella asks, "Dad, you want to play catch?" Similarly, *The Natural* ends with Roy Hobbs playing catch with his uncoordinated son. In *Sandlot,* Smalls reconciles with his stepfather through a game of father-son catch.

By 1900, baseball had become codified with a set of written rules, but on the sandlots, pastures, and streets the number of players and the vagaries of the playing field necessitated kids making up their own rules. If there were too few to choose sides, "knocker" (one-knocker, two-knocker, or three-knocker) became the game of choice. Hitting was the object and if a kid were good enough he could bat all day, but every player had a chance to become a hitter. Catch a fly and you were up. Otherwise, with each out, kids moved up in orderly progression from outfield to third base to second to first to pitcher and, ultimately, to batter.

When enough players showed up at the sandlot, street or pasture, it became possible to choose up teams. Such games always started with two captains picking their teams in turn. Captains might be the biggest or strongest, but were usually the best players or natural leaders—the alpha male about whom no one argued. Choosing sides always began with the ritual bat toss from one captain to the other, then the two going hand-over-hand up the bat to the knob; the one whose hand held the knob picked first. The last player selected could always look forward to the command "go out to right field." Baseball was and is a hard game.

Real teams, as opposed to choose-up teams, were hard to come by. Youth baseball did not yet exist—no Little League, Babe Ruth League or American Legion teams. In some cities Boys Clubs or YMCAs sponsored leagues, but these usually lacked the most vital component of a real "team": uniforms. Those hot, sweaty, wool flannels were the gold standard of sandlot baseball. When a boy got to play on a team with uniforms he had crossed the Rubicon.

Graduating to a uniform usually meant a youngster had made the town team, or, depending on the location, "company" or "mine" team. Every town, hamlet or village had a team. Baseball served as a cohesive agent in each locality, building a sense of community. In the dugout and in the stands, ethnic rivalries and class differences became moot. They did not disappear, but they did not define the player or fan. The mill owner and laborer, coal operator and miner, Hungarian and Irish, or Protestant and Catholic were all on the same side. It should be noted, however, that baseball in that era seldom reduced the overriding importance of race.

The ideal for a town team was to have an enclosed field on which to play. That meant teams could charge admission to games. With paid admission, teams were moving from amateur to semi-professional. On some teams, all players shared in gate receipts, but usually the best player or players got the largest share. Seldom were any players under contract or paid a salary. Semi-pro baseball did require a local organization. People were needed to man the ticket booths, take charge of the money, make sure the field was in order, order uniforms, arrange games, and make travel arrangements. By World War I, many of these organizations had become quite sophisticated. In the hinterland of Pittsburgh, dozens of semi-pro teams had enclosed grounds. Some had local organizations supporting the team; Elks Park in Uniontown was only one example. Others evolved into stock companies, which sold shares to the community and built their own ballparks.

Professional baseball, as opposed to semi-professional, had since 1903, meant playing within the structure termed "Organized Baseball." Through the peace treaty between the National League and the upstart American League, known as the National Agreement, the "major leagues" (National and American) recognized "minor leagues" and their teams. Crucial for the minors, all teams within the new structure accepted the territorial monopolies of the minor league teams, agreed to recognize the contracts of all teams within the structure, and granted minor league clubs the right to "reserve" players on their roster from one year to the next. The minors then formed their own administrative organization, the National Association of Professional Baseball Leagues (NAPBL), commonly referred to as the National Association. The NAPBL created a minor league hierarchy by designating leagues as AA (the highest rank), A, B, C, and D. Later the designations were changed to AAA for the International League, Pacific Coast League and American Association, and AA for the Southern Association and Texas League. A new agreement in 1921, in the wake of the Black Sox Scandal, gave sweeping powers to a commissioner of all of Organized Baseball. Judge Kenesaw Mountain Landis served as czar of baseball until his death in 1944.

The first years of the twentieth century had been boom times for minor league baseball. A higher percentage of the nation's population attended professional baseball games than at any time before or since. Some 43 minor leagues had operated when hostilities broke out in Europe in 1914. The Great War, however, all but killed the minor leagues. Only ten leagues survived by Armistice Day. After the war, the minors began to come back. By 1922, the number of leagues reached 30 and appeared as if they would stay at that level for the foreseeable future.

With the future of minor leagues looking promising, the postwar economy booming, and the jazz age sweeping the country, the mid–1920s appeared to be a promising time for creating new leagues. One man who saw such an opportunity was a Pittsburgh sportswriter named Richard "Dick" Guy. When the *Pittsburgh Leader* folded in 1924, Guy, who had been that paper's sports editor, decided to become a sports promoter, starting with a professional baseball league of his own. "Guy never got rich by promoting sports, but he never stopped trying." The main chance for him always existed in the next enterprise. Early in his sportswriting career, he had doubled as president of the Class D Pennsylvania-Ohio-Maryland League (POM) from 1906 to 1907. After that he found he could free up time from his writing to coach baseball at East Liberty Academy and Carnegie Tech in Pittsburgh. In summers, beginning before 1910, he operated the Pittsburgh Collegians, the fastest white semi-pro baseball club in western Pennsylvania, Ohio, western Maryland and northern West Virginia. He also operated a minor league ice hockey team in Pittsburgh. Long before the word "networking" came into use, Guy had perfected it, having established a broad spectrum of contacts within the sports communities of four states.[1]

Guy saw the chance of reviving the Central League, which had operated as a strong Midwestern loop back before World War I, but had failed to regroup after the end of hostilities. He hoped to organize a league for 1924 consisting of the Ohio cities of Akron, Canton, Youngstown, Springfield, and Dayton, as well as Erie, Pennsylvania, Wheeling, West Virginia, and Fort Wayne, Indiana. He stirred up a bit of interest, but not enough to translate into a league.[2] By the winter of 1924–1925, Guy gained a steady income from the *Pittsburgh Gazette-Times* and new optimism for his minor league plans. When he renewed his efforts at reorganizing the Central League, he decided to reserve the Erie franchise for himself. A former player of Guy's at East Liberty Academy, Raymond Archibald, had done well in the oil business and agreed to operate a franchise in Wheeling. Another former player on the Pittsburgh Collegians, Wilbur Good, wanted a team and offered to operate a club in Johnstown, Pennsylvania. In early January, Guy announced that he had found backers in Youngstown, Canton and possibly in Altoona, Pennsylvania. He still hoped to entice supporters in Akron, Dayton, Springfield or Fort Wayne. He expressed confidence that even if he could not make a league from those, that Uniontown, New Castle or Washington, Pennsylvania would fill out his roster of teams. Finally, he let it be known that Cumberland, Maryland, Parkersburg, West Virginia, and Greensburg, Pennsylvania, remained on his "possible" list.[3]

Guy's plans came apart in March 1925. The Ohio cities dropped first after failing to find sufficient financial backing. At that point, James F. "Jimmy" McGuire, who had managed the Cumberland Colts against Guy's Collegians for five years, urged Guy to reduce his vision. Rather than shooting for a Class A league centered in Ohio, McGuire argued, that he should settle for a league formed from the area where Guy's Collegians had played and where Guy personally knew the baseball people. McGuire was looking for a league for his Colts and had approached the Class D Blue Ridge League before Guy let it be known that Cumberland could have a place in his league. McGuire and his partners were delighted. In McGuire's mind, Cumberland, Wheeling and Johnstown would provide a core for Guy's league. McGuire pushed for the inclusion of Fairmont, West Virginia, which had a strong baseball tradition dating back to the beginning of the century. If Fairmont joined, then Clarksburg, West Virginia, 26 miles up the West Fork River, would be a logical addition. In prewar leagues, Fairmont and Clarksburg had been paired for scheduling purposes and had developed a heated rivalry. Guy wanted to keep Erie, where he planned to operate the franchise, but McGuire argued for a tighter territory to reduce travel costs, and his logic prevailed. McGuire wished to include Uniontown, a short distance from Cumberland. Guy countered with Scottdale, and/or Kittanning-Ford City, both smaller Pennsylvania towns. Neither had a history of professional baseball, but both had solid semi-pro teams, which led Guy to believe either town would do as a one-year fix until larger cities could be brought into the fold.[4]

By mid-March 1925 a league began to take shape. Guy called an organizational meeting to be held at the Hotel Henry in Pittsburgh. Another trip to Erie, plus McGuire's arm twisting, had convinced Guy to drop the city on the lake. Representatives of six cities—Wheeling, Cumberland, Johnstown, Fairmont, Clarksburg, and Scottdale—answered the call with forfeit money in hand. Archibald represented the Wheeling franchise. McGuire was accompanied by his co-owners of the Cumberland Colts, Irving "Babe" Millicent, a real estate dealer, and pharmacist Dr. James K. Ford. Fairmont already had an organization which had run the local semi-pro club, the Marion County Baseball Association, and backing from wealthy coal barons Brooks Fleming and James E. Watson. Fred L. "Joe" Doringer, who would later spend ten years in the West Virginia House of Delegates, was president of the Fairmont group and its representative at organizational discussions. S. Quay King, the mayor of Scottdale, and Russell Hockenbury, both officers of the semi-pro team, represented their little city. There had been a change in the Johnstown leadership necessitated by the condemning of rickety Point Park, the traditional ball ground. So instead of Good, the franchise would go to Frank B. Cook, who operated Ideal Park, a large amusement park outside the city. Doringer claimed to speak for Clarksburg interests, but baseball men in that city had not yet organized. No one showed up from Kittanning-Ford City. When both Guy and McGuire were nominated for league president, the representatives decided to a step back for a few days, even before electing a president and deciding a myriad of details.[5]

When the founders met five days later, Guy came with a surprise. He had given up on Erie, but he still wanted to have his own team. He announced that he had decided to operate the franchise in Wheeling, the nearest of the league cities to Pittsburgh. Perhaps as a sop to Archibald for relinquishing Wheeling or as a means of finessing McGuire, Guy now argued that the league president should not be a club owner. Archibald was his man. To placate McGuire, Guy supported Millicent, one of the Cumberland owners, to be the league secretary-treasurer. For the same reason, Guy proposed to give the Clarksburg franchise to Blake "Spook" Lytle, a good friend of McGuire's from Keyser, West Virginia.[6]

The group agreed to name the organization the Middle Atlantic League. The new loop would play a 96-game schedule beginning in early May. They limited the size of rosters to 15, including the manager, thereby assuring that managers would be playing-managers. The owners established a salary limit of $2,650 per month. Managers usually received the highest salary, $300 a month being common. That left an average of $167 per month for players, a good monthly salary for 1925, but there was no guaranteed employment; players could be released without pay if they became injured or did not perform. At best, players had four months of employment.[7]

Archibald, Guy's hand-picked league head, would not prove to be the best choice. Following his graduation from Pennsylvania State College, Archibald had played professional baseball for Jamestown (1912), Dallas (1913), Buffalo (1914) and Warren, Pennsylvania (1915), where he also managed. After that he played for Guy's Pittsburgh Collegians and also played basketball for the Pittsburgh East Ends, all while getting started in the oil business. What Archibald seemed to lack was the temperament for dealing with the egos of owners and managers and the time or inclination to mend fences, build relationships, and convince people to invest their money and their time in baseball. He rather quickly fell out with both Guy and McGuire, the two most influential personalities in the league.[8]

Before the league could even begin, Archibald faced his first crisis when Scottdale dropped out of the league in April. The franchise had been granted to Mayor King, who had not counted on the opposition of C.E. Gilchrist, the chief of police, who just happened to double as manager of the town's strong semi-pro team, the Milltown Yanks. The chief claimed that a professional team would kill the semi-pro team and that his team, which had won the Westmoreland County championship in 1924, was better than a Class C team. Besides, a pro team would also deprive Gilchrist of $7 a game, which he earned as manager. Archibald, Guy and McGuire went to Scottdale but could not placate Gilchrist and his local supporters. In this standoff, the police chief bested the mayor.[9]

Archibald scurried to find a replacement, but in mid–April he had to acknowledge his failure. The five remaining clubs were left with the choice of disbanding or going ahead with five teams. They chose the less than ideal five-team league rather than admit failure. The initial quintet consisted of Wheeling, Fairmont and Clarksburg, West Virginia, Cumberland, Maryland, and Johnstown, Pennsylvania.

Johnstown, with a population of around 67,000, was the largest city in the new league. The city would always be known as "Flood City" after the 1889 catastrophe that took 2,200 lives and caused $40,000,000 in damage. A generation after the flood, Johnstown was an industrial city producing chemicals, textiles, bricks and lumber, but the most important economic engine was steel. The massive Cambria plant of Bethlehem Steel dominated the city's economy, employing nearly 15,000 people and stretching nine miles through the city. The city prided itself on being modern; radio station WJAC went on air the same year the Middle Atlantic League went live.

Wheeling began the decade as the largest city in West Virginia with over 56,000 inhabitants. Its line of tobacco products gave its baseball team the nickname Stogies. Big, black Marsh Wheeling cigars and Block Brothers' Mail Pouch chewing tobacco gave Wheeling national recognition. Steel, iron and tin plate had actually passed tobacco in local importance. Their plants filled the Ohio River valley with sooty haze and acrid odors at a prodigious rate. The city was not new to baseball; Wheeling had been the site of the first game in West Virginia following the Civil War, and had hosted pro teams in various leagues between 1887 and World War I.

Fairmont had enjoyed strong pro teams dating back to a team called the Coalers in 1906 and continuing until World War I. After that the city continued to have strong semi-pro teams, The city was enjoying enormous growth, increasing its population by 80 percent in the second decade of the twentieth century, and another 30 percent in the '20s. Despite this growth, its 1920 population was only 17,851. Although it had seen a growth in small industries, especially glass, its economy still depended on coal. The Consolidation Coal Company, the largest in West Virginia, made its headquarters there.

Clarksburg and Fairmont vied for domination of north-central West Virginia. The seat of Harrison County, Clarksburg had moved beyond being dependent on coal for its economic wellbeing. Although coal still played a role in the economic life of the community, Clarksburg by 1920 had become the industrial center of the region. Its population had exploded between 1910 and 1920, increasing by 200 percent to 27,869. It was home to major glass companies such as Republic Glass, Hazel-Atlas, Owens, and Akro-Agete Marble Company, the world's largest producer of marbles. National Carbon, forerunner of Union Carbide, had a chemical plant outside of town.

To the east of Fairmont and Clarksburg on the Baltimore and Ohio Railroad main line, Cumberland was going through its own growth spurt in the '20s. The city, in the mountains of western Maryland on the banks of the Potomac River, dated back to 1750. George Washington's ill-fated expedition against the French in 1753–1754 began from a fort there. Coal from nearby mountain sides moved east first along the National Road, then the Chesapeake and Ohio Canal and later on the Baltimore and Ohio Railroad to Washington and Baltimore. Locals liked to refer to their city as the "Queen City," the second largest in Maryland with a population of nearly 30,000 (Baltimore was the "King").

The first task requiring the attention of these new franchises was finding a place to play. Locating a site, renting a park, or building stands and fences often determined whether or not a city could field a team. In Johnstown, Frank B. Cook's Ideal Park was part of an amusement park located five miles outside the city limits, just across the county line in Somerset County. The park that had given Cook his franchise was far from ideal for baseball, even by the primitive standards of the time. It had no grandstand, just wooden bleachers. The field had the worst playing condition in the league; its infield had no grass, and visiting players complained about ruts in the infield and the overgrown outfield grass. It lacked a clubhouse. Cook offered players the opportunity to dress in the swimming pool bathhouse, but he charged the players the regular admission price to use the facility. Most Johnstown players, understandably, dressed where they lived, usually a boarding house, and hitchhiked in uniform to and from the park. Visiting teams knew to arrive in uniform.[10]

Other parks varied in quality. Mid-City Park in Cumberland was the newest, just two years old, having been built by the owners of the semi-pro Colts. The Colts built on land rented from the Chesapeake and Ohio Canal Towing Company at what had been the terminus of the C&O canal. The all-wood park sat 6,000 customers. It had a covered grandstand which began ten feet above the playing field; that allowed for dugouts and clubhouses under the stands. A high fence surrounded the structure. Fans found the park convenient to reach because of its downtown location. Although most fans walked or came by streetcar, the park had parking for 300 cars.

Other playing grounds were not as new. Fairmont's South Side Park (a.k.a. Traction Park) had been one of the first steel and concrete minor league parks when the local streetcar company built it before World War I. It sat 3,000 in the baseball grandstand and another 2,000 in seats that had been added for football down the right field foul line. The Clarksburg club rented Norwood Park, a racetrack oval at the Harrison County Fairground. Located outside the city limits in a village called Nutter Fort, the park was accessible from downtown by trolley. It lacked good sight-lines. The diamond, laid out in the infield of the track, was some distance from the grandstand. Unlike Clarksburg's Norwood Park, Wheeling's Fulton Park, locally called Stogie Park, possessed splendid sight-lines. It dated from pre–World War I years, but remained in good shape in the mid-'20s. It was a model of the old wooden parks with covered grandstand, dressing rooms beneath, bleachers down the foul lines, and a symmetrical playing field. Its problem was its location across the Ohio River in Martin's Ferry. Promoters of the baseball team always noted that the park was just a short trolley ride across the Ohio River; this might be true, but nonetheless it was across the river in another state.[11]

After settling on a park, teams needed to fill out their player roster. None of the Middle Atlantic teams had a formal affiliation with a major league team that would provide the minor league club with players. In the days before farm systems, it fell to the local team's manager to find his own players. Although teams often had business managers (the term "general manager" would not come into use for another decade) the holder of such positions normally did not deal with player recruitment, at least not in the 1920s. Veteran managers depended on their contacts in the baseball world to find players. All teams held tryouts, usually at their own park, before the season started. In the initial MAL season, many of the players came from the semi-pro circuit in the region. Cumberland retained seven players from its old semi-pro Colts. All teams, but the Colts in particular, signed players from the Class D Blue Ridge League. Major league teams, and International League teams, did option a few players to Mid-Atlantic teams.[12]

In those days, teams traveled by automobile. Fairmont's initial capitalization allowed it to buy a bus to transport players, but no other team owned a bus. Players generally piled into three cars. Distances between league cities were not great and by 1925 most main roads were paved. Clarksburg to Fairmont was just 26 miles. The road from Fairmont to Wheeling ran parallel to the Baltimore and Ohio Railroad track for 68 miles. In two years the road would be known as U.S. 250. Wheeling to Cumberland along the National Road (soon to be designated U.S. route 40) was 132 miles, and the last leg over Big Savage Mountain was fraught with dangers from hairpin curves and steep drops without guard rails. To Johnstown from Wheeling was about the same as to Cumberland, but navigating through the streets of Pittsburgh slowed the trip. From Johnstown to Cumberland was under 100 miles. Since all games were played during the afternoon, players with their heavy, sweaty flannel uniforms piled into cars to return home each day. This saved the team the cost of hotel rooms. The roads they traversed, which were not yet numbered, were narrow, curvy two-lane roads over mountainous terrain. Maximum speed limit was 35 miles per hour, but teams were anxious to get to the game or to home, so drivers seldom worried about posted limits. Flat tires and car problems were more common than not. Travel was often an adventure.[13]

The league got off to a promising start. May's weather, which can be iffy in the mountains, cooperated with baseball. Fairmont drew a capacity crowd of 5,000 happy fans for its opening game. All the other clubs drew well in the first few weeks. As the weather heated up and play moved into June, Cumberland began to attract larger crowds than Fairmont. Johnstown gained the advantage over the other clubs when the Pittsburgh Pirates sent two highly touted rookies from California, named Joe Cronin and Ed Montague, plus power-hitting Mike Martineck, to Johnstown. Those three players made the Johnnies the pre-season favorite, and, indeed, the eventual league champs.[14] With a strong team, Johnstown was pulling in fans despite the dreadful park and the long trolley ride out from the center of town.[15]

In early July, Scottdale, belatedly, decided to join the league after all. By late June it had become clear that baseball fans in Scottdale were voting for pro ball with their feet by staying away from the local semi-pro games. On July 4 when Scottdale's semi-pro Yanks played Clarksburg in an exhibition game at Scottdale, the MAL club gave the locals a "thorough trouncing." That game destroyed the townspeople's belief in their town team. It allowed Mayor King to finally regain control of the town's baseball fortunes. The directors of the semi-pro outfit decided to apply for admission to the MAL. It would have been understandable if the original five teams had told Scottdale to get lost, but they welcomed King's team back into the fold. The league quickly revised its schedule, increasing the number of games to 100 from the original 96. Moreover, to accommodate Scottdale, the owners decided to adopt a split-season format. They declared the standings on July 3 to be the first half, even though at that date, the teams had not reached the midpoint in the original schedule. The second half of the season commenced on July 4. The league championship would be determined by a playoff between the winners of the two "halves" following the regular season.[16]

Scottdale was by far the smallest city in the league, and would be so as long as it was in the MAL. With a population under 7,000, it was easy to wonder what it was doing in a Class C league in the first place. The next smallest city in the league, Fairmont, had 20,000 residents. Scottdale seemed to pride itself on being a dirty, smoky, mill town. Although small, Scottdale bustled with industrial activity. The town was the birthplace of Henry Clay Frick, whose H.C. Frick Coke Company made its headquarters there. Coal and coke ovens and a steel pipe manufacturer filled the town with dirt, grime

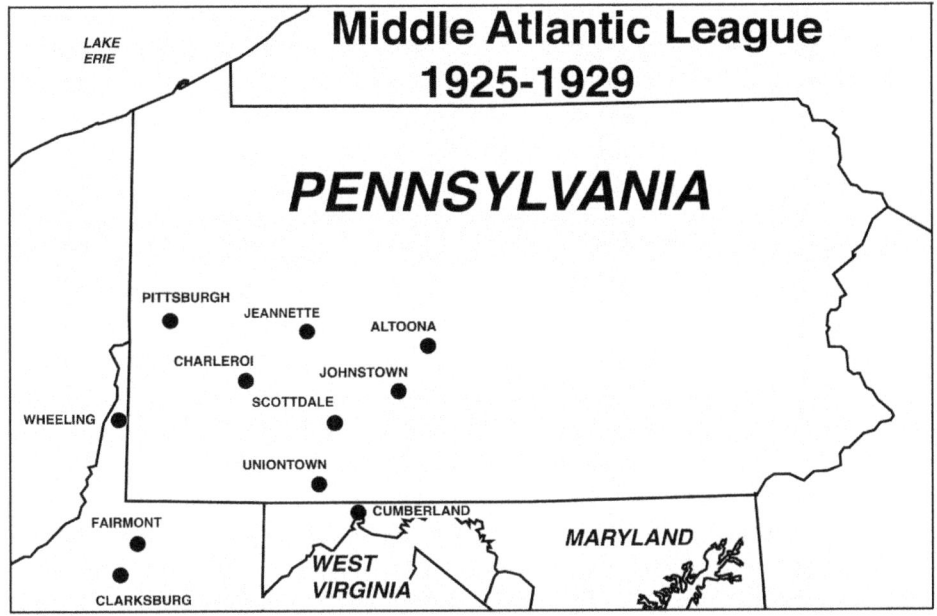

The Middle Atlantic League began as a tightly clustered group of industrial cities centered in southwestern Pennsylvania. All games were day games, allowing teams to return home after each game (Michele Duncan).

and smoke. Rather than complain, residents embraced the industries, calling their dirty little city "Milltown" with unconcealed pride. When outsiders complained about the foul air and odor, local residents replied that to them it "smelled like jobs." The local semi-pro team, which morphed into the MAL Scotties, had long been called the Milltown Yanks, and locals continued to use that nickname even though sportswriters preferred the alliterative "Scottdale Scotties." The MAL team played on grounds named Idelewild Field, but commonly known as Athletic Park. A multipurpose facility, its rectangular shape made the left field fence 320 feet from home, but right field was an imposing 425 feet away and dead center field a hopeless 470 feet. A grandstand sat 1,200 fans, and bleachers extending down the first and third base lines brought the capacity to at least 3,000. There were no dressing rooms, so players used the local YMCA and walked the short distance to the field.[17]

"Yanks" or "Scotties," the team never had a chance in its new league. King and the other Scottdale baseball men had believed their Yanks to have been far better than they showed themselves to be. Their initial optimism was quickly deflated. The Scotties fielded a few decent players: catcher Jack Smith batted .333 and hit with some power, Bill "Lefty" Phillips batted .371

in limited action, and Joe Brophy, a third baseman acquired from Fairmont, hit .298 and would be a fixture in the league for several years. Most of the old semi-pro Yanks, however, were just overmatched. They would be gone after 1925. The team finished with 18 wins and 42 losses. Scottdale went through four different managers, but none made any difference in the team's on-field performance.

Johnstown dominated the entire season. The Johnnies won the first half by a wide margin and did not let up, finishing the season with 61 wins, well ahead of second-place Cumberland. The Johnnies were loaded. Left-handed pitcher John Schmutte won a league-best 19 games. First baseman Mike Martineck led the league in batting with a .372 average. He not only hit for average, he also hit for power, slamming out a league-high 18 homers. At age 19, he seemed the MAL's best prospect for future major league stardom. The second baseman, 5-foot-5, 18-year-old Cuban Jose Olivares, was on option from Baltimore and hit .323.

Shortstop Joe Cronin, playing his first year of pro baseball, was the player destined for greatness. He batted .312 on the season. Cronin came from San Francisco along with third baseman Ed Montague, and the two roomed together in a Johnstown boarding house. Montague was the only infielder who did not bat over .300, but he was good enough to make the major leagues in three years. In the outfield, versatile Nat Hickey, one of the finest professional basketball players in the country, batted .330, the second-best average on the team.

Jimmy Collins covered center field for the Johnnies. He hailed from a colorfully named town in the Altoona, Pennsylvania, area called Nanty Glo. Collins, who hit .327, would later acquire the nickname "Ripper" and become an integral part of the St. Louis Cardinals' Gas House Gang of the 1930s, where he played on two world championship teams in 1931 and 1934. In 1934 he led the National League in home runs, slugging, and total bases, and he batted .367 in the World Series. When he joined the Johnnies, he had already lived a hard-scrabble life, having quit school after the fifth grade to work in the coal mines. Even though he stood just 5-foot-9 and weighed 160 pounds, he was tough; neither teammates nor opponents chose to mess with him.[18]

Cronin's career dwarfed that of the other 1925 Johnnies. When he arrived in Johnstown out of high school, he was a tall, skinny (6-foot, 150 pounds) kid of 18, but the Pittsburgh Pirates had high hopes for him. Pirates scout Joe Devine had signed both Cronin and Montague in San Francisco. Cronin's signing had involved a bidding war with the hometown San Francisco Seals. The Seals offered Cronin $300 a month while Devine could only counter with $200. To make the deal, Devine promised Cronin a $400 salary for 1926.

Clearly, the Pirates expected big things from Cronin, and would move him quickly up the baseball ladder. At the end of his second year of professional baseball, after hitting .320 at Class A New Haven, the Pirates called him up to the big club. He did not post impressive numbers for Pittsburgh, but his potential was not lost on Washington scout Joe Engle, who arranged for the Senators to purchase Cronin for the unheard of figure of $250,000. He went on to a 20-year major league playing career in which he compiled a .301 batting average, won a Most Valuable Player trophy, and was named the best shortstop in the American League seven times by *The Sporting News*. He also managed for 15 years, winning championships with the Washington Senators in 1933 and the Boston Red Sox in 1946. After his managerial career, he served as president of the American League from 1959 to 1973. He became the first MAL alum to be inducted into the Baseball Hall of Fame when he was elected in 1956.[19]

Despite Cronin's promise, in 1925 Martineck put up much more impressive numbers. He appeared to be the Johnnie destined for stardom. The next year, Martineck struggled in the Class B New York-Pennsylvania League, while Cronin starred in class A, but in 1927 while Cronin road the bench for Pittsburgh, Martineck led the New York-Pennsylvania league with a resounding .366 average and 186 hits. Moving up to Class A in 1928, he continued to hit over .300. By 1937, he had batted over .300 for ten consecutive years, but somehow he never got to the major leagues.

No other team came close to Johnstown on the field, and only Cumberland (56–40) stayed within shouting distance of the Johnnies. A former semi-pro Colt, John Byrnes hit .312 and would remain a fixture at first base into the 1930s. Another keeper from the Colts' semi-pro days was shortstop Jesse "Shine" Cortazzo. The 5-foot-3 Cortazzo would never be a Joe Cronin, but he was a sure-handed fielder, consistent hitter and colorful, hustling player who became a fan favorite around the league. Cumberland pitcher Paul Secrist posted a 10–1 record and threw the league's first no-hitter, against Scottdale on the last day of the season. Clarksburg was never a threat to Johnstown, but managed to finish above .500 (48–45) thanks to the play of two locals with major league experience, pitcher Harry "Pop" Shriver, who won 15 games, and infielder Lee King, who batted .330. Fairmont changed managers in midseason, putting Ira "Rat" Rodgers at the helm. The former West Virginia football All-American pumped life into the team; they nosed past Clarksburg in the second half, but finished fourth (47–53) overall.

The best that could be said of Wheeling (39–62) was that it finished above Scottdale in the standings. Local sportswriters blamed Guy's "aloofness" and operating on the cheap. A Cumberland writer described Guy's approach to player development as "he signs poor material at reduced prices." His approach seemed to have been to run a revolving door, bringing in lots of players, mostly from the Pittsburgh-area industrial leagues, in the hope of finding quality out of quantity.[20] The Stogies went through more players than any other team. Guy had little success in his talent search, although one, outfielder Jack Cummings, hit .315 and did make the majors. The Stogies finished 28 games out of first place and lost money for Guy.

Guy's two best players came off the Pittsburgh sandlots. These tough Irish Catholic kids who grew up above their father's saloon, were named Art and Dan Rooney. Both had played football and boxed, Art more seriously than Dan. Previously, they had played for Guy's Pittsburgh Collegians. Art had barnstormed with Guy since 1919, and played college football and baseball at Indiana (Pennsylvania) State Normal School, Duquesne, and Georgetown, as well as a stint in professional baseball with Flint, Michigan, in 1921. Dan joined the Collegians in 1921, and attended Duquesne College in the winters. Dan became the Wheeling Stogies' catcher, but moved to third base when Guy brought in a veteran minor league backstop. The bigger of the two, Dan became one of the MAL's power hitters. He led the league with 35 doubles and slammed 18 home runs to tie for the league lead with Johnstown's Martineck. He also hit an impressive .359 batting average. Art, the oldest of nine children, with flaming red hair, was considerably shorter than Dan. While Dan had power, Art brought speed to the diamond. He led the league with 58 stolen bases and 143 base hits. He also finished second in batting with a .369 average. Only 24 years old, Art even managed the Stogies for part of the season.[21]

Judging by their outstanding performances in Wheeling, both Rooney brothers appeared to have unlimited prospects in baseball, but they had other plans. Before the conclusion of the 1925 season, each decided that professional baseball was not for him. Dan did come back to play eight games for Cumberland in 1926, but then he opted for the Church. He entered Saint Bonaventure College in 1927 and became a Franciscan priest, known in the order as Father Silas, in 1928. Dan/Silas became well known as the athletic director at Saint Bonaventure College in Olean, New York. Not surprisingly, under his direction the Bonnies became a small-college football power, sending several players to the National Football League. The order later sent him to China as a missionary.[22]

Art never wanted to be far from Pittsburgh. A born hustler, he preferred to promote more than to play. He attempted to get a MAL franchise of his own in 1926, and was rumored to be in line for the managerial job in Cumberland in 1927. He did continue to play semi-pro baseball in Pittsburgh for another five years, and operated a semi-pro team of his own through the '30s. By the late '20s his primary interest shifted to football. He operated a semi-pro club, the Hope-Harveys, from 1926 through 1932, serving as owner, coach and halfback. Then he purchased a franchise in the newly formed National Football League. Art's team, first known as the Pirates and later in 1940 as the Steelers, faired only slightly better than the 1925 Stogies until they became a dominant power in the 1970s. Fortunately, Art lived to enjoy the success. In 1974, Rooney's 41st year as owner, the Steelers finally won a Super Bowl championship. They become the ruling dynasty of the decade following their 1974 triumph with Super Bowl victories in 1975, 1978 and 1979.[23]

Fans in Cumberland and Fairmont quickly developed a passion for their teams. The Cumberland Colts topped all the others at the gate, attracting over 42,000 to Mid-City Park. Fairmont drew 41,000 fans, over twice the population of the city. Despite the play of the Rooneys, Wheeling's last-place finish assured that the Stogies would be a disappointment at the box office. Wheeling drew just 21,000 spectators, less than its semi-pro team had attracted in 1924, and only 37 percent of the city's population. In contrast, Johnstown, despite its park problems, attracted about 36,000 people. Tiny Scottdale, in half a season, drew 9,000 people. Clarksburg brought in only 20,000 paying customers, joining Wheeling and Johnstown in drawing fewer fans than its total population. Nevertheless, league secretary-treasurer Millicent reported that all teams made a profit in their first season, although Dick Guy disputed the accounting.[24]

Despite the relative success of the league's inaugural season, the Middle Atlantic League faced major issues. The greatest of those was an irreconcilable split between the league president and key owners. Following the season, Doringer of Fairmont took the lead in trying to oust Archibald. Guy and McGuire had been the prime movers in organizing the league and in electing Archibald as president, but they too found themselves at loggerheads with the league boss. The specific issues that divided them are not clear. Doringer and the Cumberland owners complained that Archibald had little time to attend to league issues. The *Cumberland Evening Times* sports editor noted in September that Archibald had not been to the Maryland city since Opening Day. One specific issue was McGuire's desire to have his own franchise in Uniontown, and Archibald's opposition. Guy, losing money in Wheeling, and looked to Archibald for help in finding a buyer for the Stogies, but he found the president unresponsive. The dissidents decided to depose Archibald.[25]

Guy called a league meeting in September without Archibald. At that meeting the owners awarded franchises to McGuire and to Art Rooney. Each would have to find a city in which their franchise would play. To no one's surprise, McGuire claimed Uniontown, Pennsylvania. Rooney wanted Altoona, but was never able to get financial backing to complete the deal or to gain access to a playing field. The admission of Uniontown assured that a majority of clubs supported Archibald's ouster. After voting to outs Archibald, James Ford, now the majority stockholder in Cumberland, moved that Guy be elected league president. To the surprise of most at the meeting, Guy declined.

Still the most influential man in the MAL, Guy had come to the meeting with his own candidate for president in the person of Elmer Michael Daily. Guy, Doringer, and Ford applied enough pressure on the Scottdale representatives, King and Hockenbury, to swing their vote to Daily, thus giving Daily four votes, enough to carry the election.[26]

Daily had been well known in baseball circles in western Pennsylvania and northern West Virginia before World War I. He made friends easily and had lots of them in the region. The son of an Irish immigrant father, he had been born near Washington, Pennsylvania, but grew up in Waynesburg where he starred in three sports in high school. He attended Waynesburg College before transferring to Bethany College in West Virginia. Between 1909 and 1913 he tried his hand at professional baseball, playing for teams in Williamsport, Shamokin and Altoona, Pennsylvania, and in Wilmington, Delaware, Salem, Ohio, and Fairmont, West Virginia. Later, after World War I, he played for the Allegheny Steel team in the semi-pro Pittsburgh Industrial League. Never more than an average player, he had more success on the coaching and managing side of the game. In his last year of pro ball, he managed Fairmont in the Class D Pennsylvania-West Virginia League. Following his playing career, he coached at Fairmont Normal College, West Virginia Wesleyan College, Bethany College, Waynesburg College and Windber (Pennsylvania) High School. At Wesleyan, his 1914 team won the school's only state championship. During the Great War he served in the Army Air Corps as a balloonist in France and coached the base team at Fort Omaha. After the war, he married Mary Elizabeth Schultz and opened a grocery store and general mercantile business in Acosta, Pennsylvania. When Guy contacted him about becoming league president, Daily had just experienced tough times. He had campaigned for sheriff of Somerset County and lost. Then his store burned to the ground. He did open another store in Windber, Pennsylvania, but the prospect of a baseball job was as much of a rush as a home run.[27]

The admission of Uniontown at the September meeting created its own problem, leaving the league with an odd number of teams. Rather than wait for Rooney to find another location, Daily quickly went to work trying to find another city for the MAL. By the beginning of 1926 he had a solution.

He called a MAL meeting for January 3, at which time the league granted a franchise to Jeannette, Pennsylvania. Businessmen J.P. Birk and Ward Greenwalt headed the Jeannette operation.[28]

After three months of inactivity, Archibald took action to regain his job. He declared the fall meeting illegal, and attacked McGuire and Doringer for turning against him. He charged that he had been "railroaded out of office." Archibald appealed his ouster to Michael H. Sexton, president of the National Association. To the surprise of the MAL owners, Sexton sided with Archibald. Sexton reinstated Archibald as league president, maintaining that his initial appointment ran for a year which did not end until March 22, 1926. Sexton also voided all actions taken at the two league meetings when Archibald was absent. That meant that Daily's election as the new league president was void, as was the awarding of new franchises. Sexton also notified the owners that he would send a representative to the next MAL meeting in order to assure that Archibald was in the chair and that owners followed proper protocol.[29]

Observers expected "verbal pyrotechnics" at the next meeting, which was held on March 26 at the Henry Hotel in Pittsburgh. The meeting turned out to be subdued. Archibald, having made his point and seeing the writing on the wall, resigned before the meeting. He cited lack of "harmony" with some owners. That was an understatement. Daily was officially elected league president for a two-year term. Guy then supported Russ Hockenbury of Scottdale for secretary, apparently as a *quid pro quo* for Scottdale's support in the ouster of Archibald. Ford, however, successfully lobbied Johnstown, Fairmont, and Clarksburg to join him and McGuire to support the reappointment of Irving Millenson. The league also kept the salary cap at $2,650 per month and the roster size at 15. They added a rule that teams could have a maximum of three "class men," players who had played at a classification higher than Class C, and a maximum of three players optioned from higher classification teams; the owners did not want to become farm clubs of some major league team. Finally, the owners increased the schedule from 100 games to 120.[30]

Having survived its first year and a tumultuous offseason, the MAL prepared to open the 1926 season with a full complement of eight teams with the addition of Uniontown and Jeannette. Known as "The Glass City," Jeannette, 27 miles east of Pittsburgh, was home to seven major glass factories of which Chambers and McKee Glass, established in 1889, had been the first. Others included Fort Pitt, Pittsburgh Lamp, American Saint Gobaon, Westmorland Glass, and Brass and Glass. Its 1920 population was only 10,627, but its economy was booming and its population growing by 50 percent in the decade. In Uniontown, the town's 15,000 residents depended mainly on coal and coke for their livelihood. In the years shortly before and after the turn of the century, it had been the center of violent industrial strife. By the 1920s it had become home for a large number of wealthy coal barons, whose residential area and rapidly growing downtown put a patina of respectability on the city. Located halfway between Cumberland and Wheeling on the National Road, Uniontown had easy access to the other league cities.

One of McGuire's first public relations moves in Uniontown was to stage a "name the team" contest. Fans were asked to submit names for the team. When the ballots were in, McGuire announced the team would be called the "Cokers." Team nicknames in the minor leagues were just beginning to become formalized. Traditionally, sportswriters or headline writers bestowed such team names. Often the scribes just identified the team with the manager. In 1925, the Fairmont club was called the "Fairies" after the team manager, Cy Ferry. Clarksburg had been labeled the "Ghosts" after manager Blake "Spook" Lytle. Others were diminutives of the city name; thus, Johnstown became the "Johnnies" and Scottdale the "Scotties." Some were just alliterative. Cumberland teams had been "Colts" since 1915 when the city had a team in the amateur George's Creek League. The new Jeannette team adopted the "Jays." City fathers liked to think of a professional baseball team as an advertisement for the city. In this vein, team monikers often reflected the city's identity. "Cokers" appealed to Uniontown's pride in its coke ovens. When the Fairmont club got a new manager for 1926 named Joe "Hooker" Phillips, it became apparent that a new team name was in order. "Black Diamonds" was a logical choice for a city whose economy revolved around coal. Wheeling teams had been known as "Stogies" since the 1890s. The Marsh Cigar Company, located in Wheeling, made big black cigars that had been favored by teamsters and pioneers going west on the National Road in big Conestoga wagons. Clarksburg jettisoned the appellation "Ghosts" in favor of "Generals," to reflect the city's pride in being the birthplace of Civil War general Stonewall Jackson.

When the 1926 season got under way, Johnstown and Fairmont battled each other for the top notch the entire season and through the playoffs. The Johnnies started fast, as they had done in 1925, capturing the first-half crown, with Fairmont four games behind. Phillips drove his Black Diamonds to a first-place finish in the second half, winning going away. Johnstown slipped badly, playing just .500 ball after July 10. Fairmont (68–44) claimed the regular-season title with a two-game lead over Johnstown (63–43) when all games were counted.

Johnstown benefited from holdovers from its 1925 championship team. Martineck, Schmutte, Olivares and Cronin had moved up the baseball ladder, but plenty of talent remained. Ed Montague, who had come east with Cronin, returned to Johnstown for a second season, batted .317 and became the league's all-star third-baseman. All three regular outfielders hit over .300. Nat Hickey led the MAL in stolen bases and hit .327. Jimmy Collins batted .313 with a team-high 14 homers. Left-handed-hitting Carl Frey compiled a .317 average. Ironically, Hickey and Frey garnered all-star selection, while Collins, the only one of the three to make the major leagues, was not selected, an oversight that remains hard to explain. Jack Matthews moved up from number two man on the pitching staff to the ace, posting an 18–11 record. He, Joe Hartman (16–8) and Jimmy Devine (16–9) each pitched over 200 innings.

Hickey excelled in basketball as well as baseball. Professional basketball was just in its infancy, but Hickey was one of its brightest stars. He played in the first year of the American Basketball League, which started with a questionable future in 1925. Hickey, described by the *Reach Basketball Guide* of 1926 as a "fleet footed forward," was only 5-foot-11, but that was in the days before giants entered the game. He joined the Cleveland Rosenblums and helped them to a 13–1 regular-season record. In the playoffs against Brooklyn, Hickey led the Rosenblums in scoring in each game of a three-game sweep for the league championship. Hickey would continue playing pro basketball until the 1947–1948 season when he became the oldest man to play in a National Basketball League game. When coaching the Providence Steamrollers, he inserted himself into a game on January 28, 1948, when he was just two days shy of his 46th birthday.[31]

The big news in 1926 for Johnstown was the opening of a brand new, state-of-the-art park, Point Stadium. Baseball had been played at "The Point," the confluence of the Little Conemaugh River and Stoney Creek River, since a park was built there for the Tri-State League team in 1910. After the dilapidated old wooden grandstand was condemned by city engineers, Johnstown's mayor, Louis Franke (1924–1928), adopted a plan for a new park. Franke thought big and got things done. He paved streets and built bridges, doubled the sanitary sewers, built a public safety building, raised retaining walls of the rivers in order to reduce the likelihood of flooding, pushed through the city's first zoning ordinance, started municipal garbage pickup and installed the first traffic light. After the Johnnies won the 1925 MAL championship, he focused attention on the need for a new ballpark. In November 1925, voters approved a bond issue for $250,000 to pay for the new structure. The contract was signed on February 10, 1926 and less than four months later, on July 5, 1926, the park opened.

The new Point Stadium was built entirely of steel, as befitted a steel-producing city. The main grandstand had 28 rows of seats, topped by a small second deck, and covered by a freestanding roof that slopped toward the

Point Stadium in Johnstown, Pennsylvania, was built in 1926. With its extended stands for football, it could seat 17,000, making it the largest facility in the Middle Atlantic League (author's collection).

field. Uncovered concrete stands for football were added down the right field foul line, and fewer down the left field line. When finished, Point Stadium had a seating capacity of 17,000. The location between the rivers and city streets gave the field strange dimensions for baseball. Down the left field line was only 251 feet and right field stretched just 262 feet. Dead center field would have been well over 400 feet, but the Johnnies erected a snow fence at the 380-foot mark. To reduce cheap home runs and to keep costly baseballs in the park, the club added a monstrous fence, fifty feet high, at the left field wall. At the park's opening, the Johnnies drew a league record 10,000 fans for a doubleheader against Clarksburg.³²

Despite their slide in the second half of the season, the Johnnies got a chance to redeem themselves in the playoffs against second-half champion Fairmont. The Black Diamonds lacked the talent of Johnstown, but made up for it with hustle and determination. None of their regulars would make the majors, and not a single player was even selected for the MAL all-star team. They did have a bunch of players who just wanted to play ball and would play in the minors for as long as they could. Second baseman Lafe "Red" Byard hit 12 dingers to go with a .349 batting average. Third baseman Tony Cyran and outfielder Orrel Holand played in every game and would continue to play in the MAL for another six years. Outfielder-pitcher William "Chick" Helmick, just a year removed from the Uniontown Elks semi-pro club, batted .314 and won 11 games; he would play for Fairmont as long as the Black Diamonds lasted. Outfielder Ray Flood, who batted .318, went on to compile a .303 average over 15 minor league seasons. The Black Diamonds also had the league's first 20-game winner in Art Cousins, who won 21games against only seven losses. Cousins' won-loss record gave him the best winning percentage among MAL pitchers for the year.

Johnstown came back from its second-half slump to best Fairmont in the 1926 playoffs. The first two games were pitchers' duels. Elbert Hammock bested Helmick, 2–1, in the first game even though Helmick allowed only two hits. Collins' first-inning triple was the big blow for the Johnnies. In game two, Johnstown squeezed out a 3–2 win thanks to relief pitcher Jimmy Devine bailing out Jack Matthews from a ninth-inning jam. The Johnnies appeared to run away with the series by whipping Fairmont, 8–2, in the third game. Fairmont, however, did not go down easily. They came back to win game four behind Helmick's pitching and Flood's two-run homer. Flood homered again in game five to help Cousins notch a 6–4 victory. The Fairmont comeback ran out of steam in the sixth game when Matthews pitched a shutout for a 2–0 Johnnies win. Collins again tripled to score the deciding run. The victory gave the Johnstown their second straight title.

On paper, Cumberland (62–48) looked to be a better team than either Johnstown or Fairmont. The Colts posted a league-leading .301 team batting average. Sportswriters selected tiny Jesse "Shine" Cortazzo as the league's most valuable player. He hit .307, and in the field his quick reaction, good hands, and a strong and accurate arm made him the top shortstop in the MAL. Outfielder Dennis Southern led the league with a .374 average. The Colts sold him to the Philadelphia Phillies at season's end. First baseman John Byrnes and catcher Gus "Mike" Thompson were selected as all-stars after batting .338 and .355, respectively. Third baseman Joe Buskey and pitcher Warren "Pete" Rambo (13–9) went up to the Phillies with Southern for a "cup of coffee" in the majors following the Colts' season. Cumberland's roster also included two former major leaguers, outfielder Lee King and pitcher Pat Ragan. Unfortunately, as often happens with hard-hitting teams, their pitching let the Colts down.

The remainder of the teams had lackluster seasons. Clarksburg did finish with a winning record (56–51), as outfielder Dewey Stover led the MAL in hits. Scottdale (51–61) could boast of pitchers John Hopkins (11–12), who led the league in strikeouts (193), and Tracy "Dick" Barrett, who later spent five years in the majors. Jeannette's pitcher Waldo "Rusty" Yarnell went up to

Philadelphia to pitch one game for the Phillies before the conclusion of the 1926 season. Uniontown's tiny Elks Park proved a haven for home runs. The Cokers (47–61) led the league as a team with 98 four-baggers, and catcher Jack Smith had the most (28) of any individual. Pitcher Joe Drugmond (17–12) was the best lefty in the league. The Wheeling Stogies (44–64) had little to cheer about as they again finished last in the standings. They did manage to sell outfielder-catcher Jack Cummings (.368) to the New York Giants, a transaction that allowed the Stogies to avoid losing money on the year.

The season was not without challenges for Daily in his first year as league president. In the lower minors the margin between profit and loss was razor thin. Often, men who put up their money to attract or support the local team became disenchanted when losses piled up. Guy and McGuire were promoters who saw their main chance in owning a MAL franchise without putting up much money of their own. Just as the season opened, Guy managed to find buyers for his Stogies that allowed him to walk away from Wheeling with a tidy profit. Daily helped to find a new ownership group to take control from Guy. The investors, headed by Gibson Bradfield, a banker and old baseball hand in Barnesville, Ohio, across the Ohio River from Wheeling, paid Guy close to $10,000 for the club. Bradfield's group included local retail businessman George Phillips and wealthy dairyman Charles Holloway as minority owners. Bradfield served as president and Phillips, who had been vice president in 1925, continued in that position.[33]

By Independence Day, McGuire had soured on his Uniontown franchise. When the team stumbled out of the starting gate, McGuire took the managerial reins himself. From his start as manager of the Cokers, McGuire had a running battle with umpires that invariably led to Daily imposing fines on the fiery manager. In late June, McGuire stepped down as manager, and announced he would be willing to sell the team. He claimed to be out $1,643, of which $1,415 came from the initial purchase of uniforms and equipment. Maurice Meinert, a sporting goods salesman and the largest stockholder in the Uniontown Baseball Association, also let it be known that he wanted to cut his losses. Daily went to Uniontown in order to resolve the crisis. By July 8, Daily and Meinert had orchestrated a reorganization of the team. A.W. Dick, owner of a sporting goods store in Uniontown, became the primary owner of the team, with businessman James H. Dunn as president of the club. They insisted that McGuire stay on as manager, at least for the present.[34]

Neither McGuire nor Guy was the type of man to look for an eight-to-five job. Rather they looked for new baseball opportunities. By December 1926, McGuire was back in Cumberland where he purchased the stock that his former Cumberland partners, Ford and Millicent, held in the Mid-City

Baseball Association. That $5,200 investment gave McGuire controlling interest in the Colts. He took over as president of the reorganized club.[35]

Guy, for his part, tried to start another league of his own. In January 1927 he began making the rounds of towns around Pittsburgh to line up investors in his proposed class D league. He hoped to find backers in McKeesport, Braddock, Greensburg, Latrobe, Donora, and Charleroi. None stepped forward and Guy's plan fell to the floor like so much quicksilver. He did, however, uncover a potential investor in John "Scissors" McIlvaine, a Charleroi sporting goods store owner, former minor league pitcher and operator of the local semi-pro team.[36]

It turned out that McIlvaine was more interested in the Middle Atlantic League than in Guy's proposed venture. As it happened, a franchise was available. In Uniontown, Meinert, an original investor in McGuire's Cokers, had managed to buy the club at a rock-bottom price in December 1926. When the opportunity to sell arose, he was delighted to sell and walk away with a profit. Before the MAL winter meeting in mid–January 1927, McIlvaine completed the purchase of the Uniontown franchise from Meinert. At the league meeting, owners approved the transfer of the franchise from Uniontown to Charleroi.[37]

The MAL's January 1928 meeting proved lively for President Daily. During the 1926 season, Daily and McGuire had tangled numerous times over McGuire's behavior as the Uniontown manager. Early in the season Daily had suspended McGuire two games for extended arguments with umpires. In July, following a ruckus with umpires in Clarksburg, Daily fined the manager, but McGuire refused to pay. At the next game in Fairmont the umpires held up the start of the game until McGuire paid his fine. When McGuire refused, Fairmont president Joe Doringer decided to take the fine out of the visiting team's take of the gate receipts. McGuire was livid but the game was played. At the MAL meeting, McGuire, now the primary owner of Cumberland, launched a verbal attack on Daily. Then Uniontown sportswriter Dan Albright, who represented the Cokers, challenged the reappointment of Daily. This was, presumably, at the behest of McGuire. Albright understood he lacked the votes, but he wished to embarrass Daily for his "mistreatment" of McGuire. Then McGuire went after Daily on a different front. He proposed to abolish the ten percent tax on gate receipts that went to the league. That income paid for the league's expenses, including umpires and, of course, Daily's salary. That motion also failed. Then McGuire pushed to raise the league salary cap from $2,650 per month to $3,550, but he lost that vote as well. At the end of the day, McGuire had accomplished little.[38]

Charleroi, as the newest member of the league, took the nickname

"Babes." That was not a strong start. Charleroi was a small city of 11,516 located on the bank of the Monongahela River, but the city of Monessen, just across the river, had a population of over 20,000. That gave McIlvaine a sizable fan base. Charleroi's economic well-being depended on glass manufacturing. Pittsburgh Plate Glass had one of the world's largest glass factories there, employing over 1,000 people. Across the river, Monessen was a steel and tin manufacturing center. McIlvaine brought in Warren "Cowboy" Comstock as player-manager of the Babes. The team had only one holdover from Uniontown, pitcher Joe Drugmond who had been the Cokers' best player. Unfortunately, with the Babes, his record dropped to 10–18, down from the 17 wins he recorded in 1925. The new players performed no better than those of Uniontown had done, while some were worse. McIlvaine's frustration with his team led him to take the managerial reigns himself in mid–June. He also tried his hand at pitching. On the mound, he mirrored the Babes' season, winning only one game while losing seven. The Babes finished dead last (42–75).

McIlvaine did find a couple of prospects. Outfielder Fred "Fritz" Lucas batted .371 in half a season. He would go on to play for the Phillies in 1935. Following his taste of major league life, Lucas continued playing and managing in the minor leagues until 1940 and then became president of the Cambridge, Maryland, club in the Eastern Shore League. After World War II he became president of the league.[39]

Charleroi pitcher Bill Thomas would not make the "bigs," but became, arguably, the most successful minor league pitcher of all-time. Just 22 years old and in his second year of pro ball, Thomas compiled a 16–17 record for Charleroi. That was not impressive until compared to the remainder of the pitching staff, which had a 26–58 record. Thomas had a sharp 2.73 ERA. Always a workhorse, at Charleroi he pitched more games (41) than any other MAL pitcher. Between 1929 and 1943 he pitched for Milwaukee, Indianapolis, Portland, Seattle, San Diego and Hollywood at the highest level of the minor leagues, but big league clubs never gave him a chance to show what he could do on baseball's biggest stage. By 1946 he had fallen to Class D ball in Houma, Louisiana, but he won 35 games. As late as 1950, at age 45, he won 23 games. Thomas kept on pitching until 1952 when he was 47. Along the way he had stops in places named Brownsville, Lafayette, Texas City, Lake Charles, Owensboro, Greenville, El Dorado and Houma. In his 24 years of minor league pitching, Thomas set numerous records, including the most games pitched (1,015), most innings pitched (5,987), most wins (383) and most losses (347). If there were a Minor League Hall of Fame, Thomas would be one of the chosen few.[40]

McGuire, rebuffed at the winter meeting, got his satisfaction on the field in 1927. His Cumberland Colts (66–47) had an outstanding season, their best ever. Their first baseman, John Byrnes, later remembered the 1927 season as "one of the greatest in the history of the Middle Atlantic League." It is not surprising he thought that way because the Colts won the first half of the split season, posted the best overall record, and ended Johnstown's ownership of the championship by capturing the playoffs. Byrnes described the Colts as "an alert club with a never say die spirit." Major league scouts, he claimed, told him that Cumberland was capable of beating any Class A team.[41]

In late May, while the entire country was mesmerized by the accomplishment of Charles Lindbergh, the Colts made a shambles of the first-half race. "Lucky Lindy" took off from New York on May 20, flew solo across the Atlantic and landed at Paris the following day. Newspapers around the country ran banner headlines for an entire week and printed extra editions to cover Lindbergh and his plane, *Spirit of St. Louis*. The day Lindbergh landed in France the Colts won their sixth straight game and then won two more games to make it eight in a row. Ed Conley, Frank Gleich, and Byrnes tore up the league during the streak.

For the season, player-manager Gus "Mike" Thompson, who caught and batted .331, led the Colts. The outfielders all batted over .300: Bill "Cy" Morgan hit .306, veteran minor leaguer Gleich chipped in with a .306 average, and young Conley batted .301 and knocked out a team-high 16 homers. The infielders fielded brilliantly. First baseman Byrnes, second baseman Dave Black, and third baseman Joe Conti all led the league in fielding. Cortazzo, who started the season as Cumberland's shortstop, but was injured in June and traded to Johnstown, also led the loop in fielding. Future major league pitchers Pete Rambo (11–9) and Irving "Stub" Rase (14–7) posted double-digit victories. The Colts could also be cocky and feisty. During the season Black, Conti and Cortazzo were fined at various times for altercations with umpires.

Johnstown remained serious about winning. In December 1926 wealthy coal operators John C. Cosgrove and Harry J. Meehan, who was also president of Johnstown Brick and Tile Company, purchased the Johnnies from the club's original owner, Frank Cook. The Johnnies had captured the league titles in 1925 and 1926 and the new owners intended to give fans a three-peat. Expecting attendance at expansive Point Stadium to enrich the team coffers, they felt confident in hiring a big-name manager. Meehan went to St. Louis and came back with Charles "Babe" Adams, who had recently been released by the Pittsburgh Pirates. Adams had pitched for the National League champion Pirates in 1925, albeit not effectively. He had won 194 major league games over his career. Unfortunately, Adams lacked the knack for managing. The Johnnies were an embarrassment to their fans in the first half of the season. They finished in seventh place, only one-half game from the basement. Not only did they play bad baseball, they showed no spark or hustle.[42]

In mid-season the Johnnies made crucial changes. The team replaced Adams with another former major league pitcher, Charles Albert "Chief" Bender. One of the dominant pitchers in the major leagues in the first two decades of the century, Bender had won 212 games. He was at his best in the big games, winning six World Series contests, including pitching three complete games in the 1911 Series. His ability to come up big in the most important games, perhaps more than his wins, led to his selection to the Baseball Hall of Fame in 1953. Unlike Adams, Bender had experience managing and dealing with personalities on a team. He had managed in the minors with New Haven (Eastern League) in 1920–1921, and Reading (International League) in 1922. He then coached the baseball team at the United States Naval Academy. So, when classes at the Academy ended, Bender was available. He brought discipline and spark, and pretty good pitching to the Johnnies. He announced his arrival by pitching a one-hitter against Jeannette. In July an umpire ejected Bender from a game in Charleroi for arguing a call. Fans threw pop bottles onto the field, and after the game "dozens" of police were required to prevent a "riot." In a game at Fairmont an obnoxious fan with a megaphone rode Bender and the Johnnies in a manner that Chief thought crossed the line. He demanded that the umpire eject the fan. When he got no satisfaction from the ump, Bender pulled his team off the field. Finally, Fairmont officials removed the fan and the game continued. Bender's enthusiasm and desire to win proved infectious to his players.[43]

In addition to bringing in Bender, the club revamped the Johnnies lineup with mid-season acquisitions. They purchased veteran second baseman Lafe "Red" Byard from Fairmont. He had batted .349 in 1926 and continued hitting for Johnstown. He hit .333 for the Johnnies and garnering the league most valuable player award that came with a $100 prize. As a double-play partner for Byard, they acquired Shine Cortazzo from Cumberland. Although Cortazzo had been the 1926 Most Valuable Player, he was available because he had suffered an injury which required Cumberland to find another shortstop. McGuire decided John Boyle, Cortazzo's replacement, would handle the position until the end of the season. At the time of the deal, it was not clear whether Cortazzo would recover from his injury, so sending him to Johnstown seemed safe for Cumberland because the Johnnies were playing so poorly. The Johnnies also picked up outfielder Peter Gallupe from Wheeling, outfielder Ray Floyd from Fairmont, catcher Dick Vassey from Clarksburg, signed pitcher Jimmy Devine, who had been released by Fairmont. In half a season, Bender won seven games, while losing only three, and posted a league-best ERA of 1.33. With their new lineup and attitude, the Johnnies finished first in the second half of the split-season, belying their overall 57–55 record

Despite Johnstown's second-half surge, the 1927 playoffs belonged to Cumberland (66–47). In the first playoff game, the Colts got to Bender for a 5–3 win. Johnstown came back to win a pitching duel, 1–0, in game two as Russ Robertson (10–7, 2.17) bested Sam Wernke. After the Johnnies came back from a 3–0 deficit to take a 6–3 win in game three, Johnstown appeared to be on its way to a third straight MAL crown. The Colts then tied the series with a 4–2 win in game four. Byrnes collected three hits for the winner. Cumberland gained the upper hand by taking pivotal game five by a 7–2 score behind the pitching of Rambo. In the sixth game, played at Johnstown, the Colts took the lead when Byrnes hit a monster home run to the deepest part of Point Stadium. Johnstown tied the game in the sixth on Peter Gallupe's homer. Then Cumberland came back to score three runs aided by sloppy fielding by the Johnnies. Had there been a series MVP it would have been Byrnes who batted .500 for the playoffs. The series remained Byrnes' fondest baseball memory. "Never did I get more personal satisfaction," he remembered.[44]

The three West Virginia teams, Fairmont (64–50), Clarksburg (63–55), and Wheeling (59–55), finished in the first division of the 1927 season. The Black Diamonds featured Chick Helmick, whose 18 wins were the most in the league. Wheeling had two future major league pitchers, lefties Elon "Chief" Hogsett and Fritz Ostermuller, but their best hurler was Claude Gillenwater, whose ERA of 1.66 was the league best, as was his 13–3 record, a winning percentage of .812. Stogies first baseman Karl "Doc" Weber, who attended dentistry school in the offseason, led the league with .340 batting average and 33 doubles. Clarksburg, managed by Earle "Greasy" Neale, better known in football than in baseball, led the MAL in batting but ranked last in fielding.

The three remaining Pennsylvania teams, Scottdale, (57–54) Jeannette (48–65), and Charleroi (42–75), continued to be also-rans. The Scottdale Athletic Association went through a reorganization that moved Quay King out of the leadership position and replaced him with James L. Reynolds. With Clarence "Moose" Maxwell as manager and leading hitter (.343), the Milltown team did have its first winning season. Jeannette went through three managers, but the problem was not the manager, just the lack of talent. Before the season ended, McIlvaine sold his Charleroi team to a group of local businessmen. Dr. Albert S. "A.S." Sickman led a new ownership group. They had chartered a corporation that sold stock as a means of raising the funds to purchase the team. Sickman was elected president, and Steve Woodward, the mayor of Charleroi, who had run the old semi-pro team there, agreed to become vice president and business manager.

The transfer of the Charleroi club from McIlvaine to Sickman's group highlighted the contrasting ownership arrangements in the league. McIlvaine had been the only individual to own a team outright. Cumberland's primary owner, Jimmy McGuire, had invested a good deal of his own money to gain control of the club, but he shared ownership with minority stockholders. When Guy formed the league, his first step was to contact "baseball men" in towns where his Pittsburgh Collegians regularly played. These men had operated the local semi-pro teams. In several cases they already had a stock company to finance the semi-pro club. This vehicle could be expanded to acquire the capital necessary to go professional. This was the case with the Mid-City Baseball Association in Cumberland, the Marion County Baseball Association in Fairmont, the Uniontown Elks Baseball Club, and the Scottdale Athletic Association. Now it was the case with Charleroi. Fairmont did benefit from having two of the wealthiest coal barons in West Virginia supporting the club behind the scenes. In Johnstown and in Wheeling, well-to-do locals created partnerships that purchased the club from the original franchise owners. Clarksburg differed because there the local economic elite got behind professional baseball. The key was Virgil Highland, who owned the Empire National Bank, the largest bank in the city, and the two newspapers. He did not have to work hard to bring in others of the local power structure. The list of team officers and directors read like the who's who of Clarksburg: D.E. "Dan" McNichol, owner of McNichol Pottery, president, prosecuting attorney William E. Stathers, vice president and William O. Merrills, owner of a printing and engraving business, secretary-treasurer. When McNichol stepped down, T.B. Cain, president of West Virginia Business College, eagerly took the top position.[45]

In addition to the ownership, the first years of the league resembled the old semi-pro brand of baseball on a slightly larger scale in other ways. Until MAL teams established working agreements with major league clubs, many of the players were local. Even if they were not from the immediate area, fans could identify with players because they became familiar, since parks were small enough to allow fans to banter and chat with players. Around the league, fans got to know opposing players because they stayed in the league for a number of years. Sam Thomas played nine years in the MAL, all with Johnstown, where he had a career batting average of .329. Venerable Nat Hickey played in the league in eight different seasons, mostly with Johnstown. Three other players logged in eight years: pitcher Tom "Ace" Roberts, who played for Fairmont, Cumberland, and Johnstown; infielder-outfielder Bill Prichard, who had stops at Clarksburg, Wheeling, and Johnstown; and Bill "Chick" Helmick, who played at Fairmont, Cumberland and Charleston. Lafe "Red" Byard, John Byrnes, Tony Cyran, and Peter Gallupe played seven seasons. In addition, eleven others played at least five years. In the first years of the league the MAL was not known for producing major league talent, nor did the major league teams farm many prospects to the MAL

In the first years of operation some teams continued to wear the uniforms of their semi-pro forefathers. Cumberland's uniforms looked sharp with a "C" on either side of their uniform breast; inside the "C" on a player's right side were the words "cumb" while on their left the "C" surrounded "colts." However, most uniforms were anything but snazzy. Photos of Johnstown's championship teams of 1925 and 1926 show dirty, mismatched uniforms. Sleeves were three-quarter length, and sweatshirts were of the wearer's choosing. There were not enough home whites to go around so some players had to wear road grays all the time. On the road, the heavy flannel uniforms got sweaty but did not get washed so they remained dirty and pungent. Pants were often too baggy or oversized, giving players the appearance of a man needing suspenders.

Keeping a league of eight teams together was not an insignificant accomplishment in the low minors of the 1920s. The Mid-Atlantic might be composed of dirty, gritty, smoke-infested towns in the hinterland of Pittsburgh, but the eight cities that comprised the MAL were actually nearing their peaks of prosperity and population. They might depend on coal, coke, steel, and glass, but so did the United States. These towns and small cities epitomized industrial America.

Because the world outside the tight confines of the Middle Atlantic League was changing, the cities of the MAL could not escape. Nor did they wish to escape the changes. The Jazz Age was in full swing as the 1928 season approached. Local elites and workers in mines and mills knew they were in a modern age and wanted nothing more than to be a part of this modern world. The United States highway designation protocol was approved in November 1926. Signs proclaiming U.S. highways began to sprout. The Lincoln Highway became U.S. 30. The National Road was now U.S. 40. Henry Ford finally succumbed to pressure and brought out a new model car, the Model A. General Motors outdid Ford by offering a model for every price range, all with a choice of colors. General Motors Acceptance Corporation existed to help customers purchase their new cars. In October 1927, the first talking movie, *The Jazz Singer,* made its debut. The following summer, the first all-talking film, *Lights of New York,* appeared, and by 1930 all motion pictures were talkies. Local movie houses competed to see which would be first to install Vita Phone sound equipment. Sound of a different sort was moving into homes in the form of radios. Westinghouse station KDKA in Pittsburgh began the commercial radio craze, and by the mid-'20s could be heard throughout the MAL area. Stations WTAC and WGBK began broadcasting in Johnstown in 1925. Jeannette's station, WGM, went on the air in August 1926, followed by WWVA in Wheeling, which went live in December 1926. These early stations had limited power and generally broadcast at night. Since MAL games were all played in the afternoon, radio would not be competition to baseball until the 1930s.

The league faced trouble even before the 1928 season started. Despite his having a championship team in 1927 and drawing well at the box office, McGuire had accrued a significant debt, including a debt to the league. In February 1928 Daily went to Cumberland, and after investigating, gave McGuire ten days to settle up or to dump the franchise. At the eleventh hour, after several evenings of public meetings at City Hall, and dozens of private sessions with Cumberland political and business leaders, a local businessman, John W. Snyder, came forward with a check to Daily to cover the Colts' debt. As unlikely as it sounds, McGuire somehow managed to hold on to his control of the club. That would not be the end of Daily's McGuire problems.[46]

Cumberland, as league champions, began the 1928 season with great fanfare. On Opening Day a grand parade from City Hall to Mid-City Stadium, consisting of bands, a fire brigade, and open cars carrying political and business dignitaries and the uniformed Colts, preceded the game. Maryland governor Albert C. Ritchie was there to raise the 1927 MAL pennant. With manager-first baseman John Byrnes leading the way, the Colts got off to a fast start. They won more than any other team in the first half, but in a twist of fate still finished one game behind Wheeling, which played three fewer games. By the end of the season Cumberland came to despise the split-season format. The Colts finished with a record of 75 wins and 49 losses, considerably better than second-place Fairmont's 70–51 record. Byrne, who hit .359, and outfielder Ed Conley, a .350 hitter who led the league in runs and triples, were all-stars. Yet, the Colts were closed out of the playoffs because Wheeling won the first-half title and Fairmont captured the second-half by winning a doubleheader on the final day of the season. In each half season Cumberland finished one and a half games back.

Pitching carried Wheeling. The league's official scorers selected Bill Thomas as the best right-handed pitcher of the year and Gowel "Lefty" Clastet

The umpires and president of the Middle Atlantic League in 1928. Sitting (L-R): Frank Delahanty, George McNally, Elmer Daily (president), Red Robinson, Bill Ragon. Standing (L-R): Danny Friend, Dennis O'Keefe, Sam Richardson, Charley Schmidt (John Wiseman).

as the top left-hander. Thomas, who was piling up career victories, won 15 games against nine losses with a 2.75 ERA. Clastet went 14–11 with a 2.47 ERA. In addition to the two at the top of the rotation, Isadora "Izzy" Goldstein and Bill "Kid" Gwathmey each had 12 victories. George Dresher (9–8) pitched the league's only no-hitter. The Stogies picked up the league's top hitter, Bill Prichard (.370), from Clarksburg shortly before the playoffs. Fairmont countered with a balanced club. Orrel "Apples" Holland had 20 home runs and 96 RBIs to lead the league in both categories. Cousins won 18 games, John "Ace" Roberts notched 14 victories, and Helmick chipped in 12 wins. Roberts, who pitched a no-hitter against Charleroi, held opposing batters to a .213 average, making him the most difficult pitcher to hit.

In the all–West-Virginia playoffs, Fairmont emerged on top. Thomas won two games for Wheeling and Prichard led the series in RBIs, but it was not enough for the Stogies. After the series was tied at two games each,

Helmick won game five with the aid of three hits from Julian "Moose" Solters. Roberts then nailed down the series in game six. Following the MAL playoffs, the Black Diamonds then went on to win a postseason series against Hanover, Pennsylvania, champions of the Blue Ridge League, in four straight games. Fairmont topped-off its glorious season by beating the Chicago Cubs, 4–0, in an exhibition game.[47]

To the surprise of everyone around the league, the perennial bottom-enders, Jeannette (65–54) and Charleroi (62–60), finished 1928 with winning records. Pitcher Joe Drugmond led Charleroi with a league-best 23 wins and 149 strikeouts. The workhorse toiled for 307 innings, a workload never surpassed in MAL history. Strangely, he was not named an all-star pitcher, but he was voted the league's Most Valuable Player for 1928. In an effort to recapture the fever of 1926, Johnstown (55–59) brought back Chief Bender to manage the second half of the season. He turned the club into winners but not enough to make the playoffs. The Johnnies double-play combo of Byard (.330) and Cortazzo (.317) were again all-stars. Scottdale (40–76) continued its woes, finishing last once again.

Several teams experienced serious financial difficulties. In July, Cumberland's newspaper, *The Evening Times,* reported the league is "not likely to finish out the season." A Fairmont newspaper, *The West Virginian,* summed up the 1928 season this way: "a black cat must have crossed their pathway ... there has been nothing but grief for club owners." Daily tried to squelch the rumors that the league was coming apart, but he knew most of his clubs were in trouble. For the second half of the season Daily's time was taken up with shuttle diplomacy, traveling from one city to another to find ways to keep teams afloat. Despite its on-field success, Fairmont had experienced financial trouble since the start of the season. The Opening Day crowd of 800, the smallest in the four years of the franchise, foreshadowed the trouble to come. By July, the club fell $4,500 in debt. Fortunately, a $5,000 infusion of cash from an anonymous donor, thought to be Brooks Fleming, paid off the debt. Daily was in Clarksburg in June and again in July to arrange for a reorganization of the ownership group and then the sale of the Generals to Clarence "Dutch" Langenbacker of nearby Bridgeport. In Jeannette, the Jays managed to finish the season thanks to a generous $8,000 donation from the local Chamber of Commerce. McGuire's trouble continued in Cumberland. Despite the Colts' winning ways, fans failed to support the team as well as they had done in the first three years. By August, the Colts were in a neck-and-neck race for the second-half title, but financially the club was in "precarious condition." One league newspaper reported in early August that Cumberland was "in danger of throwing in the sponge." Daily admitted at the time that

Cumberland might quit. McGuire wanted out, but he insisted on being bought out. Daily implied that the problem was McGuire's mismanagement.[48]

Much of the decline in attendance could be blamed on the bituminous coal strike. In the soft coal industry a collective bargaining agreement covering the northern coal fields, the Jacksonville Agreement, had been put in place in 1924. Coal, however, remained a cut-throat industry, composed of hundreds of small competing operations. The industry had not gone through the consolidation process that characterized most other industries. After the Jacksonville contract, mines in cheap-labor, non-unionized, southern fields of southern West Virginia, Kentucky, Tennessee, and Alabama began to undercut the price of unionized coal. Then coal operators in southwestern Pennsylvania, northern West Virginia and eastern Ohio began losing markets and money. When Andrew Mellon's Pittsburgh Coal Company broke the Jacksonville Agreement and began cutting wages, other companies followed suit. In March 1928 the United Mine Workers of America called the miners out on strike. Over 100,000 miners responded to the strike call. The strike continued through most of the summer. Many small mines shut down. Others brought in strike-breakers, as was the case in Charleroi. Either way left miners without work for the summer. The union had little choice but to accept lower wages. By August most miners were returning to work, but "King Coal" did not soon return. For the coal industry the Depression had begun well before the stock market crash.[49]

"Financially," the *Charleroi Mail* concluded, the 1928 season "for the most part, was a failure." That the league held together "speaks well for the executive ability of President Elmer Daily." Fairmont, which had won the MAL championship and the postseason playoff against Hanover, still managed to lose an estimated $6,000. The club recouped much of that through the sale of the Black Diamonds' top players, Roberts and Holland. Team president Doringer had no choice but to announce an austerity budget for 1929. Doringer had just become the program manager for Fairmont's first radio station, WMMN. Broadcasting games remained in the future, but he announced that the station would report the league schedule of games daily as a means of increasing attendance. In Clarksburg, Langenbacker, who had taken over the club during the season, decided to bail out following the season, raising doubt whether the city could reorganize for the 1929 campaign. Virgil Highland, the most powerful man in town, was not ready to give up on baseball. His employee, Harless L. Clark, a teller at Highland's bank, took over as president of the club.[50]

The most significant offseason development involved two MAL teams for the first time becoming farm clubs for major league teams. Scottdale had always been the weak sister of the league. The smallest city had finished last two of the four league seasons. Like most other teams in the league, Scottdale lost money. The exact amount of the losses was unclear; one estimate had it at as low as $2,000 while another claimed the losses were $10,000 over two years. Quay King had been forced out as club president during the 1928 season, in part because of the finances. Michael J. Petonic, the official scorer, took over until the season concluded. Then Harry E. Cramer became president with Petonic as his vice president. The two decided that only a working agreement with a major league club could save the franchise. They first approached Detroit and then Newark, then a Class AAA International League team. Detroit showed interest but decided it wanted to affiliate with a larger city.

Petonic headed for the major league meeting in Toronto to find a club to hook up with his Scotties. He sought out the most logical man, Branch Rickey, vice president of the St. Louis Cardinals and the father of the farm system. Rickey, always the most imaginative man in baseball, made an unusual proposal. St. Louis did not want to purchase the Scottdale franchise; they already owned seven minor league teams. Nor did he offer the usual working agreement where the major league team would send some players to the minor league club in exchange for the first choice of players from the minor league team at the end of the season. Rather, he proposed that St. Louis would run the team. The Cardinals would stock the team's entire roster of players and the manager, pay their salaries, and absorb whatever losses might accrue for a fixed price of $7,500 that Scottdale would pay St. Louis. In addition, the locals would provide and maintain the field. The deal was an attractive one for Scottdale because it protected supporters from unlimited losses and offered the prospect of better players. The head of the Scottdale group would remain as club president, but Rickey would assume the title of vice president. Rickey also promised that the parent Cardinals would play an exhibition game in Scottdale. Petonic and Cramer raised the necessary money by late February. Thus, Scottdale became the first MAL team to have a major league affiliation. Rickey also insisted that Scottdale take the Cardinals name. This was also a MAL first.[51]

Wheeling also lost money in 1928. One estimate placed the losses at $5,000. Despite the losses, Charles Holloway willingly bought out his two partners, Bradford and Phillips. Initially, he announced his desire to move Wheeling to a league in a higher classification in the belief that a faster level of baseball would attract more fans, but his flirtation with the Central League failed to provide him an alternative to the MAL. He then set out to affiliate with a major league club. He found a partner in Detroit. Having rejected

Scottdale, the Tigers were happy with Wheeling. Holloway's agreement with Detroit was a loose one that favored the Tigers, who were free to put as many or as few players as they wanted in Wheeling, and take the best of the Stogies players. At least Detroit allowed Wheeling to keep its traditional nickname.

Before Daily could finalize plans for the 1929 season, he had to deal with one more crisis. Cumberland's McGuire wanted someone to buy his controlling interest, 81 percent of the stock, in the Mid-City Baseball, Inc. By the MAL winter meeting in February, he had no takers and Cumberland was without a representative at the meeting. The sticking point for potential buyers was the club's debt of $6,440. That figure included a $2,000 loan to tide McGuire through 1928, $1,068 in back salaries, and $1,525 owed to McGuire's former partners, James Ford and Irving Millicent. In early March Daily went to Cumberland where he stirred Mayor Thomas Koon into action. With Daily at his side, the mayor kicked off a subscription drive. Before the end of March the sale was made. McGuire was out and a new organization, Community Baseball, Inc., with Dr. Homer B. Waller as president, controlled Cumberland's baseball fortunes.[52]

Few people in the league were sorry to see McGuire go. Irwin "Skeet" Flaharty, sports editor of the *Wheeling Independent,* penned an obituary. McGuire, Flaharty allowed, "knew baseball better than any other man in the league," but he was "stormy, hot headed and obstinate." No one argued with his conclusion that McGuire "has been a thorn in the side of many of the club owners ... pulled a lot of 'fast' deals in the league ... [and] practically ran the league sub rosa." Not surprisingly, the paper concluded, "it is doubtful if there was another manager or club owner in the league who would admit that he liked Jim McGuire."[53]

Although he wanted to continue as league president, Daily made changes in his personal life. He took a job at Saint Francis College in Loreto, Pennsylvania, where he coached both basketball and baseball, and served as athletic director. Clearly, the demands of a full-time job limited his time for the Middle Atlantic League, but the owners' confidence in him did not waiver. They gave Daily and secretary-treasurer Hockenbury votes of confidence.[54]

Once the 1929 season began, Charleroi surprised everyone. It was without argument the most improved team in the league. In fact, Wheeling and Charleroi finished 1929 with identical records; Charleroi won the first half and Wheeling the second half. The club ownership, the Charleroi Athletic Association, perhaps realizing the team had grown in stature, changed Charleroi's nickname from Babes to Governors or "Guvs" for short. Without any major league affiliation, the Governors roster included only one player,

Fred "Fritz" Lucas, who would reach the big leagues. Manager Bob Rice, who hit .340, had logged in time in the majors. He coaxed a team of MAL veterans to outdo themselves. Rice enjoyed a strong supporting cast of Class C players. First baseman Eddie Sobb (.270), outfielders Peter Gallupe (.282) and Lew Phillips (.310), and pitcher Joe Drugmond (12–7) had all played in the league since its inception.

Lucas, in his second year with the Guvs, was the league's outstanding player. The New Jersey native had performed well in 1928, hitting .328, but in 1929 Lucas put together a monster season. He became the MAL's first .400 hitter, with an eye-popping .407 batting average. He also became the first to capture the triple crown, slugging 21 home runs and 113 RBIs. He became the first player in the league to drive in over 100 runs in a season. He also led in hits (178) and doubles (34). After his playing career, Lucas settled on the Eastern Shore of Maryland where he served as president of the Cambridge team, president of the Eastern Shore League, Cambridge County treasurer, and a delegate to the Maryland House of Delegates.

Charleroi had other hitters. The Guvs' team batting average reached an unprecedented .307. The absurdly short right-field fence at Athletic Field allowed the Governors to became the first team to collect over 100 home runs in a season. Scottdale also compiled a team batting average over .300. The offensive production stemmed in large part from the MAL's decision to use a less expensive baseball, known as the Worth ball. Introduced as a money saving move, the new ball brought unintended consequences. The ball had a thinner and tighter horsehide cover than the Spalding ball, so it wore out quicker. Because the stitches were lower, pitchers could not grip the ball as well, making it difficult to break off curveballs and throw other breaking pitches. That meant balls were easier for batters to hit.

While Charleroi had the hitters, Wheeling relied on pitching, fielding and timely hitting. The Stogies led the MAL in fielding percentage with three infielders leading at their position. Three of the Stogies would wear Detroit Tigers uniforms in the near future. Outfielders Frank "Dolle" Doljack (.270) and Gerald "Gee" Walker (.373) would be in the Motor City the next year, with pitcher Tommy Bridges (10–3) the year after. The Detroit-Wheeling affiliation seemed to pay dividends for both.

In the playoffs, hitting dominated as Wheeling managed only one win, when Bridges threw a three-hitter in game three. For the Governors, Rice led the way with a .526 average in the playoffs, followed by Lucas who hit .476. Drugmond got the win in two games. Following their victory over Wheeling, Charleroi took on Hagerstown, winner of the Blue Ridge League, in the Tri-State Series (Maryland, Pennsylvania, and West Virginia) sponsored by the

Baltimore Sun. In a series dogged by dismal weather, Drugmond picked up two more wins in Charleroi's four-games-to-one series triumph.

The most interesting team in 1929 was Scottdale (57–58). Unlike Wheeling's experience as a Detroit affiliate, the St. Louis Cardinals completely stocked Scottdale. The young Cardinals roster included nine players who would make the majors, ten if manager-outfielder Eddie Dyer were counted. No previous MAL team had ever had more than five future big leaguers in any season. Despite these prospects, Scottdale finished the season in fifth place. That was because St. Louis had loaded the roster with rookies in their first year of pro ball. Of this initial group of Young Cardinals, pitcher Mike Ryba had the best season (10–1) and the most distinguished major league career.

Every team had something to brag about. Third-place Cumberland (65–53) boasted about Stub Rase (22–5), the league leader in win and earned run average (2.63). Rase was the only 20-game winner. Sportswriters selected him as the league's most valuable player, although it was not clear how they overlooked Lucas, the MAL's first .400 hitter. Fairmont (58–55) came on strong in the second half of the season and missed the playoffs by just two games. The Black Diamonds' Julius "Moose" Solters tied Lucas for the league lead with 21 home runs. He would enjoy a nice nine-year major league career. Clarksburg (53–63) faded in the second half after finishing second in the first half of the season. A graduate of Holy Cross College, Joe "Jo-Jo" Morrison hit .354 for the Generals. Jeannette (50–67) played terribly, but the Jays had two future major leaguers who had outstanding seasons. Jimmy Ripple batted .336 and legged out a MAL record 24 triples. Phil Voyles hit .326; he would step up to play a few games with the Boston Braves after the MAL season ended. Johnstown (44–72) had fallen a long way since capturing the MAL's first two pennants. The Johnnies were the only team without a future major league player.

Breaking even financially remained the biggest challenge for most minor league clubs. League champion Charleroi demonstrated, as Fairmont had done in 1928, that winning was no guarantee of financial success. Johnstown, Wheeling, Cumberland, and Fairmont outdrew the league champions. The Governors sustained losses for a second consecutive year. Teams counted on selling players to higher classifications to offset losses, but Charleroi had only Lucas to deal. Scottdale, because of its deal with St. Louis, did not have to worry about losses.

Cumberland's new owners also found ways to close the gap between income and expenses by finding other sources of income. They managed to pay off the debt of the former owners and renovate the park and still break even. In February they held a ball at the State Armory as a fundraiser. They rented out the park to the Christy Brothers Circus, the National Reiss Shows, Sparks Circus, and the American Legion Drum Corps. Throughout the winter and the playing seasons they conducted a variety of raffles. These ventures added over $5,000 to the income side of the ledger and represented 12 percent of all income, clearly the difference between profit and loss.[55]

At the close of the 1929 season, one newspaper thought "the 1929 campaign has been most hazardous," but in reality the league seemed to have reached maturity. For leagues in the low minors, survival remained the first order of business. The Middle Atlantic League had not only survived for five seasons, but had achieved relative stability. The original five members completed the first five-year span. For the last three years the league was composed of the same eight cities, an unusual feat for the low minors. True, the one problem the league and its members had not solved was how to turn a profit year in and year out. All of the eight clubs had dealt with financial difficulties that left them teetering on the brink of bankruptcy at one time or another. Reorganizations and turnover in ownership had been commonplace, but franchises had been able to regroup and move on. Much credit for the league's survival went to president Elmer Daily and secretary-treasurer Russell Hockenbury, both of whom worked tirelessly to hold the league together.

The affiliation of Wheeling and Scottdale with major league teams indicated the growing respect for the MAL in the larger baseball world. Affiliation with major league teams, limited as it was in 1929, pointed to an altered future. Most players who had appeared on league rosters in its first five years could not dream of playing in the big leagues; they were glad to keep playing the game and to be paid more during the season than they would make in the mines or mills of industrial America. That perspective would change in the next decade.

2

Expanding in the Depression Years
The "Mad-Atlantic League," 1930–1933

The 1929 season hardly finished when the Stock Market Crash began America's economic descent into the Great Depression. On what came to be called "Black Thursday," October 24, panic set in on Wall Street as investors began selling off stock as quickly as possible. Efforts to stabilize the market appeared to work over the weekend. Then, on "Black Tuesday," October 29, the market crashed. The downward slide of stock prices continued for three more years.

Confidence in the economy dropped but not as fast as the stock market. President Herbert Hoover spoke confidently about the economy well into 1931, but he was losing touch with economic reality as well as with the people of the country. Banks and brokers called in loans thus tightening credit. Investment was drying up; retailers cut their inventory, which led manufacturers to cut back industrial production and to lay off unneeded workers. People ran to the bank to liquidate their account. Banks began to fail. The Depression continued to deepen through the winter of 1932–1933. By then millions were struggling, poor, destitute and homeless. Upwards one-quarter of industrial workers joined the unemployed. Out-of-work men and women looked for soup kitchens, took to the road, and poured into "Hoovervilles," shantytowns on the edges of cities.

The Crash and the Depression affected minor league baseball almost immediately. In the last pre–Crash year of 1929 the minors consisted of 25 leagues. When the 1930 season began, only 21 leagues made it to the starting gates. As the Depression continued to worsen through 1931, the number of leagues continued to dwindle. By 1932 minor league baseball reached the all-time low of 13 operating leagues.

Having struggled for the last two seasons of the 1920s, owners of Middle Atlantic League franchises were hardly in an expansive mood as they looked to the 1930 season. Across the league, clubs tightened their belts and prepared for austerity. At their winter meeting in Pittsburgh, the budget cuts became positively draconian. The MAL had always employed eight umpires, two for every game. Now, the league's powers decided the game would survive with one salaried, full-time umpire employed by the league; the home team could provide a second ump. Salaries, being the largest single expense of teams, needed to be reduced as they were in other labor-intensive industries. The maximum monthly payroll went from $3,250 per team down to an even $3,000. While they were in the cutting mood, the "moguls" reduced the salaries of the league officers, Daily and Hockenbury. President Daily's salary went from $1,500 to $1,200, while Hockenbury's salary was chopped by $200. Daily's expense account fell from $1,000 to $750, while Hockenbury's dropped from $250 to $200. As a means of taking salaries down further, teams were required to carry two first-year pros and three players with only one year of professional experience. The owners also agreed to continue using the less expensive Worth ball, despite its rabbit-like qualities. Non-playing managers now seemed a luxury that few teams could afford. Fairmont's "Hooker Joe" Phillips became the first manager to lose his job to the new economic reality. The Depression had come to the MAL even before the calendar turned to 1930.[1]

Despite all the concern about costs, the 1929–1930 offseason saw fewer teams go through reorganization than in the past. In Charleroi, according to the *Charleroi Mail*, the Governors had "lost contact with its public" for the past two seasons. Whether or not the Guvs no longer related to its public, the team's investors looked to cut their losses. Dr. Sickman and his fellow stockholders in the Charleroi Athletic Association found willing investors in the most unusual place, the local fire company. Back in the early days of baseball, the New York Mutuals, thought by some historians to be the first professional team, albeit under the table, were owned by the Mutual Fire Company. That fire company, however, was bankrolled by Boss Tweed. The Charleroi Volunteer Fire Company lacked such a patron, but, nevertheless, it took over the franchise. The new ownership group had volunteers who installed new dugouts and press box, and repaired the fence. They could do nothing, however, about the right field wall, which stood just 251 feet from home plate.[2]

Avoiding massive financial losses loomed as a greater issue in 1930 than at any time in the league's existence. Cumberland, which seemed to have found an answer to the profit-loss problem by renting its park, nearly had the financial props cut off. The C&O Canal Towing Company, the leaseholder for Community Park, saw the Colts' income from rentals and demanded half the rental fees. Colts president Nelson W. Rucker threatened to forfeit the franchise if his Colts lost the rental fees. The Canal Company gave in, apparently deciding its $1,200 rent on the park was better than nothing.[3]

From its creation, the Jeannette franchise had been a shoestring operation. In past seasons, Jeannette had managed to stay alive by keeping its payroll low, but it needed help. President James W. Bugher believed he found that assistance in the form of a working agreement with the Montreal Royals of the International League. In exchange for becoming a Montreal farm, the Canadian club would contribute $4,000 to the Jays' budget. The Jays also figured to capture additional income from three pre-season games against the Homestead Grays. This strong Negro League team from the Pittsburgh area was always a better draw than were any of the MAL opponents. Since the start of the league, teams often played preseason games against the Grays and the House of David team, a barnstorming outfit composed of ostensibly Jewish players wearing long beards. Now the Grays found their dance card full. In addition to Jeannette, the Grays also played Scottdale, Wheeling, Charleroi, Fairmont, and Clarksburg in pre-season contests.[4]

Not surprisingly, the decision to reduce the number of umpires led to more than the usual arguments and complaints about umpiring. Earle "Greasy" Neale, Clarksburg's manager, never let a call he did not like go by without an argument. He quickly became the favorite target of fans in all the parks around the league. Neale never went so far as to take his team off the field, but Scottdale's fiery manager Eddie Dyer did just that in a June 11 game at Johnstown. After an extended argument with the umpire, Dyer was ejected from the game, whereupon he pulled his team. For that action, Daily fined Dyer $350 and suspended him indefinitely. Daily later reduced the suspension to twelve days.[5]

As the Depression became more of a reality, teams in some of the smaller towns struggled to make it to the end of the season. Fairmont felt the need to cut salaries. One way was by releasing its non-playing manager "Hooker Joe" Phillips and appointing Del Gainer, a former major leaguer who lived in the area, as player-manager. Jeannette lacked both the external support that limited Scottdale's losses, and the new enthusiasm, willing hands, and a desire to succeed found at Charleroi. At midpoint in the season, Jeannette became the league's problem franchise. After a solid first half on the field, the Jays played dreadful ball from July 4 until season's end. To make matters worse, the Jays began cutting payroll and selling off quality players to other league teams; pitcher Pete Beam (15–10) was shipped to Fairmont while

Hall of Fame outfielder Joe Medwick was not known as "Ducky" in 1930. Rather, he went by Mike or Mickey King during the first half of the season in a futile effort to preserve his amateur status. He hit a resounding .419 for Scottdale, the highest batting average in MAL history (National Baseball Hall of Fame Library, Cooperstown, New York).

pitcher Orville Jorgens, good enough to make the majors, went to Clarksburg, and shortstop Augustus "Gus" Daviu (.344) was sold to Cumberland. By mid-August the Jays began the practice of transferring their home games to other parks, especially Cumberland and Johnstown, in the hope of attracting a larger audience than they could expect in Jeannette. Those franchises quickly grew tired of taking the Jays' games without time to advertise them and suffering through games with nearly empty stands.[6]

Scottdale demonstrated the advantage of being part of a flourishing chain-store enterprise The "Young Cardinals," as Scottdale fans sometimes called the team, were not as deep in 1930 as they had been the year before, but they were good enough to lead the MAL in team batting with a whopping .314 average. Seven Scottdale Cardinals would go on to the majors. Dyer would take the managerial helm of the parent Cardinals in 1946, just in time to lead the team to the pennant and a World Series victory over the Red Sox. Mike Ryba, who split time between pitching (3–3) and catching (.356) in 1930, would enjoy a productive ten-year major league career. Pitchers Ed Chapman (19–9) and Clarence "Lefty" Heise (16–12), first baseman Dick Attreau (.317), and shortstop Emmitt "Heinie" Mueller (.275) also got a taste of the major leagues.

None of the Young Cardinals matched the exploits of their outfielder, Joseph Michael Medwick, either in the Mid-Atlantic League or later in the majors. He would become the third MAL player to be enshrined in the National Baseball Hall of Fame, following Cronin and Bender. By 1932, after a stop in Houston, Medwick graduated to the wacky St. Louis Cardinals team dubbed the Gas House Gang. Medwick went on to a glorious big league career in which he compiled a lifetime batting average of .324 in 17 seasons and played in ten all-star games. He became the last National League player to win the triple crown, which he did in 1937 with a .374 batting average, 31 homers, and 154 RBIs. For his accomplishments that year, he received the National League's Most Valuable Player Award.

Medwick went by his boyhood names, "Mickey" or "Mike," while in Scottdale. He did not acquire the nickname "Ducky," the moniker by which major league fans knew him, until he played in Houston in 1931 and 1932. He never liked that name, but did not mind being called "Muscles," which some Scottdale teammates used. In 1930 he got off to a late start because he had to graduate from high school before reporting to manager Dyer. Only 17 when Charley Kelcher signed him for a $500 bonus out of Carteret (New Jersey) High School, the underage youngster decided to play under an assumed name, Mike King, in the hope of maintaining his amateur status in order to play college football. This charade lasted until late June. Medwick then signed a new contract, which his parents co-signed, making his contract legal. When Medwick arrived in Scottdale he was ready to hit and to play the game hard. His 5-foot-10, 180-pound frame housed "bulging forearms and biceps, piercing black eyes, and a hair-trigger temper." From his first game at Scottdale, he played a hard-charging, aggressive style of baseball. He also arrived with a $200 a month contract, more than any other player on the Young Cardinals team. Clearly, the Cards expected much of Medwick when he reported to Scottdale.[7]

He did not disappoint. Medwick put together a marvelous year in 1930. In 75 games, he slugged 22 home runs, drove in 100 runs, and batted .419. That batting average, which topped Fred Lucas's .407 average from the previous season, would stand forever as the highest average in Middle Atlantic League history. Following the 1930 season, the sportswriter for the *Connellsville Daily Courier* saw clearly when he wrote: "Mickey King Medwick showed every sign of being a classy performer in the major leagues."[8]

Johnstown (64–53) assembled a veteran team that averaged 30 years of age, old even by the standards of minor leagues. No other MAL team averaged more than 25 years of age. The Johnnies' average was pulled up by 44-year-old player-manager Wilber Good (.362) and 40-year-old pitcher-outfielder Bill Bishop (10–10, .344), neither of whom showed his age on the field. Outfielder Sam Thomas, who would play nine years with the Johnnies, batted .357, led the league with 41 doubles, 94 walks, and 125 runs. Fellow outfielder Bill Prichard smacked 29 homers and hit for a .364 average. The Johnnies captured the first-half title with seeming ease, but then slipped badly in the second half. To counter the tendency of teams to ease up in the second half, once they were assured of a playoff spot, the league had offered $1,000 to a team that won both halves of the split-season. That incentive failed to motivate the Johnnies, who plunged all the way to seventh place in the second half.

Clarksburg and Fairmont battled for the second playoff spot down to the last day of the season. In Clarksburg Neale had assembled a team of hitters. His Generals batted a collective .301, with seven of their regulars topping the .300 mark. The pitching, on the other hand, consisted of Richard "Red" Proctor and a batch of would-be hurlers, all of whom posted losing records. The 30-year-old Proctor, who once enjoyed a brief stay with the Chicago White Sox, won a Middle Atlantic League record 24 games. The workhorse also topped the loop in innings pitched (279) and games pitched (46).

The Generals and the Fairmont Black Diamonds were natural enemies. The two cities had competed in high school football and basketball as well as in baseball since the start of the twentieth century. Since the Civil War they had fought for the economic and cultural dominance of north-central West Virginia. Both teams had struggled along with losing records in the first half of the 1930 season. For Fairmont, the arrival of 44-year-old Jimmy Walsh, a hard hitting manager-outfielder, turned things around. The club found new life and spirit under Walsh. They began winning. Walsh hit .357, and second baseman Stan Ripp, who some thought was the MAL's second-best major league prospect, batted .334. Pitcher Cecil "Cy" Slaughter, who threw the only MAL no-hitter of the year against Jeannette, won 16 games and posted the league's best earned-run-average (3.23). Fairmont picked up pitcher Pete Beam, a 15-game winner, from Jeannette to help down the stretch. Fairmont's acquisition of Beam touched off major turmoil. Clarksburg protested that Fairmont's acquisition of Bean violated the league rule that prohibited transfers in the last 30 days of the season. The Generals demanded that Bean's two wins be stripped from Fairmont's record. Fairmont countered that Clarksburg had violated the league's "rookie" requirement that teams must carry five players with one year of professional experience. The Black Diamonds wanted five Clarksburg wins taken away. Daily sided with Fairmont. Then, in an unprecedented move, Clarksburg appealed to the league owners. By a 6 to 0 vote, the owners overruled their president, leaving the five disputed games in the win column for the Generals, and taking two games away from Fairmont.[9]

The struggle for first place came down to the last day of the season. In an unusual scheduling move, Labor Day found the two clubs playing three games, one in the morning in Clarksburg and a doubleheader in the afternoon in Fairmont. Slaughter pitched the Black Diamonds to a 4–1 win in the morning game to pull Fairmont even with the Generals. A crowd of 5,000 filled South Side Park for the afternoon contests. Clarksburg won the first game, 4–1, behind George "Pepper" Barry's home run. Jim Urinscho pitched into the ninth and got the win, but when he got into trouble Neale took no chance, bringing Proctor in to pick up the save and preserve the victory. Now, Clarksburg was one game ahead, so the season came down to the final game. Fairmont pulled an ethically questionable move by obtaining pitcher Andy Bednar from Pittsburgh on a 24-hour recall. Bednar, a Pirates rookie, had won 18 games that season at Wichita. Neale again called on his ace. Proctor was up to the task. The Generals squeezed out a 4–2 win and the second-half flag.

That title proved to be Clarksburg's finest hour in the Middle Atlantic. The 1930 club is still remembered with pride in Clarksburg. Neale managed the club, roamed center field, and batted .330. A graduate of West Virginia University, Neale had married a local girl; that made it easy for Clarksburg to think of him as their own. He had enjoyed a brief but productive major league career, having batted .357 to lead Cincinnati to their tainted victory in the 1919 World Series. His eight-year big league career had ended in 1924. Even before that, Neale, a two-sport star at WVU, had started coaching football. In 1921 he guided tiny Washington & Jefferson College to the Rose Bowl. Ultimately, he would gain more fame as a football coach than as a baseball player or manager. His coaching success at W&J, Virginia, West Virginia and Yale led to his induction into the College Football Hall of Fame in 1967. After his college coaching years, he led the Philadelphia Eagles to their greatest seasons. Neale took the Eagles to three NFL championship games, in 1947, 1948 and 1949. His Eagles captured the title in 1948 and 1949. The Professional Football Hall of Fame inducted Neale in 1969. Neither as a football coach nor as a baseball manager was he a "rah-rah" leader. He was not much for making rules. He treated players as responsible adults, expecting them to do their jobs, but when they failed to perform, he lit into them with profanity-laced diatribes.

Neale's Generals had momentum going into the playoffs against Johnstown. Clarksburg jumped out to the lead taking game one, 5–4, thanks to Mickey Noonan's four hits. After Johnstown captured game two in a 17–14 slugfest, Neale's team won game three behind Proctor's overpowering pitching. The Generals took game four by the slimmest score 9–8, a game featuring the hitting of Noonan and Barry. This gave the Generals a seemingly commanding three-games-to-one lead.

Then it was Johnstown's turn. Pitchers Harvey "Tommy" Thompson, who won 18 regular season games, and Tom "Ace" Roberts, who notched 15 victories, were at their best in the playoffs. In game five, Thompson limited Clarksburg to five hits and Thomas contributed three base hits in a 4–2 Johnstown victory. The turning point came in game six. Neale sent Proctor to the mound with the expectation he would close out the series before the home fans. Proctor, however, was literally knocked out of the game by a line drive off his knee. Clarksburg's relief pitchers could not stop Prichard and his teammates, who racked up a 9–4 win.

The Flood City had been fortunate off the field as well as on it. Not until the fall of 1930 was there general acknowledgement of a depression in Johnstown. The massive Cambria Steel Works did its best to support President Hoover's request that industry maintain employment and wages. So fans there still had money in their pockets. For the deciding game in Johnstown, 7,265 fans paid their way into Point Stadium to cheer the home team. The Johnnies rewarded their fans with a 9–3 win and the 1930 MAL championship.[10]

Besides the exciting pennant races and Medwick's great season, the MAL could take pride in other individual highlights. Charleroi's short fences and the lively Worth ball allowed the Governors to club a record 125 home runs. Big first baseman Hal Stricklin accounted for 31 of those, making him the first MAL player to top 30 round-trippers. Stricklin also led the league with 108 RBIs. Wheeling's lineup included three outstanding prospects. First baseman George McQuinn would enjoy a 12-year big league career that included two World Series and six all-star games. Outfielder Ervin "Pete" Fox, who batted .339 in 1930, played 13 years in the majors with Detroit and Boston (AL), appearing in three World Series and compiling a .298 career batting average. Frank Doljack, kept in Wheeling for a second season, hit a resounding .386, with league-leading 176 hits and 41 doubles.

Daily allowed that 1930 seemed the "longest season since he has [sic] been chief executive." Even so, he could be optimistic about the future because of the arrival of night baseball. The *Cumberland Evening Times* stated flatly that lights "saved the situation." Lights for night baseball at league parks was not only the biggest news in the MAL, it was the greatest sensation of the season for all of baseball. Lights swept across the minor league world much as the dust storms were currently engulfing the agricultural heartland of the country. Barnstorming teams, especially the House of David and Kansas City Monarchs, had used portable lighting systems for several years in the 1920s, but they were crude systems with floodlights mounted on moveable 20-foot towers. On May 2, 1930, the Des Moines Demons of the Western League played the first night game in Organized Baseball. The game attracted nationwide attention, touching off a widespread adoption of lights. By mid-summer, the *New York Times* claimed there were more night games than day games being played in the minors.[11]

In the Middle Atlantic League, Wheeling led the way to night baseball. In late May, Stogies owner Charles Holloway announced that Western Electric would install a light system at his ballpark. He justified his $9,000 cash expenditure as "a sound business investment." With the 90-foot light towers in place, generating 180,000 watts, the Stogies played the first night game in the MAL on July 15, 1930. Daily and the region's greatest player, Honus Wagner, were among the 4,000-plus in the stands to witness the first MAL game under lights. Industrial workers, Daily opined, now had the opportunity to attend a baseball game after a hard day's work. The Stogie's 9–2 win over Charleroi seemed unimportant.[12]

Johnstown and Cumberland turned on their lights in early August. Cumberland purchased its system from Giant Lighting at a cost of $10,142, but the club put down only $1,700, having arranged to pay for the system "on time." A Colts victory over Jeannette delighted the overflow crowd at the first game. The fans and press had nothing but positive comments about playing baseball at night. Most noted the advantage lights gave to workers who could never attend day games.[13]

Johnstown's lights did not enjoy quite the same universal approbation. The lights at Point Stadium were of lower quality than those of either Wheeling or Cumberland. The first night game at Point Stadium on August 5, 1930, in fact, was played under temporary lights costing only $2,500. The worst part of the evening was that the bus carrying the visiting Wheeling team broke down on the way to Johnstown. The Stogies eventually arrived but play did not start until 10:30. The game turned out to be a slugfest, which Wheeling won by a score of 17–13, keeping fans in the stands until the wee hours of the morning.[14]

In Charleroi, the Governors shared their field with the high school whose football and baseball teams played there. That proved to be an advantage because the fire company, owners of the baseball team, and the school board agreed to share the costs of lights. West Penn Power Company installed the lighting system, which was ready to go on August 14. The local newspaper exuded: "Local owners, fans and players have been alike in their jubilant acclaim of the success of the nocturnal sport in Charleroi." The sports editor was certain that "nothing will popularize the game again so speedily as night ball." Even Jeannette ordered a lighting system, but the team ran out of money before the arc lights could be installed.[15]

While Daily understood that night ball would help the financial situation of MAL teams, he believed it would not be enough to assure the league's survival in hard times. Before Christmas arrived in 1930, rumors began to spread around the league cities that the MAL would expand to ten teams. Wheeling's Holloway seemed to be the source of the rumors, although the *Cumberland Evening Times* believed Holloway was a stalking horse for Daily. Holloway was on record as wanting changes. During the previous two seasons he had floated feelers to the Central League in the hope of gaining admission to that league for Wheeling. By December the rumors gained traction. Initially, the talk was of two Pennsylvania cities joining the league. Altoona plus either Greensburg or Washington seemed the most likely candidates. The MAL's small Pennsylvania cities of Scottdale, Charleroi and Jeannette expressed support for such a move.[16]

Holloway, however, wanted the league to enlarge its population base more than the number of its franchises. Instead of small cities within the footprint of the existing league, he proposed the West Virginia cities of Charleston and Huntington. Walter "Watt" Powell, who had operated a semi-pro team in Charleston for over a decade, wanted into Organized Baseball.

Huntington was a logical pairing with Charleston. Former major league pitcher John Stuart ran baseball in Huntington. Both men had owned and managed teams in the independent or "outlaw" Tri-State League in 1929 and 1930, but they feared that league would not answer the bell in 1931. Powell and Stuart were baseball lifers. Powell came to Charleston as a player in the old Ohio State League in 1916 and stayed for the remainder of his life. His team, the Senators, played in city-owned Kanawha Park. The wooden structure, built in 1916, had recently been equipped with lights. Stuart took pride in having had major league experience, even though his 20–18 pitching record during the 1922–1925 period was modest at best. After winning only two games for Oakland of the Pacific Coast League in 1926, he understood the need for other work. He gladly signed on with Marshall College in Huntington as baseball coach and assistant football coach. In summers he ran the Huntington Boosters, a fast semi-pro team in 1927–1928, before he took the club to a professional league in 1929.[17]

Powell and Stuart made a strong case for their cities. Both had drawn well in the Tri-State League. Both played in decent, if not new, parks. Both played Sunday ball, no small consideration since Pennsylvania still outlawed Sunday baseball. The two cities would greatly increase the league fan base. Only Johnstown and Wheeling had more than 30,000 people. Huntington, having surpassed Wheeling in population, was now the largest city in West Virginia. It would be the largest city in the league with its population of 75,572. Charleston, the capital of West Virginia, had 60,408 inhabitants with another 6,000 living in South Charleston. The inclusion of the two would give the league four cities in excess of 60,000 people.

On the other hand, strong arguments existed against bringing Huntington and Charleston into the league. Ten-team leagues had existed before, but that number defied baseball culture and accepted wisdom that eight-team leagues were the ideal. It certainly made scheduling difficult. The strongest argument against admitting the southern West Virginia cities was distance. Johnstown to Charleston was 250 miles on narrow, winding mountain roads. Cumberland's Nelson Russler calculated the driving time from his city to Huntington at 12 hours, and he was being optimistic. Nevertheless, he supported admitting the two distant cities. Not surprisingly, the Pennsylvania franchises, Johnstown, Charleroi, Jeannette, and Scottdale, objected. The transportation and hotel costs would more than eat up the guarantee to visiting teams. This consideration was real. Although some teams had abandoned the practice of returning home when playing away games, the cities closest to each other continued the practice. Jeannette, Charleroi, and Scottdale were less than two hours apart. Only 30 miles separated Clarksburg and Fairmont. The addition of Charleston and Huntington meant not only long trips but added hotel costs as well. The small Pennsylvania cities also feared that the next step would be to lop them off in order to make an eight-member league.[18]

The proposal to admit Huntington and Charleston came to the MAL winter meeting in January. Fairmont's president, Joe Doringer, who had made the league schedule since 1926, offered to develop a schedule that would minimize travel in time for the next meeting. When pushed, his best estimate was that teams would have to travel around 5,000 miles if Charleston and Huntington were in the league. That did nothing to alter the opposition of the Pennsylvanians. The members appeared deadlocked. Rather than bring the issue to a vote, Daily deferred action on league expansion until a February meeting.[19]

Daily then focused on Johnstown's concerns. Johnstown had long complained about the league rule requiring the home team to split general admission ticket sales with the visiting team. Rather than split the general admission revenue, Daily proposed that the home team would pay visiting teams a flat guarantee of $100 for weekday games, $125 for night games, but 40 percent of the general admission gate for Sunday and holiday games. Such a change would, of course, favor teams that drew well at home. The proposal satisfied Johnstown. Jeannette and Scottdale were not happy, but then other league cities, especially Johnstown and Wheeling, made no secret of their unhappiness with the visitor's take from the small Pennsylvania towns. Before the next league meeting, Daily felt confident enough to assure Powell that admission of Charleston and Huntington "was a done deal."[20]

Things became even more complicated for Daily and the MAL prior to the February meeting. The Blue Ridge League, a Class D circuit that had operated just to the east of MAL territory since 1915, collapsed in early February as did so many leagues in 1930–1931. Hagerstown, Maryland, had been the strongest franchise in that league. A city of just over 30,000, it could be reached from Cumberland in two hours on the National Road, and less than that on the Baltimore and Ohio Railroad. Hagerstown owner Joe Cambria had just entered Organized Baseball in 1930 by purchasing the "Hubs," as the Hagerstown team was called. He was a force to be reckoned with. An immigrant from Messina, Italy, Cambria had built a commercial laundry business in Baltimore, Bugle Coat and Apron Company, into a thriving enterprise. In 1928 he bought a small field, which he named Bugle Field, and entered a semi-pro team in the Baltimore city league. Now, in 1931, he had a team in Organized Baseball, with a promise of help from Washington Senators owner Clark Griffith, but he had no league in which to play.

Cambria contacted Daily with a request to join the MAL. To cover all the bases, he also applied for membership in the Class B New York-Pennsylvania League, but that league had no interest in expanding below the Mason-Dixon Line. Cambria, who later gained fame as a scout for Griffith, was a hard man to say "no" to, as attested to by his nickname "Jabbering Joe." Cumberland gladly supported the application of its sister city, but a league with an odd number of teams created a scheduling nightmare; an 11-team league would not work. Daily tentatively agreed to Cambria's request, on the condition that another city could be found to balance Hagerstown.[21]

Daily was willing to support a 12-team league. He had always been anxious to get Altoona into the league and now floated that possibility. Unfortunately, the Pennsylvania Railroad controlled Cricket Field, the best ballpark in Altoona, and the railroad made it clear that it would not lease it to a professional franchise. Powell and Stuart suggested approaching Dr. Doff Daniels, a former player of Daily's at West Virginia Wesleyan College back in the 1910s. Daniels and his partner Aubrey O. Smith had run the Beckley, West Virginia, team in the Tri-State League in 1929 and 1930. Before that, Daniels operated a coal mine team in nearby Eccols, where he served as the town physician. Beckley had no experienced in Organized Baseball, but it had drawn well the past two years, and did have a field, Raleigh Mining Institute (RMI) Park, with lights. Even though Beckley's population of 9,357 was less than that of the other league members, excepting Scottdale, Daily offered to support membership for Daniels. All the original West Virginia teams—Wheeling, Fairmont and Clarksburg—supported Beckley. Cumberland could be counted on to back membership for Beckley in order to gain approval for Hagerstown.[22]

The 1931 configuration of the Middle Atlantic League was decided at the February 12 league meeting in Pittsburgh. Going into the meeting, Charleston and Huntington seemed assured of membership, but the chances of a 12-team league appeared slim. Not surprisingly, the meeting proved the most contentious since 1926. Daily opened the meeting after lunch and it lasted to midnight. First, Doringer presented his proposed schedule for a ten-team league; it called for travel days to accommodate trips to and from southern West Virginia. Then the eight member clubs voted to admit Charleston and Huntington by a 6–2 vote; Daily had earlier brought Johnstown around to support the expansion, but Scottdale's support was a surprise; Charleroi and Jeannette were the "no" votes.[23]

Then the now ten-team league took up the subject of further expansion. Cambria needed to be his most persuasive in order to get a franchise. He took his first-ever plane ride to get from Baltimore to Pittsburgh for the meet-

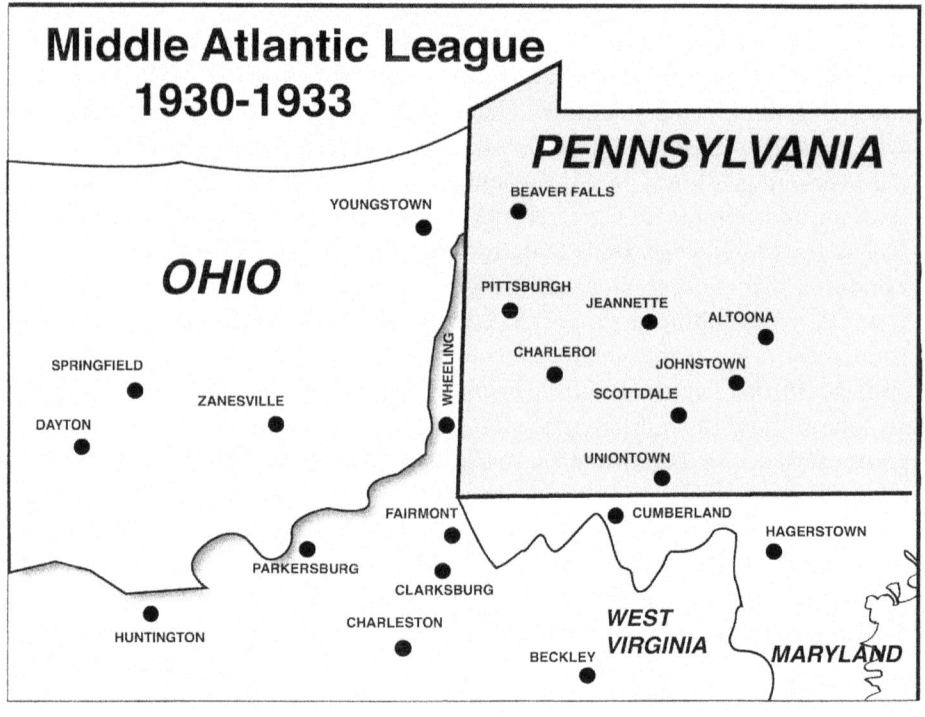

No longer a tight little league in the 1930s, the MAL spread over four states, experimented with a 12-team league and began to develop farm-team affiliations with major league clubs (Michele Duncan).

ing because, he said, MAL membership was so important to him. Before he began to make his case, he only had only the support of Cumberland. Cambria, however, refused to take "no" as an answer, maintaining that "no" was just the beginning of the discussion. Daily, for his part, admitted his fear that several teams would fold during the coming season, so he came to support further expansion as a hedge against the loss of teams. When the five West Virginia teams decided to support Beckley, which meant Hagerstown as well, the tide turned. In the end, the league voted to admit Hagerstown and Beckley, with the only "no" votes coming this time from Scottdale and Charleroi. Frank Colley, sports editor of the *Hagerstown Daily Mail,* lauded Cambria's "untiring efforts." Doringer headed a committee that drafted a schedule of 132 games with offdays for travel to be followed by a doubleheader.[24]

Baseball's establishment took notice of the no-longer-little Middle Atlantic League. As Holloway opined, the MAL "having bucked the recent business depression, had reinforced its position by expansion." *The Sporting*

News ran the story on page one. Daily's photo, with a big cigar clamped between his teeth, appeared in "the Baseball Bible." The expanded MAL was seen as a "tribute to the ability of President Elmer M. Daily." The league's population entitled the loop to a Class A classification, not its current Class C rating, although Daily opposed changing the designation. A league with a dozen teams seemed a grand experiment, perhaps "without precedent." There had not been such a venture in Organized Baseball since the Central League operated with a dozen teams in 1912. To many baseball men, the idea of a 12-team league appeared to be the height of heresy, if not insanity. Sportswriters began labeling the league the "Mad-Atlantic" or "Madlantic" League.[25]

Daily saw other developments as signs for optimism. Sportswriters around the league formed the Middle Atlantic League Baseball Writers Association. Irwin "Skeets" Fluharty of the *Wheeling Intelligencer* headed the 31-member group. Charleroi finally put up a screen above its short right field fence 252 feet from home plate, taking away the cheapest homers in the league. Work on installing lights continued in the spring. Newcomers Hagerstown, Charleston, Huntington, and Beckley either had lights or kept their promise to equip their parks for night baseball. Jeannette and Fairmont, already in debt, nevertheless, invested in lighting systems. So when the season opened only Scottdale and Clarksburg had to play day games; both firmly opposed the installation of lighting systems.[26]

League teams increasingly found help by becoming part of a farm system. The New York Yankees signed a working agreement with Cumberland in February. The Yankees promised to ship 19 players to Cumberland for spring training, and super scout Paul Krichell recommended other prospects for Cumberland to sign. Cumberland would have no regrets with the arrangement. The St. Louis Cardinals continued to supply a bountiful crop of prospects to Scottdale. Wheeling maintained its working agreement with Detroit, no matter how unsatisfactory it had been for the Stogies. Larry McPhail, general manager of the Cincinnati Reds, would not sign a formal working agreement, but promised to help Beckley with players. Linkages with high minor league clubs offered some hope to MAL teams, but seldom proved satisfactory. In addition to receiving players from Cincinnati, Beckley also got players on option from Montreal (Class AA) and Memphis (Class A). Montreal, however, terminated its arrangement with Jeannette on March 26, leaving the Jays management feeling abused. Even so, Stuart was excited to sign a working agreement for Huntington with Louisville of the American Association (Class AA). He got far less benefit than he expected.[27]

The league also gained in the on-going fight to play on Sundays. In the spring, the Maryland legislature approved Sunday ball in Hagerstown. The

West Virginia cities, now half of the league members, had no trouble playing on Sundays. Pennsylvania's Blue Law, which prohibited Sunday ball, had long been a scheduling nightmare for the league. At various times, Johnstown tried to find a way around the law by playing at Ideal Park, outside the city limits. That sometimes worked, but at other times had led to the arrest of players and team officials. Johnstown now found a place, Crystal Beach, to use as a Sunday park safe from prying law enforcement officials. Doringer, the schedule maker, had only to move Sunday games from Charleroi, Jeannette and Scottdale to Johnstown, Cumberland or Wheeling.[28]

In 1931 the 12-team MAL consisted of six West Virginia cities (Wheeling, Fairmont, Clarksburg, Huntington, Charleston and Beckley), four teams in Pennsylvania (Johnstown, Scottdale, Charleroi and Jeannette), and two from Maryland (Cumberland and Hagerstown). No sooner had the season started than Daily's enthusiasm for his expanded league turned into a nightmare. Jeannette became the first casualty. Around the league everyone knew that Jeannette "always has had financial difficulties." James Bugher, president of the Jeannette Athletic Association, understood his organization was overcommitted before the season started, but he had expected to recoup the debt carried over from 1930 from the Montreal Royals. The Jays believed their agreement with Montreal required the Canadian team to reimburse the Jays for paying the transportation costs for players coming to Jeannette and a bus ticket home when released. The Royals refused to honor this past expense; when Bugher appealed to the NAPBL, he was rebuffed. So the Jays started the season in debt, and they had just invested in a lighting system. To make matters worse, the team got off to a horrible start on the field, winning only once in their first dozen games. Not surprisingly the Jays' few fans more or less abandoned the team. Only 50 people showed up for what would be the Jays' last home game. On May 16, Bugher, citing a $4,000 debt and an inability to meet its payroll, returned the franchise to the league.[29]

The league president needed to act quickly in order to preserve his 12-team league, and he committed himself to that goal. Until Daily could find a new home for the Jeannette team, the league would operate the Jays as a road team with Hockenbury in charge. Daily made trips to Martinsburg, West Virginia, favored by Cambria and the Hagerstown newspapers, and to Monessen and Washington, Pennsylvania, supported by Charleroi and Scottdale. His trips failed to flush out backers willing to commit money for the Jeannette franchise. Even though he had been rejected in Altoona earlier in the year, Daily returned to the railroad center. This time he convinced James P. "Big Jim" Lamont to take the team. Daily knew Lamont because both operated hotels in the region. Lamont, a burly 40-year-old sporting a trim beard, ran a hotel in the small town of Nanty Glo near Altoona, and had served that hamlet as its mayor.[30]

Lamont still lacked a place to play. Possible locations in the city were either controlled by the Pennsylvania Railroad, the city parks system, or the school board. All three refused to lease their facilities, wishing to protect their flourishing city amateur teams and leagues. Lamont, however, found a place to play at the Altoona Speedway. The track was a sharply banked oval made of wood. Built in 1923 but rotting by 1927, the track was on the verge of being abandoned. Lamont could lease it on the cheap, but for several reasons it had no chance of sustaining professional baseball. First, it had no grandstand; race spectators at the oval stood at the top of the track or in the infield. For baseball, fans had the choice of standing or sitting on the board track. Second, the track was 12 miles north of Altoona in the village of Tifton with almost no public transportation from downtown Altoona. Daily and Lamont apparently believed they could leverage an acceptable playing field once the city saw the benefits of a team in Organized Baseball. So on May 23, Daily announced the transfer of Jeannette, with its pathetic 1–11 record, to Altoona. The team, now called the Engineers, needed to continue playing on the road for a week until the lighting system in Jeannette could be moved to Altoona and a semblance of a field created at the Speedway.[31]

Daily's Altoona experiment quickly ended. Daily and Lamont, apparently, had hopes of convincing the Veterans of Foreign Wars to absorb the debt and take over the team. When that plan failed, Daily lobbied the school board to open its Maple Avenue field. He, again, met unyielding opposition. Following Altoona's first home game on May 28, the *Altoona Mirror* gave more coverage to local amateur games, Altoona Merchants vs. Altoona Works and Penn Central vs. Mohawk Giants, than it did to the Engineers' unusual 21–3 win over Charleroi. The lack of support from the local media, the distance to the park, poor conditions at the park, and the Engineers' woeful play assured slim crowds at the Speedway. When a handful of fans turned up for the scheduled June 12 game between Altoona and Huntington, they found the gates locked and "no trespassing" signs posted. Players had not been paid since the team moved to Altoona and the club's debt had mounted to $7,500. That was more than Lamont's yearly income in 1930. Lamont and his group of backers cut their losses and returned the franchise to the league. Daily spent the week in Altoona conferring with civic boosters and local businessmen. He brought Pittsburgh Pirates owner Barney Dreyfuss to town to help sell the folks of Altoona on a professional baseball team, but Dreyfuss had no more success than did Daily. All their efforts were for naught. At midpoint in the season, the league was the owner of a franchise with no place to play.[32]

Unlike Jeannette, where the Jays got off to a terrible start, Hagerstown played well, going 26–20, which was good enough for fourth place, when Cambria became unhappy. Despite the team's on-field success, and the sterling play of several holdovers from the 1930 Blue Ridge Hubs, Hagerstown fans did not take to the Middle Atlantic League. In the defunct Blue Ridge League, where Hagerstown had drawn well, all the opponents had been natural rivals from cities within a 50-mile radius, especially Frederick, Maryland, Martinsburg, West Virginia, and Chambersburg, Pennsylvania, all less than 30 miles from Hagerstown. The MAL opponents, except for Cumberland, held little interest for Hagerstown fans. Cambria had no loyalty to Hagerstown and was not one to sit still and lose money. He threatened to move the team to Martinsburg if attendance did not pick up, but Martinsburg's park had burned and possible investors in baseball there had been tapped-out by their Blue Ridge's Blue Sox. On June 23, without forewarning, he announced he was moving his club to Parkersburg, West Virginia. He cited a debt of $8,000 as the reason for packing up and moving.[33]

Parkersburg was a strange choice for Cambria. Although its population of 29,625 was large enough to support a professional team and its location on the Ohio River and the B&O railroad made it convenient to other league cities, Parkersburg had never been a good baseball town. Cambria's club, now dubbed the "Parkers," opened in their new home, South Side Park, on June 28, 1931. No bands played to welcome the club. There was no parade, no reception from city officials, and very little support from the local newspaper. Manager/business manager John "Polk" Whalen attempted to promote its star, Ernest "Babe" Phelps, who was on his way to becoming the MAL's third .400 hitter in three years. Unfortunately for Whalen and Cambria, neither Phelps nor the Parkers impressed Parkersburg. At the first doubleheader on June 30 only 200 customers came through the gate. Cambria knew he had made a mistake in moving to Parkersburg. After less than three weeks in town, Cambria, on July 10, informed Daily that he wanted out of Parkersburg.[34]

At the close of the first half of the split-season, the league operated the Jeanette/Altoona team and Hagerstown/Parkersburg faced the choice of moving or declaring bankruptcy. If that was not enough to keep Daily up nights, Charleroi added to his woes. The Charleroi Fire Company threatened to give up the franchise on July 10 but agreed to postpone a decision until Daily could meet with local business and political leaders. He was, of course, already working to find a place for Altoona. The *Charleroi Mail* moaned that the team was "going to be lost," because of poor attendance and a growing debt. "The Depression," the paper concluded, "has laid them low." People in

Charleroi did not have 50 cents for admission to games, much less money to invest. On July 16 the firemen turned the franchise back to the league. Daily and Hockenbury descended on Charleroi. Hockenbury, leaving veteran manager Joe "Hooker" Phillips to run the Altoona road club, took over operation of the Governors. Daily wasted no time before twisting the arms of local leaders. He knew that compared to other operations around the league, a $2,500 debt was not much. Charleroi Burgess (mayor) Steve Woodward worked with Daily, but they failed to find investors.[35]

On the field, Cumberland, Charleston and Beckley dominated the first half of the season; each of them posted over 40 wins, the only clubs to do so. The New York Yankees, true to their word, placed quality players in Cumberland. Pitchers Vito "Lefty" Tamulis and Marvin Duke, both of whom made the Yankees, were all-stars. Yankee farmhands Don Paiement (.357), Merritt McCloy (.322), and Dan "Buddy" Hall (.312) hit over .300. The new clubs in southern West Virginia relied on veteran players, many from the coal mine teams that dotted the region and the old Tri-State League. Hard hitting continued to characterize the league. Phelps of Hagerstown/Parkersburg did hit over .400 for the year. Frank "Bugger" Welch, a former big leaguer who had played for Beckley in the Tri-State League in 1930 and who stayed in town, showed prodigious home run power for Beckley's Black Knights.

Daily called a league meeting in Wheeling to consider the league's options at midpoint in the season. Cambria, after searching Ohio cities and visiting Frederick, Maryland, decided to transfer his club from Parkersburg to Youngstown, Ohio. Owners were more than happy to approve such a move; it was one less immediate worry. Holloway, who had been an original supporter of expansion, now urged the league to contract by cutting Altoona and Charleroi, a move that made perfect economic and logistical sense. Daily, however, would not retreat from his 12-team concept. Despite all the evidence to the contrary, he still believed he could find investors in Charleroi. Altoona, he knew, would have to move, but he asked for more time to find a new home for the team. Meanwhile, the Engineers would continue as a road team. Daily had the support of the small cities and the southern West Virginia teams. Holloway, with support from Cumberland and Johnstown, then urged the league to close its season early. They complained about the small crowds in Scottdale, Fairmont, Charleroi, and Clarksburg. All the teams except Charleston and Beckley were losing money at the midpoint of the season. The league itself had taken on a $7,000 debt when it took over the Altoona franchise. Wheeling seemed to be the hardest hit of the remaining clubs, with Clarksburg and Scottdale close behind.[36]

Cambria, indeed, moved his club to Youngstown. The territory had opened up in spring 1931 when the Central League folded. Youngstown's population of 170,000 dwarfed that of all other MAL cities. The inclusion of Youngstown expanded the footprint of the league, but only slightly. The Ohio city was only 15 miles from the Pennsylvania border. A thriving industrial center in the 1920s, the steel furnaces of U.S. Steel and Republic Steel defined the city's economy and its air quality. The Depression, of course, led to reduction in steel production and cutbacks in the labor force. Locals came to see Youngstown Sheet and Tube as a better city icon than steel, hence the nickname "Tubers" for the team. Despite Youngstown's population, Cambria must have believed he had made another terrible decision when only 600 fans showed up for his Tubers' first home game. Determined to hold on to this potentially lucrative territory, Cambria could only cut costs to reduce his losses, and salaries were the largest expense. As he turned to players who commanded less salary, the team began to plummet through the standings from fourth at the conclusion of the first half to tenth at the end of the season.[37]

A week after the Wheeling meeting, Daily finally faced the reality that the Charleroi franchise was broke. On July 15, the Charleroi Fire Company lacked the funds to pay salaries. The players, understandably, went on strike. Hockenbury convinced the players to return after two days. Daily and Hockenbury agreed to operate the team themselves. After a week, when the local coal miners went out on strike, Daily lost all hope of sustaining baseball in Charleroi and announced that the Governors would become a road team operated by the MAL. In giving up, Daily lamented, "I always thought Charleroi was in good condition. I never expected trouble here."[38]

In mid–July, the Altoona debacle finally got resolved. Daily had tried to place the team in various locations ranging from Akron, Ohio, to New Castle, Pennsylvania, before settling on Beaver Falls, Pennsylvania. An industrial town of 17,000 producing china, metal and cork products, Beaver Falls was located 80 miles north of Pittsburgh. The team, now called the "Beavers," played at the Beaver Falls High School field. As a cost-saving measure, Ed Harvey, leader of local investors, replaced Joe Phillips, a non-playing manager, at the helm of the club. Not surprisingly, his charges fared no better than they had in Altoona or in Jeannette. The Beavers compiled a record of seven wins against fifteen losses. Nor did the team draw more fans than it had done in other locations. The highlight of the Beavers' short stay in the MAL came on September 3 when they pulled off a triple play against Beckley, the league's first. After a Beckley batter struck out with runners on first and third, the runner on first tried stealing, but was thrown out. Then the runner on third was cut down at the plate trying to score.[39]

2. Expanding in the Depression Years   63

Just when Daily thought he had resolved all the problems, a new one sprung up, this time in Fairmont. In late July, manager Frank Walsh and six of his players struck for back pay. They claimed they had not been paid since July 7. Doringer replaced Walsh as manager with veteran Tony Cyran and signed replacement players from the local amateur league. That move always proved costly; the new players simply were overmatched. Daily met with Brooks Fleming, who was the son of a former West Virginia governor, assistant to the president of the largest coal company in the state, and chairman of the National Bank of Fairmont. A great city booster, Fleming believed the city needed the team. He arranged for the club to go into trusteeship with Fred A. Kraft, head of industrial relations for Consolidation Coal Company, and J. Ray Smoot, vice president of the Fairmont National Bank, to serve as trustees. They determined the club needed to raise $4,300 to pay back salaries and to cover the team debt. Before they could raise the money, Frank Ice, a local sporting goods dealer, attached the team uniforms for failure of the team to pay its back debt to him. A local civic leader did come forward, perhaps Fleming again, to clear the debt, but Doringer let it be known that he had been told this would be the last time a philanthropist would bail out the team.[40]

All the shuffling of franchises and the financial crises took attention away from play on the field. Too bad, because the 12-team league saw plenty of excellent hitting and some outstanding pitching. Ernest Gordon "Babe" Phelps, the catcher from Cambia's traveling circus, hit a resounding .408. This was the third straight year a MAL player had topped the magical .400 mark. The big 6-foot 2-inch, 235-pound, left-handed hitter had been signed by Washington Senators owner Clark Griffith in 1930. Optioned to Hagerstown, he had batted a resounding .373 with 19 homers, but because Washington had such a thin farm system, Phelps found himself back in Hagerstown in 1931. Before the end of the season, Griffith recalled the burley catcher for a late-season trial with the Senators. It was the beginning of an eleven-year big league career in which he compiled a .310 career batting average playing for Washington, the Chicago Cubs, Brooklyn, and Pittsburgh. Seven years of his big league career were spent with the Dodgers, where he made three all-star games.

The other batting star, Frank "Bugger" Welch, the stocky player-manager of Beckley, clubbed 38 home runs to lead not only the MAL but all the minor leagues. No MAL player would ever again hit as many homers. Welch also batted .364 and drove in 122 runs, just three behind league-leader Bill Prichard of Johnstown. Welch's Beckley outfield of Holt "Cat" Milner (.360), a fan favorite, Fern Bell (.350) and Bailey Groseclose (.344.) all had banner years with the bat.

Johnstown's outfield pair of Sam Thomas and Bill Prichard continued to pound the ball and run the bases with abandon. Thomas followed his .357 batting average in 1930 with a .355 mark in 1931. He always showed discipline at the plate; in 1931 he became the first MAL player to draw over 100 walks (104) in a season. He also led the league with 122 runs and 59 stolen bases. Those numbers garnered him a well-deserved all-star recognition. Prichard's batting average dropped a bit, down from .364 in 1930 to .329. He pounded 27 homers and led the circuit in doubles with 34 and RBIs with 125.

The 1931 version of the MAL boasted four 20-game winners for the first time. Charleston's Ed Marleau, who had his best year of 16 minor league seasons, led with 23 victories and 256 innings pitched. Lefty Bill Lee of Scottdale also notched 22 victories and struck out a league-best 256 batters, the most by any MAL pitcher to that point. Johnstown boasted the duo of Harvey "Tommy" Thompson and Tom "Ace" Roberts, stars of 1930, both of whom notched 20 victories

The Charleston Senators, under manager Dick Hoblitzel, a former Boston Red Sox and Cincinnati Reds first baseman, nosed out Beckley and Johnstown for the second-half title. That entitled the Senators to a shot at first-half winner Cumberland. On the season, Charleston (82–44) and Cumberland (82–46) were the two best clubs. Charleston lacked a .300 hitter, but had strong pitching headed by fire-balling Marleau (23–8, 2.36) backed by Melvin Miller (17–7) and Joe Martin (14–6)

Cumberland also possessed a deep pitching staff headed by veteran Bill "Chick" Helmick, whose record of 18–4 was the MAL's highest winning percentage. Behind Helmick the staff included three future Yankees: Vito Tamulis, who compiled the league's best earned run average of 1.92 and won 15 games, Marvin Duke, who also notched 15 victories, and Jimmy Densmore who won 17 games. The Colts were loaded with .300 hitters: first baseman Max Posnack (.333), second baseman Don Paiememt (.357), third baseman Merritt "Jake" McCloy (.322), outfielder Dan "Buddy" Hall (.312), and catcher Leo Mackey (.338).

In the playoffs, Cumberland fell behind before reeling off three straight wins to take the title. Charleston drew a team-high 5,500 fans to see the Senators take the first game. After splitting the next two games, Charleston held a two-games-to-one lead. In game four, before a capacity crowd of 4,500 enthusiastic fans, Helmick drove in the go-ahead run and outdueled Martin to propel the Colts to a win. In game five, the Colts slugged their way to a 7–5 win and a 3–2 lead in the series thanks to shortstop Gus Daviu's three RBIs. Teenager Tamulis then closed out the series for Cumberland by pitching a 6–0 shutout. After the final out, the *Charleston Gazette* reported

2. Expanding in the Depression Years 65

The 1931 MAL champions, the Cumberland Colts. Front: batboy. Kneeling (L-R): Jimmy Densmore, Vito Tamulis, Dom Paiement, Merritt "Jake" McCloy, Dan "Buddy" Hall, Bill Solomone, Harold "Pat" Shea, Emil Moscowitz. Back row (L-R): Augie Daviu, Bill "Chip" Helmick, Bob Walsh, Bernie Connell, Leo Mackey (manager), Nelson "Colonel" Russler (president), Marvin Duke, Max Posnack, Bob Synnott (John Wiseman).

that the Cumberland fans reacted as if their team had just won the World Series, "rushing on to the field and carrying their heroes off on their shoulders."[41]

The Middle Atlantic League's experiment with a 12-team league had ended in a financial bloodbath. Only Charleston showed a profit, while Beckley claimed to break even. The city of Charleston had enjoyed prosperity and growth in the 1920s. The 20-story Kanawha Valley Bank, the sparkling new Boone Hotel, and the new state capitol building bore witness to the city's prosperity during the booming 1920s. Powell ran a tight and efficient ship. Before the season began he had raised $11,000 in stock sales to pay for installing lights at Kanawha Park. With that start, Charleston, unlike most other clubs, did not have to go into debt to pay for the lights. The Senators' on-field success brought fans through the turnstiles.[42]

During the season, Daily, at times, worked without pay, put in many a night on the road, jawboned, cajoled, and pleaded with investors and potential investors. He had to deal with Joe Cambria, as well as failures in Jeannette, Altoona, and Charleroi. He also, as one newspaperman said, did it "without sleep." Years later, Daily remembered 1931 as "the toughest time I ever had." Despite the red ink, Daily could take pride in somehow getting the league through the season as a 12-team league.[43]

After the season, Cumberland's Puerto Rican shortstop Gus Daviu organized a barnstorming team called the Middle-Atlantic All-Stars. A minor league barnstorming team was highly unusual, but Daviu believed the publicity generated by the 12-team league would pay off. His team consisted of first baseman Frank Crist (Fairmont), second baseman Tony Cyran (Fairmont), third baseman Jack McCloy (Cumberland). Shortstop Daviu, outfielders Buddy Hall (Cumberland), Harold "Pat" Shea (Cumberland) and Ed Boland (Scottdale), catchers Dick Vassey (Clarksburg) and Bill Rae (Scottdale), pitchers Bill Wallace (Youngstown) and Chick Helmick (Cumberland). The MAL club played against army, navy and marine teams in Puerto Rico and Panama.[44]

The MAL was hardly alone in experiencing troubles. Nationally, President Hoover and business leaders continued to flail at the Depression without knowing what to do to restore prosperity. In February 1932 the Hoover administration rolled out its new weapon. The Reconstruction Finance Corporation was empowered to give loans to banks, railroads and insurance companies to keep them afloat. Its loans, however, went mainly to big banks and corporations, and did little to protect banks in small cities. Over 5,000 banks countrywide closed their doors by March 1933. In Johnstown, the two largest banks went into receivership. Johnstown's largest employer, the Cambria Works, began laying off workers and reducing wages. The city electorate responded by electing a radical mayor, Eddie "Red" McClosky, who attacked the "Cambria-business complex" and invited the Bonus Army of World War I veterans to use Johnstown as a staging area. Other cities around the MAL experienced similar reduced wages and high unemployment.[45]

The bottom of the Great Depression was not an auspicious time for minor league baseball. Only 21 leagues had survived through 1930, and in 1931 there were just 16. In 1932 the number of leagues would fall to 13. Only two other Class C leagues existed: the Piedmont League and the Western Association. The Piedmont would not answer the bell in 1932 and the Western Association would not make it through 1933. The difficulties of the minor leagues led to action at the December 1931 meeting of the National Association of Professional Baseball Leagues. The membership deposed Michael H. Sexton, who had presided over the National Association since 1902. A committee was selected to run the Association's affairs for one year.

As leader of the only team to show a profit, Watt Powell considered himself entitled to advise Daily and his fellow owners on league affairs. Powell, probably correctly, believed that fans had interest in seeing only three or four other teams, some natural rivalries. Charleston-Beckley-Huntington had competed against each other in baseball, for population, and for status over many years. Other rivalries developed over time from the competition, but the 12-team league did not allow rivalries to develop. Travel expenses were another consideration, having plagued all teams in 1931. The answer, Powell thought, was a six- or eight-team league with a balanced schedule. Further, he wanted each series during the season to be no more than three games, with teams never playing more than six consecutive days at home or on the road. Powell's proposal for a geographically tighter league was a six-team West Virginia circuit. In this, he had support from Huntington and Beckley, but Wheeling, Clarksburg, and Fairmont wanted to remain in a league that included Johnstown and Cumberland. Noting the on-going hastle visiting teams faced in collecting their guarantee, Powell proposed a straight $100 guarantee to visiting teams for all games.[46]

Despite the financial disaster of 1931, when Daily called a league meeting for Pittsburgh in January 1932, eleven teams sent representatives to organize for the coming year. Of the teams that finished the 1931 season, only Charleroi, which had turned its franchise back to the league, failed to show. Before the meeting, Daily floated the possibility of a 12-team league but with two six-team divisions. Even thought that arrangement would have allowed for Powell's six-team West Virginia circuit, the suggestion went nowhere. Everyone understood the league needed to contract in 1932. At the January 17 meeting, the owners voted to reduce the league to eight teams, without reference to which teams would leave. They also agreed to reduce maximum monthly salaries from $3,000 to $2,500 for the 14-man rosters. There still remained the issue of which teams would be included; that sticky issue was postponed until the February meeting.[47]

The task of reducing the league would take a couple of months. Beaver Falls clearly lacked the fan or monetary support to maintain a team. Scottdale had developed a core of loyal supporters, but, unfortunately, there were not enough of them. The Young Cardinals had cost the parent St. Louis Cardinals $8,000 in 1931. Branch Rickey, the man in charge at St. Louis, did not like to lose money. The St. Louis pullout from Scottdale, rumored since midseason 1931, became official the end of February. Hockenbury, a resident of Scottdale, tried to drum up interest among local baseball enthusiasts, but by March he recognized the impossibility of Scottdale going it alone and thus turned the franchise back to the MAL. Even before the February meeting it was clear to everyone except Hockenbury that Scottdale would not be fielding a team in the 1932 MAL.[48]

At the February meeting, Daily proposed dropping "financially embarrassed" Fairmont in order to achieve an eight-team league. Doringer made "an eloquent plea to have his club kept in the league." Unfortunately, he lacked a convincing plan that would allow the Black Diamonds to stay afloat for another year. Doringer found that only Clarksburg would vote to keep Fairmont in the league. At the conclusion of the meeting, Daily thought he had an eight-team league lineup for the coming season. Four charter members remained—Johnstown, Cumberland, Wheeling, and Clarksburg. The three southern West Virginia newcomers—Charleston, Beckley, and Huntington—had weathered the 1931 season in good shape. Cambria's operation, now in Youngstown, likely would be a headache, but for the moment Cambria appeared prepared to go forward.[49]

It was not long after the February meeting that Daily's plans began to unravel. In Wheeling, Holloway was in poor health, and because of his failing health his family pressured him to retire. The Stogies had been a "hobby" for Holloway; despite losing money on the Stogies in 1930 and 1931 he had not complained. Local sports editor Tom Hopkins wrote that Holloway "for the last two years took it on the chin financially." Holloway had been the first to install a lighting system, and had spent heavily to upgrade Fulton Park. Following the 1931 season, he ended the Stogies' working agreement with Detroit. After all, that arrangement had left Wheeling with a tenth-place finish in 1931. Daily contacted several major league teams about coming to Wheeling's assistance. The Boston Braves and Brooklyn Dodgers showed initial interest, but then declined the opportunity. Daily thought he had the New York Giants lined up to either purchase or operate the Wheeling franchise; Holloway offered the Giants what he described as a "sweetheart" deal, but those negotiations broke down. As he looked at the deepening economic conditions, Holloway decided in early April to throw in the towel.[50]

Cambria cast his eyes on the vacant Wheeling territory. He quickly opened negotiations with Holloway about renting Fulton Park. Having seen Cambria operate in 1931, Holloway did not trust his fellow owner, who had shown no loyalty to any city. Cambria claimed that Holloway demanded more for rent than he had been prepared to offer the Giants. Holloway, for his part, was prepared to let baseball die in Wheeling before he would bring Cambria into his city. Wheeling business manager Earl Klemer promised he would back Wheeling in 1933, but the city was done for 1932.[51]

Always the wheeler-dealer, Cambria had plans B, C and D ready to implement. Zanesville, Ohio, struck him as a likely next stop for his Youngstown franchise. Daily and Hockenbury also had their eyes on Zanesville as a league city. Hockenbury claimed to have thirty Zanesville businessmen willing to pony up the necessary money. The Zanesville Chamber of Commerce threw its moral support behind a team in Organized Baseball, but was reluctant to join forces with an outside owner. Cambria returned to Baltimore where he purchased the Baltimore Black Sox to play in his Bugle Park. He left business manager Tony Citrano in charge of the Youngstown operation. At the same time, Cambria was talking to people in Altoona about transferring his franchise there. Likely, this was a smokescreen to put pressure on people in Zanesville and Wheeling, because Altoona still lacked an adequate playing facility. Cambria was also reportedly in conversations with baseball people in Dayton, Lima, Canton, and Springfield, Ohio.[52]

With Wheeling gone, the MAL was reduced to seven teams with less than a month before the scheduled start of the 1932 season. Cambria made one final attempt to reach a deal in Wheeling, but that also failed. He then decided to transfer his Youngstown operation to the reorganized Central League. The MAL owners made no effort to stop the move. The Ohio-based Central League would crumble after the 1932 season, but it served Cambria's needs for that year. The MAL would proceed with half the number of teams it had the previous year. Since Daily and Hockenbury had invested considerable energy in Zanesville, they promised to welcome that city into the league in 1933, assuming another city could be found to balance its addition.

The league changed in other ways. For the first time, half the clubs were farms for major league teams. After Wheeling cut its ties with Detroit, the Tigers signed a working agreement with Huntington, where the Tigers farm hands continued to underperform. Johnstown was pleased to get a working arrangement with Pittsburgh. The New York Yankees stuck with Cumberland. The Yankees provided the Colts with $750 for training camp, $1,000 toward salaries for each of the four months of the season, a manager in Leo Mackey, and 24 prospects for the start of spring training. The Yankees wanted to build a system to challenge the complex that Branch Rickey had constructed for the St. Louis Cardinals. In 1932 the Yankees system consisted of Newark, New Jersey (Class AA), Springfield, Massachusetts (Class A), Binghamton, New York (Class B), Erie, Pennsylvania (Class B), and Cumberland of the MAL (Class C).[53]

Even as the Depression worsened, teams did little by modern standards to promote their games. Municipal politicians, of course, still found it politic to throw out the first ball on Opening Day. Parades with bands playing, players in uniform riding in open cars in uniforms, and politicians waving to onlookers as the procession meandered through the downtown business area on to the ballpark had been commonplace in the Roaring Twenties. They became uncommon during the lean years of the Depression. In the league's first few years, downtown retailers had regularly closed down the afternoon of Opening Day. That practice became laughable by 1930 when retailers needed every penny they could get. Night ball, introduced in 1930, became universal in 1932 when even Clarksburg, the last holdout for day baseball, installed lights. Playing games on Sundays, seen as an important way to bring fans, especially working class fans, into the ballparks, had been a problem for the MAL because Pennsylvania's Blue Laws prohibited teams from playing on Sunday. In 1932, however, only Johnstown represented a Pennsylvania city, and the Johnnies had been evading the Sunday law by playing outside the city at a place called Crystal Beach without incident for several years.

Teams offered a limited array of promotions to attract fans into their parks. Ladies Day had become an established tradition across the minor leagues by the late 1920s. MAL teams usually required ladies to be accompanied by an adult male to gain free admission. By 1932 most clubs had come to stage one Ladies Day each week, usually on Tuesdays. Although radio had been around for a decade, and all league cities had their own station, none had play-by-play broadcasts. Apparently, none even used the medium to advertise their product in the 1932 season. Joe Doringer had advertised Fairmont games on his station for several years, but the financial failure of the Black Diamonds did not encourage others to follow suit. There were few giveaways, a staple of minor league life 60 years later. "Booster Nights" were common when clubs felt a desperate need to jack up admissions. Such nights usually involved raffles or the give-away of one significant product, usually a car. Cumberland, in June 1932, did introduce new ways to entice fans to the park. The Colts gave a free loaf of bread to the first 200 women into the park. It proved a popular enticement. On another night they offered a grab bag of goodies for ten cents a grab. Unfortunately, these promotions were seen as acts of desperation. No team offered the sort of between-inning entertainment that would become commonplace by the end of the century.[54]

The most tried-and-true way of getting fans into MAL parks continued to be for the home team to play exhibition games against teams that were not members of the league. The MAL from its beginnings was a segregated affair, as was the case with all of Organized Baseball. Fans, however, delighted in seeing African-American teams play their hometown heroes. The Homestead Grays lived off the MAL in April. Charleroi once scheduled no less than three spring games with the Grays. In 1932 the Grays toured all six of the league parks. In Beckley, the most southern of the league's cities, fans packed MRI Park to see the Grays. The Hilldale club, recognized by Frank Knight, sports editor of the *Charleston Gazette*, as "another great Negro team," joined the Grays in barnstorming through MAL territory. Hilldale featured Hall of Famers Martin Dihigo and Judy Johnson. White attitudes, at least judged by those of local newspapers, changed over time. Initially, the papers used easy "Sambo" stereotypes right out of the minstrel shows to describe African-

American players. Rather quickly, however, sports editors, at least, came to appreciate the ability of Negro League players, many of whom would later be inducted into the Baseball Hall of Fame. In 1932, "Smokey" Joe Williams, Josh Gibson, Willie Wells, and Oscar Charleston, who became a favorite of Beckley fans, stood out in games against MAL teams.[55]

An even more desirable exhibition for Middle Atlantic clubs was a game against a team from the major leagues. Most big league clubs were happy to pick up a few dollars on their way to their home city after spring training, or at the end of the season, or even on an offday during the regular season. The most common opponents for MAL teams were Pittsburgh and Cincinnati, cities on the edge of the league territory. Teams with working agreements usually managed to arrange an exhibition with the parent club. Games against major league opponents commonly drew the largest crowds of the season. Such games often made the difference between a team finishing in the black or the red. If neither a Negro League nor major league club could be lined up for an exhibition, the House of David's bearded Jewish team proved an agreeable alternative.[56]

The summer of 1932 was played out against the backdrop of the demise of the Hoover presidency. In May many World War I veterans, calling themselves the Bonus Expeditionary Army, began a march on Washington to demand immediate payment of bonuses which had been approved by Congress for payment in 1945. The House approved such a bill, but the Senate would not follow suit. On July 28, General Douglas McArthur led the U.S. army in routing the Bonus marchers and burning their encampment. A rump of the Bonus Army retreated to Ideal Park outside Johnstown, but the fight was out of them. Voters, however, remembered the Hoover administration's treatment of veterans.

The backgrounds of players had changed significantly by 1932. Five years earlier, in 1927, most players had been signed by the manager of the local club either from his own contacts, local tryout camps, or semi-pro teams. As a result, most players hailed from Pennsylvania, Ohio, West Virginia and Maryland. Pennsylvania dominated, providing one-third of all MAL players, followed by Ohio with one-fifth, and West Virginia with one-eighth. Only six percent came from the South. These figures are less than precise because the hometowns of many players remain unknown, but they illustrate a general pattern. As major league clubs began to sign and assign players, the pattern shifted. In 1932, Pennsylvania still had the most players, but the Keystone State's percentage had dropped from one-third to one-quarter. Ohio, West Virginia and Maryland together accounted for another one-quarter of the players. The biggest shift came in the number of Southerners on the rosters of league teams. Twenty-five percent of players now hailed from Southern states, with Alabama and Virginia leading the way.

The MAL of 1932 staged a heart-pounding pennant race. Beckley won the first half (34–25) with Charleston and Clarksburg tied for second (31–29). In the second half, Clarksburg ran into financial trouble, dumped players, and fell to fifth place, ahead of a miserable Huntington team. Charleston kept winning and got to the wire three games ahead of Beckley in the second half. The two split-season winners, Beckley and Charleston, finished with identical records (70–54).

Beckley led the league with a .303 team batting average. All eight starters batted over .300. The Black Knights also clubbed 106 homeruns; the next-best team hit only 70 round-trippers. Third baseman Lou Chiozza batted .339, led the league with 110 runs and 187 hits, the MAL's high-water mark to that date. He established a league record by hitting safely in 34 consecutive games. Manager-outfielder Frank Welch, after launching 38 homers in 1931, managed to hit only ten before the club traded him to the Atlanta Crackers of the Class A Southern Association at the end of the first half. Welch's managerial and offensive leadership passed on to Cat Milner. A product of the rugged semi-pro textile leagues of East Alabama, Milner had come to West Virginia in 1929 to play for two years in the "outlaw" Tri-State League before joining Beckley's MAL team in 1931. A baseball lifer, he would keep playing in the minors through 1942 and manage a dozen years after that. His advice to his players was quite simple: "Hit the ball and run like hell."[57]

The brightest star of Beckley, and of the league, was another Alabama lad, Fred Sington. He came to Beckley with the highest of expectations. He had achieved All-American recognition as a tackle for the University of Alabama in 1929 and 1930. Knute Rockne labeled him "the greatest lineman in the country." His 1930 Crimson Tide team had gone to the Rose Bowl, where it defeated Washington State to complete an undefeated season, which allowed it to lay claim to the mythical national championship. Sington was a big man by baseball standards, 6-foot-2 and 215 pounds, but, according to no less an authority than the nation's premier sportswriter, Grantland Rice, he possessed the "speed of a halfback." Sington would be selected for the College Football Hall of Fame in 1955. With a square jaw and a mop of dark wavy hair, he looked the part of a Hollywood star. In fact, Rudy Vallee had even written a song about him titled "Football Freddie." At Alabama he played baseball, as a pitcher and outfielder, well enough to be selected for the Crimson Tide all-century teams in both baseball and football. Following his graduation with academic honors, he chose to play baseball, signing with the Atlanta Crackers. Atlanta optioned him to Jackson, Mississippi, allowing him to start at the

2. Expanding in the Depression Years

Class D level. He struggled at Jackson, but began to get the feel for professional ball during a brief stay at High Point (Class C). The Crackers needed hitting in 1932 and optioned him to Beckley in exchange for Frank Welch.[58]

Sington put on a show at Beckley. He simply had one of the finest seasons in the history of the Middle Atlantic League. He won the triple crown of hitting with a .368 batting average, 29 homers, and 110 RBIs. He also tied Chiozza for tops in runs scored with 110. No one would dispute his recognition as the MAL's outstanding player of 1932. Unfortunately, Sington never again put up the numbers he did at Beckley. He did play six big league years with Washington and Brooklyn, compiling a respectable .271 lifetime average, but he failed to achieve the super-star status expected of him in 1932.

In addition to Milner and Sington, a third Alabamian, James Albert "Danny" Boone, led the Charleston Senators. His brother, Ike Boone, also a great minor league hitter, had established Organized Baseball's season high of 553 total bases in 1929. Already age 37 in 1932, Danny had played in the majors in 1919, 1921 and 1923 as an ineffective pitcher (8 wins, 13 losses), before he settled into a 15-year career in the minor leagues, where he hit for power and average. In a career of 1,336 minor league games, he clubbed 214 home runs, drove in 851 runs, and compiled a .356 lifetime batting average. He arrived in Charleston with four batting titles and five years of managerial experience. For the Charleston Senators, Boone batted .349—second to Sington in the MAL—clubbed 17 homers and drove in 92 runs.[59]

Boone had a strong supporting cast. Outfielder Johnny "Ty-Ty" Tyler hit .305, and shortstop Joe Longanecker led the MAL in stolen bases. Boone's top pitchers were Wayne "Icicle" LaMaster and Joe "Speed" Martin. LaMaster (17–6), a little lefty, led the MAL with a 2.27 ERA and 177 strikeouts. The hard-throwing Martin posted a 16–3 record, the best winning percentage in the league. Martin also pitched the league's only no-hitter, a feat which he accomplished on August 2 against Cumberland.

Charleston prevailed over Beckley in the all–West–Virginia playoffs. Charleston took the first two games, highlighted by LaMaster's four-hitter and Boone's three hits in game one. Beckley came back to take games three and four to tie the series. Milner's homer and four RBIs led the Black Knights to a 10–8 win in game three. Kelsey Jennings (13–11) pitched a two-hit shutout in game four. Then Charleston won the next two games to close out the series. LaMaster won and Boone homered in game five. Boone and catcher Vern Mackey had three hits each to pace the Senators in the final game. In the six-game series, Tyler batted .375 and Boone hit .350, drove in ten runs, and clubbed four homers. Milner paced Beckley with six runs batted in. Sington proved to be a huge disappointment; he collected only two singles and batted a mere .154.

As the curtain went down on the 1932 season, Daily found it difficult to be optimistic. Personally, his position as basketball and baseball coach and athletic director at St. Francis College disappeared when St. Francis abolished all sports due to the Depression. Daily had two pre-school-aged girls to support and only the meager salary he received for running the league for an income. With the help of his father-in-law, Louis Schultz, a long-time hotel operator in various western Pennsylvania towns, Daily managed to purchase the Exchange Hotel in Ebensburg, Pennsylvania. An old structure with 35 rooms and an uncertain future, it had been built in 1913 as a resort hotel catering to people who wanted to enjoy the cool mountain breezes. He changed the name to the Penn-Eben Hotel, and tried to attract travelers and salesmen to a clean hotel with very good food located in the middle of town. On the positive side, wife Mary could run the place while Elmer was on the road as he was much of the summer.[60]

Daily could take some pleasure that the league finished 1932 with all the teams that had started the season, a claim not many leagues in the low minors could make. Looking ahead, however, he would be hard pressed to exude confidence. The geographically tight little league that began in 1925 had morphed into an extended circuit with larger cities when it expanded into southern West Virginia. With good reason, the sports editor of the *Cumberland Evening Times* believed "it is barely possible that 'Miracle Man' Daily will be able to keep the MA going."[61]

Minor league baseball reached its nadir following the 1932 season, when the number of leagues fell to only 13. Assuming the Middle Atlantic League would still be standing when the bell rang on the 1933 season, it would be one of only two Class C leagues. The MAL had already seen franchises fail in a mounting number of cities: Jeannette, Charleroi, Beaver Falls, and Altoona, Pennsylvania; Fairmont, Parkersburg and Wheeling, West Virginia; Hagerstown, Maryland; and Youngstown, Ohio. Daily seemed to be running out of cities.

By the beginning of 1933, a few rays of sunshine leaked through the clouds hovering over minor league baseball in general. The National Association of Professional Baseball Leagues got a new leader after 25 years. In 1931 member leagues had created an executive committee to run the organization for one year. Now, the membership elected as president, William Bramham. The self-appointed "Judge" Bramham was a North Carolina politician and minor league promoter. The National Association also created a promotion department charged with organizing new leagues and assisting existing ones. Joe Carr of Columbus, Ohio, who doubled as president of the fledging National Football League, became the first director of the promotion department.

The election of Franklin D. Roosevelt in November 1932 may not have saved any jobs or improved the state of the economy, but it lifted the dreary mood of the country. Herbert Hoover, who had swept into the presidency in 1928, had not caused the Great Depression, but his failure to respond with sympathy to the desperate plight of Americans led to his repudiation by the electorate. Roosevelt's warmth, optimism and promise of a "new deal" engendered a sense of hope. The Democrats' campaign song, "Happy Days Are Here Again," may have exaggerated the country's reality, but not its feeling of possibility. Roosevelt had promised action, and in the first 100 days of his administration he delivered. The country digested an alphabet of legislation and programs: the Emergency Banking Act, Federal Emergency Relief Act, Civilian Conservation Corps (CCC), Public Works Administration (PWA), Civil Works Administration (CWA), Federal Deposit Insurance Corporation (FDIC), and Tennessee Valley Authority (TVA). The repeal of Prohibition ended a culture war regarding alcoholic beverages, which had consumed much energy in the 1920s.

Daily was determined to see the MAL operate in 1933 even though his six-team MAL had just managed to stagger to the finish line in 1932. Half its teams appeared ready to follow Hoover into oblivion. The three remaining founding members faced the most serious financial difficulties. Clarksburg had come close to bankruptcy in the summer of 1932. Now, team president Harles L. Clark admitted "the condition here is desperate." Cumberland, one of the strongest franchises in the first years of the MAL, had fallen into debt in 1932. Then, following the season, George Weiss decided to move his New York Yankees farm club from Cumberland to another city. To make matters worse, in December, club president Nelson W. Russler suffered serious injury in an automobile accident, leaving Cumberland with "no real leader to devote the necessary time" to organizing for 1933. The *Cumberland Evening Times* concluded it was "apparent that the city is going to be without organized ball this summer." Even in Johnstown, the league's strongest city from 1925 to 1932, red ink and pessimism dominated the hot stove baseball discussion. The *Charleroi Mail* moaned that "the outlook for organized baseball in Johnstown this summer is the gloomiest that it has been since the M. A. opened."[62]

On the brighter side, renewed interest among baseball supporters in Wheeling and Zanesville gave Daily and Hockenbury hope. Hockenbury even hinted that the MAL might grow to an eight-member circuit. Even before the calendar turned to a new year, Hockenbury let it be known that Altoona and Portsmouth, Ohio, could gain league membership if they came up with the financial backing and fields on which to play. At worst the MAL appeared assured of a six-club operation even if two clubs dropped out. Back in the summer of 1932 when it appeared likely that Clarksburg would not manage to finish the season, Daily and Hockenbury had worked hard in both Wheeling and Zanesville to find backers for a team. By October, a group of Wheeling businessmen announced the team's readiness to move forward.

Happily for Daily, Weiss' decision to pull the New York Yankees out of Cumberland did not mean the Yankees were out of the MAL. Weiss announced his plan to move his farm club to Wheeling. He had no trouble in leasing Fulton Park (a.k.a. Stogie Park) from the estate of Holloway, who had died the previous August. Would-be Wheeling investors did not fight the idea of absentee landlords, nor did Daily. The Yankees, after all, were the best team in baseball. Unlike the Yankees' arrangement in Cumberland where local officials ran the team, the Yankees would own and operate the franchise with Weiss serving as president of the Wheeling Stogies. He brought in young Earl Mann to be business manager of the Stogies. Mann, a 30-year-old Georgia native, would return to Atlanta in 1934 to begin his long career of running the Atlanta Crackers. In 1933 he just wanted to impress his Yankees boss.[63]

In Zanesville, Emmett "Turk" Reilly, a sporting goods salesman, took the lead in generating interest in a professional team. Reilly contacted his old friend Billy Evans, general manager of the Cleveland Indians, to seek assistance. Evans expressed interest in establishing a Cleveland farm team in Ohio, and put Reilly in contact with Henry B. "Buzz" Wetzel, a long-time minor league player and manager, who had scouted for Evans since 1929. Evans agreed to finance the operation and provide a core of players on the condition that the townspeople subscribe half the projected budget. Evans sent Wetzel to Zanesville to take charge. After a 30-year absence from Organized Baseball, Zanesville businessmen quickly answered Wetzel's call. Zanesville, with a population of 36,440 people, was just 75 miles west of Wheeling on the National Road (U.S. 40). The confluence of Licking Creek and Muskingum River divided the city into three distinct sections, but Zanesville's famous "Y" bridge linked the three districts. The city's factories, specializing in pottery, ceramic tile, mosaics and dishes included S.A. Weller, Roseville pottery, and Mosaic Tile Company. The city school board owned a bandbox park, Mark Park, built in 1923 at Putnam Avenue and Ontario Street. Its wooden grandstand sat 3,000 and included a cramped and musty clubhouse. The field's dimensions were tiny: 304 feet down the left field line, 386 feet to center, and a mere 265 feet to right, although a chicken-wire addition topped the right field fence. The school board agreed to lease the park to Wetzel.[64]

Daily called a February 26 meeting in Wheeling to admit the Stogies and Zanesville, and to transact other business. Admitting the two cities was *pro forma*; the problems were Cumberland and Clarksburg. Jack Marks, theater owner and head of the Clarksburg Boosters organization, and C.P. "Mike" Leatherwood, who ran a sports shop, had taken over the Clarksburg club from Clark. They worked hard to raise funds and managed to gather enough to pay off the debt, but, unfortunately, too little to offer any prospects of success. Local power broker Virgil Highland, who had believed in baseball, had died in 1930. His son Cecil was willing to let baseball die. Leatherwood, nevertheless, attended the Wheeling meeting to plead for more time. Cumberland did not even find anyone to represent the Colts. The local newspaper, noting the passing of professional baseball in town, lamented "no tears will be shed." Contrary to his past practice, Daily seemed ready to let the two troubled franchises fall by the wayside.[65]

At the beginning of April 1933 it remained unclear whether the MAL would open with six or eight clubs, although the smart money was on six. Finally some movement appeared in Cumberland, when Dr. H.B. Walker volunteered to assume a leadership role. Daily called a meeting for April 4 to approve a schedule and other business. Hockenbury came armed with two schedules, one for six teams and one for eight.[66]

Before the meeting, Howard "Ducky" Holmes, who owned the Dayton club of the Central League, had put out feelers to Daily about gaining admission to the MAL. Daily did not want to tamper with teams in another league, but he let Holmes know the precarious situation of Cumberland and Clarksburg. The Central League faced a crisis greater than the MAL. It was down to five teams with time running out. The members had agreed to an April 2 deadline. Evansville, Indiana, begged for an extension, but Holmes refused to extend the deadline and announced his intention to apply for membership in the Middle Atlantic League. Holmes got support from Alex Pisula, who had been business manager of Joe Cambria's Youngstown team, and hoped to operate a Central League team in Lima, Ohio, for Cambria. As the Central League collapsed, Pisula let it be known that he would apply to the MAL for a franchise in Springfield, Ohio.[67]

Both Holmes and Pisula attended the next MAL meeting in early April. The meeting proved contentious, as expected. This time, Cumberland sent a delegation of representatives, including two lawyers, to the meeting with a request for more time to organize support. That request found little sympathy among other owners. The Cumberland men then proposed making the MAL a 12-team league divided into two divisions of six teams. Members had not forget the fiasco of the 12-team league of 1931 and quickly voted down the proposal. The financial situation in Clarksburg remained unchanged. The most powerful man in town, banker, newspaper owner, and Republican Party stalwart Cecil Highland, blamed Franklin Roosevelt's bank holiday for the failure to raise funds. In reality, baseball had lost the support of Clarksburg's power elite and its public. Daily wanted to be done with both of the original league members and move west into larger locations. He managed to get the votes to oust Cumberland and Clarksburg. The Cumberland men stormed out of the meeting, threatening to appeal to Commissioner Landis. Bringing two more Ohio cities into the circuit, especially one as far west as Dayton, was another story. While Wheeling and Zanesville supported expansion, Johnstown strongly opposed, leaving the three southern West Virginia cities with the swing votes. It took until two o'clock in the morning, but Daily got the necessary votes to admit both Dayton and Springfield.[68]

After the stormy league meeting, Daily allowed as how he regretted losing the two original league members. "I'll bet they don't think much of me in either place tonight," Daily remarked. Perhaps so, but he looked forward to a "bright season ahead."[69] Indeed, the original, tight little league centered in western Pennsylvania and northern West Virginia had moved south and west, and grown considerably in population.

Springfield, Ohio, added 68,743 possible fans to the league. Located on the National Road (U.S. 40) 25 miles northeast of Dayton, "The Champion City" was home to International Harvester, one of the world's largest manufacturers of farm equipment, Crowell Publishing Company, publisher of *Colliers Weekly,* and the 4H clubs. Also known as the "City of Roses," Springfield claimed to produce more roses than any city in the country. The Springfield franchise went to Pisula, even though he lacked loyalty to Springfield or any other city. Pisula, who previously ran the Youngstown club of the Central League for Cambria, had owned the Central League franchise for Lima before he jumped to Springfield. The *Lima News,* with some truth, labeled him "a henchman for Joe Cambria." His patron's connection with Clark Griffith did assure Pisula of an agreement to work as a farm for the Washington Senators.[70]

Dayton, with its population of 200,982, dwarfed all the other MAL cities. Called "The Gem City" for no known reason, the city boasted of the National Cash Register Company and mammoth Wright-Patterson Air Field. Dayton owner Ducky Holmes brought color and excitement to the game. One league reporter wrote that "he gushes color in streams." Holmes liked his nickname "Ducky" so much he named his teams the Ducks. His other nickname, "the Schnooz," a reference to his rather large nose, found less favor. A catcher by trade, Holmes had played pro baseball from 1902 through 1912, getting to the major leagues for nine games with the St. Louis Cardinals in 1906. He managed in the minors for a few years after his playing career ended, and even served as a National League umpire for the 1923 and 1924 seasons. That umpiring experience did not give him any empathy for the game's arbiters. After returning to his native Dayton, he ran a grocery store in the East End before he got the Central League franchise in 1932. He purchased Young's Field from the estate of William H. Young, and renamed it North Side Field. The wooden grandstand needed much repair, but it sat 4,000 and had a cramped clubhouse under the grandstand, and unlike many parks it had a grass infield. Like most parks of the day, its dimensions were asymmetrical—370 feet in left field, 420 feet in center, but only 285 feet to the right field fence. Holmes brought with him a nice agreement with the Brooklyn Dodgers, who funded him $5,000 in addition to its farm hands.[71]

Baseball received a boost when Prohibition ended before the 1933 season began. Daily, surprisingly, announced that he was "strongly opposed to the sale of the amber beverage in ball parks," believing it endangered attendance by offending respectable people and women. The Pennsylvania Liquor Control Commission prohibited sale of beer to seated fans, but not from concession stands. That ruling affected only Johnstown. Owners, seeing dollars pouring in from beer sales, went their own way without much regard to Daily's opinions. Holmes was "especially in favor" of selling beer at his park. All other clubs followed his lead.[72]

The league clearly received another boost from the commitment of five major league clubs to affiliate with its teams. Four of the teams with major league affiliations—Wheeling, Zanesville, Dayton, and Springfield—finished in the first division of the 1933 standings. Only Huntington, which had a working agreement with Detroit, a team that seldom placed strong players in the MAL, was an exception; Stuart's club finished last. Zanesville, a Cleveland farm, won the first half of the split-season, with Wheeling a close second. The Stogies turned the tables on Zanesville in the second half with room to spare. Independents Beckley and Charleston started strong, finishing in a tie for third place in the first half, but then dropped out of the first division when the Brooklyn Dodgers in Dayton and the Washington Senators in Springfield placed more players in their farm clubs.

The additional big league connections meant the Middle Atlantic would graduate more players to the majors. Thirty-six players who performed in the MAL in 1933 went on to the big leagues. That represented a significant increase from the previous year when only 12 MAL players later made it to the big time. There were no Hall of Fame players in the lot, but several reached all-star status. Johnny Vander Meer (11–10) of Dayton later gained fame for pitching back-to-back no-hitters, the only player ever to perform such a feat. Dayton outfielder Jake Powell (.360) played 11 seasons with the Senators, Yankees and Phillies. He appeared in three World Series and was the leading hitter in the 1936 Series. Eddie Mayo (.301 at Johnstown and Huntington), a fine fielding second baseman, played nine seasons for the New York Giants, Boston Braves, Philadelphia Athletics, and Detroit Tigers.

Vander Meer had vivid memories of Dayton. The Dodgers signed him in spring 1933 and sent him to Dayton to earn $125 a month and learn from Ducky Holmes. Only the $125 was not there every month. He remembered that "when payday came around they'd say 'How much do you need to get by?'" At season's end he was owed $250. To make matters worse, Holmes recommended that the Dodgers not sign Vander Meer. Instead Holmes sold the youngster to Scranton, which is how the left-hander ended up in the Cincinnati organization.[73]

Even as the league was coming to be dominated by young prospects, there remained room for veteran players who had established a loyal fan following. Understandably, most dotted the rosters of the independent teams. Johnstown's losing record could not be attributed to the half-dozen players with five or more years in the league. George "Pepper" Berry led the league with a .361 average. Fellow outfielder Sam Thomas batted .353, hit a league-leading 42 doubles, and made the all-star team. Nat Hickey, who had played for the league champion Johnnies in 1925, batted .340. Bill Prichard, the dean of MAL players in his eighth year, who had won a batting title in 1927, hit a respectable .295. Pitcher Harvey Thompson posted an 11–8 mark, bringing his MAL record to 74 wins against 56 losses. The league home run champion of 1933, Mickey Noonan, had started at Fairmont in 1927. Beckley's Tom "Ace" Roberts won ten games, bringing his record for seven MAL seasons to 72–70. Sportswriters selected Charleston's Chick Helmick as the all-star pitcher. He compiled a record of 18–8, giving him a MAL career record of 103 victories and 45 defeats.

Zanesville's Greys possessed great pitching depth, with five pitchers posting double-digit wins. These included future big leaguers Clay Bryant, who led the way with 15 victories, followed by Steve "Smoky" Sundra with 14 wins, and Al "Happy" Milnar with 13. Elmer Hass (13–7) and Bert Grimm (10–8) rounded out a strong rotation. Milnar, the all-star lefty, led the league with 194 strikeouts. Infielders included future major leaguers Mike "Mickey" Bellande, the all-star third-baseman, shortstop Roy Hughes, who played every game and batted .322, and late-season addition Paul Speraw. The Greys' top hitter was 17-year-old outfielder Tony Fiarito, who earned all-star recognition after batting .328.

Wheeling manager Jack Sheehan possessed the league's best infield. First baseman John "Buddy" Hassett, second baseman Don Curry and shortstop Jimmy Hitchcock earned all-star recognition. The third baseman, rookie Bill

Crittenden, batted .312 and drove in a team-high 87 runs. Sheehan's favorite of the group was Hitchcock, a former All-American football player at Auburn, who led the Stogies with a .332 average. The handsome Alabama youngster ended up marrying Sheehan's daughter. The Stogies' pitching was none too shabby. Kemp Wicker, a 14-game winner, posted a skimpy 2.00 ERA, good enough to lead the entire minor leagues. It featured three future major leaguers. Joe Vitelli, won 16 games and Jim Tobin notched 13 victories. Their batterymates included Bill Holm and George "Skeets" Dickey, Bill Dickey's younger brother, both of whom went on to play in the majors.

Players of note dotted the rosters of other league teams. Young Rex McDonald of Springfield led the league with 19 wins and 255 innings pitched, but never approached those numbers again. The batting stars of 1932, Boone (Charleston) and Milner (Beckley and Dayton), would move on after 1933, but they could still hit. Boone batted .306 with 14 homers and Milner drove in 90 runs with a .343 average. The Dodgers put a load of prospects in Dayton, enough to give the Ducks more future major leaguers than any other team. These Ducks included pitchers Vander Meer (11–10) and Roger Wolff (8–7), first baseman Dick Siebert (.344), and outfielder Jake Powell (.360). Johnstown pitcher Andrew Mattis (6–6) gained notoriety of a different sort. After a tooth extraction, he contracted blood poisoning and died in August. Shortstop Frank "Fez" Oceck, who Wheeling sent to Johnstown after the arrival of Hitchcock, never made the majors as a player, but he did become a long-time coach with the Pittsburgh Pirates.[74]

In the championship playoff series, between first- and second-half winners, Zanesville demonstrated the veracity of the old adage that good pitching beats good hitting. Wheeling took game one with shutout pitching by Luther "Bud" Thomas and a home run from Hassett. Then Zanesville reeled off four straight wins to capture the championship. Milner pitched a three-hit shutout to beat Wicker in a pitchers' duel, 1–0, in game two. Zanesville took the series lead in game three when Jim Gleason connected for a two-run, walk-off home run off Tobin in the bottom of the ninth inning. Zanesville grabbed a commanding lead in game four, winning 4–1 behind the pitching of Grimm and the hitting of Fiarito, who blasted two homers to account for all of Zanesville's runs. In the final game, Bellande paced the Greys with three hits to give him a team-best .439 average for the series. Milner won his second game, to drive Zanesville to the 1933 Middle Atlantic League championship in its first season in the league.

President Daily had to be quietly proud. The league had completed the season with the same eight teams that had started the year and in the same place. Moreover, no financial crisis required Daily to spend weeks on the road trying to shore up one franchise or another. He modestly declared 1933 to have been "one of the most satisfactory seasons." In the first four years of the Great Depression, the modest little Middle Atlantic League had not only survived, it had grown. The league now covered a large swath of territory stretching from Johnstown in the east to Dayton in the west to Huntington in the south. The league had seen 20 franchise shifts in the four years since the Crash, but its population had grown from 226,000 to 599,620.[75]

3

A Minor League with Its Own Minor League
Pennsylvania State Association, 1934–1942

As the calendar turned to 1934, Elmer Daily felt good about his Middle Atlantic League. The league had survived a multitude of internal crises, franchise shifts, failures, and bankruptcies. In its first years, 1925 through 1929, the little Class C league had more nearly resembled a Class D loop. Daily had seen the MAL through the darkest days of the Great Depression, and managed to grow the league, including experimenting with a 12-team circuit. The growth always moved west and south as the geographic center of the MAL moved from Uniontown, Pennsylvania, to Zanesville, Ohio. In 1933 he had the league back to eight teams with a population befitting at least a Class B league. Major league teams showed a desire to either own or establish working agreements with Mid-Atlantic teams. Despite the continuing reality of the Depression, the future of the MAL had never looked more promising.

Better times were on the way. Across the country people had a little more money than a year before. Bank failures had virtually ended. Industrial unionism promised a brighter day for working people. As the National Recovery Administration (NRA) drafted codes of fair competition, the NRA's Blue Eagle sticker began to appear in factory and store windows. An NRA "boomlet" was underway. The Civil Works Administration was hiring the unemployed to work on massive civil works projects while the Civilian Conservation Corps was sending young men into forest camps to build recreation facilities and fight forest fires. Even if "happy days" were not yet here again, as least, the mood of the country had taken a turn for the better.

For Elmer Daily, it was time to be creative again. The man who thought a 12-team league would be a good idea was "thinking outside the box" again.

He proposed a startlingly different scheme. Why not create a Class D league to serve as a minor league for the Middle Atlantic League? Daily believed this arrangement would create a smooth flow of players from high school or the sandlots to Class D ball and then to his Class C league. Locating his new league in western Pennsylvania, it would be in close proximity to the Middle Atlantic League cities, facilitating joint tryout camps, spring training for both circuits, with the transfer of players between the two leagues.

To implement his plan, Daily would need to locate financial backers of new teams in the midst of the economic depression and to find major league teams willing to buy into his scheme and stock both the MAL and his proposed Class D league with players. In January 1934, Daily began to canvas small southwestern Pennsylvania cities. He wanted to locate franchises in cities tightly enough grouped that teams could all return home after away games. Since none of the cities would likely have lighted parks, teams would play afternoon games, making the return trip possible. He had contacts with baseball men in all of them, and with Chamber of Commerce types in most dating to his travails of the 1920s. He took to the road to seek out men willing to pony up money for a franchise in what he tentatively called the Monongahela Valley Association.[1]

He talked to men in Canonsburg, Donora, Monessen, Greensburg, Jeannette, Charleroi, McKeesport, Altoona, and Washington. He found enthusiastic interest in Charleroi and Washington. The Charleroi men who greeted Daily with enthusiasm were ones who had been involved with the Governors in the early years of the Middle Atlantic League. Former Charleroi Governors president and city mayor, Steve L. Woodward, and his associate, Dr. Charles H. Rosenblum, were anxious to try professional baseball again. They believed that Class D ball was the appropriate level for their city of 11,260.[2]

Washington, Pennsylvania, was the town where Daily had grown up. Locally referred to as "Little Washington" in deference to the national capital, the city had a population of 24,500. Located on the National Road (U.S. 40) between Cumberland and Wheeling, and some 30 miles south of Pittsburgh the city was a county seat. It was also home to Washington & Jefferson College boasted numerous glass factories and served as the commercial center to the surrounding region of coal mines, oil wells, and prosperous farms. Department store owner Ernest H. Sackville bought in to Daily's plan and took the leadership role. Although Washingtonians traditionally saw Wheeling, the nearest MAL city, as its natural rival, Sackville was delighted to work with the Stogies. George Weiss, president of the Stogies and New York Yankees farm director, quickly agreed to lend the Yankees' support to a team in Washington.[3]

By March an eight-team league appeared unlikely. Daily had found backers in Canonsburg and Donora, but neither town worked out. In Canonsburg, the only field in town stood at the base of a hill that would give free viewing to unlimited numbers of fans. No one was willing to give the product away, so Canonsburg would do without professional baseball. The St. Louis Cardinals expressed interest in placing a farm club in Donora, unrelated to any prospects in that town, but an acceptable park could not be found there either. Daily decided he would be content if he could find six solid members.

The Cardinals then agreed to support a team in Greensburg, Pennsylvania. There, another department store owner, I.F. Flynn, headed the subscription drive and attorney Maurice J.K. Davis chaired the organizing committee. Davis assumed the office of president. Greensburg, located southeast of Pittsburgh and a short trip from Charleroi and Washington, had a population of 16,000. It was home to numerous coke ovens, a plumbing supply factory, a glass factory and several other small industrial plants.[4]

Jeannette, like Charleroi, had been an early member of the MAL, but now Daily had difficulty drumming up support for a new team. At the urging of Joe Carr, Promotion Director of the NAPBL, Ray Ryan went to Jeannette to help Daily's efforts. Ryan, like Carr, a native of Ohio, was a baseball lifer. Short and squat, looking the part of a catcher grown to middle-age, which he was, Ryan had been a player and manager since the first decade of the century, but now he wanted his own team. A cigar-smoking, fast talker, he brought none of his own money but gave energy and enthusiasm to the task of garnering support for a team in a town that did not know him and had a bitter taste from its last experience with pro ball. Ryan managed, rather quickly, to succeed in finding investors. With Ryan at the helm as both president and field manager, Jeannette became the fourth city to commit to the new league.[5]

The owners with some kickback brought McKeesport into the new league. Although McKeesport's population of 54,632, twice the size of any other member, made it attractive to Daily, some members worried that its location would stretch the driving distance between towns. The city's baseball park was 30-years-old Cycler Field. Its grandstand creaked with age, its locker rooms cramped and crowded, and everything was desperately in need of repair. In the end, Daily had little choice but to take McKeesport. Theater owner John H. Harris agreed to take the team. Harris' father, John P. Harris, had been a theater mogul who opened one of the first nickelodeons in the country in 1906. By his death in 1929, he had built the palace theater in McKeesport, and owned dozens of other movie houses in western Pennsylvania. He also had been part owner of Boston's and Pittsburgh's National League teams. Entrepreneurialism, entertainment and baseball ran in the family. Further, young Harris had the money to bankroll a team.

Monessen had the disadvantage of being just across the Monongahela River from competitor Charleroi. Nevertheless, Mayor James Gold wanted a team for his town, believing that if Charleroi, Greensburg and Jeannette had teams, Monessen's self-respect demanded that it have a team. The steel and tin manufacturing city, named for the Monongahela River and Essen, home of the Krupp steel works in Germany, had a population of some 20,000. It also had a field of sorts called Tin Plate Park, on the property of the National Tin Plate Company. The park's wooden grandstand was always in need of repair, and its skinned infield always rutted. Mayor Gold organized a successful fund raising campaign and convinced Daily to accept the team in the as yet unnamed league.[6]

Daily settled on the name Pennsylvania State Association (PSA) for his new league. In its initial season the circuit consisted of the McKeesport

In one of its more creative experiments, the Middle Atlantic League formed the Pennsylvania State Association as its own minor league. Although the plan did not work for long, the Class D league lasted for a decade (Michele Duncan).

Tubers, Washington Generals, Greensburg Trojans, Monessen Indians, Jeannette Reds, and Charleroi Tigers, which were all Pennsylvania cities. Most cities were small, gritty, smoky industrial cities. McKeesport, a steel city of over 50,000, was the largest. Greensburg (16,508) was home to a variety of small industrial plants. Jeannette (15,126) had been known as the Glass City since 1889. Charleroi, the smallest city in the PSA, also produced glass. Monessen boasted a variety of metal products plants. All were within easy commuting distance. Washington to Greensburg was the only trip that took over one hour, and they were just 45 miles apart.

A change in the legal atmosphere in Pennsylvania made Daily optimistic. Pennsylvania's blue law prohibiting pro baseball on Sunday was eliminated. That limitation had been a scheduling nightmare in the first years of the Middle Atlantic League and had deprived teams of the lucrative Sunday gate. The Sabbatarian law had always been a class issue. Upper-class country club members could play golf and tennis on Sundays, but working men who depended on spectator sports were deprived of Sunday entertainment. Connie Mack, owner of the American League Philadelphia Athletics, had taken the lead in pressuring the Pennsylvania legislature to abolish the law. The lawmakers had long been sympathetic but unwilling to take on the Protestant establishment. In 1933 they tossed the issue to the voting public. In November of that year, voters approved a referendum to allow "commercial" sports on Sundays in the state.[7]

With only five other Class D leagues operating, National and American League clubs quickly lined up to affiliate with member teams just as Daily had hoped. With the help of Joe Carr, Daily made a point of linking each major league affiliation with both MAL and PSA franchises. The New York Yankees, who owned the Wheeling Stogies, worked with the new Washington Generals. The St. Louis Cardinals, already affiliated with Huntington in the MAL, established a working agreement with the Greensburg Trojans. Beckley of the MAL found an affiliation with the Cincinnati Reds, who also developed an agreement with Ray Ryan's operation in Jeannette. The Pittsburgh Pirates aligned with McKeesport Tubers and with the Springfield team of the MAL. Detroit, already linked up with the Charleston Senators, signed a pact with Charleroi. The Cleveland Indians, already affiliated with Zanesville, developed a working agreement with Monessen. In the first year, the MAL and PSA teams held joint tryout camps and shared the same spring training facility; of course, the training period usually lasted just two weeks.

Owners quickly agreed to a number of policies for operating the league. Just as in the early years of the MAL, PSA teams played all day games. Most teams, recognizing the necessity of attracting working-class fans, but not having lights, they started games at 4:30 or 5:00 o'clock in the afternoon. The starting time represented a change from the early MAL years when games began at 3:00 o'clock in the hope of appealing to middle-class and professional customers. The tight geographic proximity, all less than 50 miles apart, allowed visiting teams to pile into cars and return home every night. The owners decided on a split-season format with a postseason playoff between the winners of the two halves to determine the league championship. They wanted a bare-bones operation, so teams would be allowed to carry no more than 14 players on their rosters. Owners set the monthly salary cap at a mere $1,000; that averaged out to $71 per player per month, not much money even in the Depression, but more than players could earn in the mills of member cities. For away games, players did receive 50 cents a day for meal money. The owners had no problem in accepting Daily's recommendation that Russell Hockenbury serve as secretary-treasurer of the league. Hockenbury, of course, held the same position in the Middle Atlantic League.[8]

The 1934 season went well for the little league. Attendance was all Daily had hoped for, except at Jeannette, which faced financial difficulties as it had previously in the MAL. The league enjoyed a tight race. Manager Benny Bengough's Washington club and Ryan's Jeannette team finished tied at the end of the first half of the season. Washington beat the Jeannette Reds in a best-of-three-games series, two games to one, to determine the first-half champs. The Generals featured the hitting of Al "Dutch" Mele (.311) and all-star shortstop John Dudick (.321). The Reds countered with Jimmy Outlaw (.340) and Al Rubeling (.290), both of whom would become solid regulars in the majors. The player who ended up with the highest career major league average, however, was second baseman Jerry Lynn, who batted only .263 at Jeannette, but retired with a major league career average of .666. The trick was that Lynn played in only one game for the Washington Senators at the end of the 1937 season, getting two hits in three at-bats. He never again wore a big league uniform.

Greensburg, the St. Louis Cardinal's farm club, ran away with the second half. Then Greensburg knocked off Washington, four games to two, for the title. Greensburg's playing manager Clay Hooper (.326), beginning a 25-year managerial career, garnered manager of the year honors. He relied on PSA all-stars and future major leaguers second baseman Lynn Myers (.338), first baseman Ed Morgan (.294) and pitcher Tom Sunkel (16-5), to pace the Trojans' attack.

Curiously, last-place Monessen prided itself on having the best players. League all-star outfielders Tommy Henrich and Carl Huffman dominated the league hitting statistics. Huffman, batting in the leadoff position, led the

PSA in batting (.373), runs (93) and base hits (153). Henrich, a "sterling young outfielder" as the local newspaper labeled him, was an 18 year old from Massillon, Ohio, who clubbed 15 home runs, the highest in the league, and batted .326. After being freed from the Cleveland Indians farm system by Judge Landis in 1937, Henrich went on to help the New York Yankees to seven World Series titles. In 11 major league seasons, he gained the nickname "Old Reliable" for his clutch hitting. Huffman, however, never made the majors. That Monessen club also included Mike McCormick. Just 17 years old and away from home for the first time, the California lad struggled, batting an anemic .235, but he stuck with it and later became a productive major leaguer for ten seasons. Two pitchers, Tommy Reis and Charley Stanceu, also made the major leagues.[9]

Daily's expectation that players would flow smoothly between the Pennsylvania State Association and the Middle Atlantic League worked well the first two seasons. Cleveland, especially, used the connection between Monessen and Zanesville in the fashion Daily had imagined. Most Monessen players had been signed to a Zanesville contract and then optioned to Monessen. Eleven members of the Monessen club, including manager Earl Wolgamot, moved up to Zanesville in 1935, where, with a year of pro ball under their belt, they helped the Greys to the MAL pennant. Some 30 some players in all moved up from the PSA to the MAL for the 1935 season.

Daily hoped to expand the league to eight members, but, as was often the case in the low minor leagues, he had to scurry just to keep the same number. Ryan, who operated and managed the Jeannette franchise, lacked the personal capital to support the team, and attendance proved disappointing despite the team having the second-best overall record for the season.

Before the start of the 1935 season, Daily moved the Jeannette franchise to Butler, a small city of 23,368 north of Pittsburgh. It proved to be a good decision. John J. "Jack" Dunlevy, manager of a gas pipeline company, who had worked tirelessly to gain the franchise for Butler, would create the PSA's most successful operation, and become Daily's most valuable ally. Butler proved to be a good baseball town, regularly among the leaders in attendance. The team's Pullman Park, built in a gritty industrial area within ten feet of the Pullman Railcar Manufacturing Company plant, had the advantage of being new if not fancy. It had seating for 1,300 in stands under a free-standing roof down the first base line, and bleachers down the third base line giving it a capacity of 3,000. Concrete-block dugouts were at ground level. The park had spacious dimensions, 356 feet to left field, 351 feet to right, and 425 feet to the center field fence. The Cleveland Indians, Monessen's 1934 partner, hooked up with Butler for 1935. Cleveland continued to shuttle players back and forth between its PSA affiliate and Zanesville. For other teams there was a downside to having Butler in the league. The distance to Butler from Jeannette, Washington, Greensburg and Charleroi was greater than any team had to travel in 1934. Washington to Butler was the longest hop, at over two hours through Pittsburgh. Following games at Butler, teams would get home well after dark, but before midnight, so as life went in the low minors, this was not overly burdensome.[10]

Daily's dream of a connection between PSA teams and those in the Middle Atlantic circuit continued to work well, but began to show cracks in the second year of the Class D league. The Pittsburgh Pirates dropped their affiliation with McKeesport. Daily did his best to convince Brooklyn to take up affiliation with a PSA team. The Dodgers were the only major league team with a MAL affiliation not already aligned with a club in the PSA. Daily's best efforts failed to convince the Dodgers to adopt McKeesport. In order to get a major league sponsor for McKeesport, Daily had to turn to the Boston National League club. That shifting left McKeesport without a MAL partner, breaking the one-to-one connection between all the clubs in the two leagues.

Monessen and Washington captured the split-season flags in 1935, although Monessen, with a strong second half, finished 13 games better than Washington did for the full season. Monessen manager Milt Stock, fielded a strong cast of players. Outfielders Harry Craft (.317) and Joe Mack (.321) plus third baseman Al Rubeling (.312) made the PSA all-star team and, later, the majors. Southpaw pitcher Walt Purcey (16–6) led the league in wins. Craft topped the circuit in base hits (137) and home runs (14). Washington countered with infield sparkplug Pete Suder (.294), and outfielders Charles Harig (.320) and Mike Milosevich (.294). Monessen came out on top in the playoffs, four games to two. Craft and Rubeling carried the offensive load. Purcey won two games and saved the crucial fourth game when he entered the game with the bases loaded and none out in the ninth inning.[11]

Two other players, Mike McCormick of Butler and Ken Heintzelman of McKeesport, stood out as big-time prospects. McCormick, who had struggled against pro pitching in 1934 at Monessen, launched his career in 1935. He batted a league-best .344 with 13 triples, also tops in the league, before being called up to Zanesville. By 1937 the Indians understood he was a serious prospect, but he was out of options. After Cleveland "sold" him to Buffalo, with the understanding he would be returned to the Indians, Commissioner Landis declared him a free agent. McCormick then signed with Indianapolis, a Cincinnati Reds farm, and the following year he was in a Reds uniform. Heintzelman, a teenaged left-hander, posted a modest 10–11 record, but he struck out a league-high 147 batters. By the time he was 21, he would embark on a 13-year big league career.

In the offseason, Daily continued his efforts to expand the league to eight teams. He explored possible backers in Beaver Falls, Kittanning, Ford City, Uniontown, and Jeannette, where a local theater owner showed interest in reviving baseball in the town. After a snow storm trapped Daily in Ebensburg, postponing the winter meeting, the owners balked at expanding the league footprint because of added costs for travel and hotels.[12]

Before Daily could find additional clubs, he faced problems with the existing teams. The 1935 McKeesport Braves had played badly and attendance declined accordingly. Owner John Harris had the money to absorb the losses, but not the inclination to do so. He first announced his intent to return the franchise to the league, but then decided to transfer his club to Jeannette. He never explained the logic of leaving a city of 54,000 for one of 15,000 that had been unable to support a team in 1934. Harris did own a theater in Jeannette, which may have influenced his decision. In any event, whatever Harris' reason, Jeannette returned to the league and promptly signed a working agreement with the Pittsburgh Pirates.[13]

Trouble also appeared in Washington. The Generals had played at the Washington & Jefferson College field for two years. Now, the college informed the team it would no longer lease it to the professional outfit. Nor would the Washington school board allow the team to use the high school field. With no other suitable location in town, the club had no other choice but to vacate the franchise.[14]

With Washington and McKeesport out, leaving the league short a team, the *Monessen Daily Independent* ran the banner headline "Penn State Association Collapse." The paper had not reckoned with Daily's ability to keep leagues alive. A Class D league could not easily give up on a city with the population of McKeesport, so that was where Daily focused his energy. As he had done in 1934, he contacted Ray Ryan, who had held the Jeannette franchise two years earlier. Ryan, who had already logged in 30 years as a minor league player and manager, had spent 1935 as manager of Allentown of the New York-Penn League, but he envisioned himself as more than a manager. He jumped at the opportunity to operate a team in McKeesport. The Boston National League club, with its own financial problems and a name change from Braves to Bees, continued its relationship with McKeesport, but provided little in the way of help.[15]

Although the PSA again opened with six teams in 1936, Daily's hope for linkages between PSA and MAL teams was slipping away. The Yankees, Cardinals, and Indians each held tryout camps and spring training for both their MAL and PSA affiliates at the same location. The Cards' PSA affiliate trained in Portsmouth, Ohio, throughout the 1930s. The Yankees' Gene Martin, who served as business manager of their affiliates in Wheeling and then Akron, moved players between the two leagues with regularity. The Pirates and Tigers broke the connection between the two, and the Braves had no affiliate in the MAL. Increasingly, the only connection between the two leagues was a common league president.

PSA teams, like those of the MAL, loaded up with exhibition games. Always a good draw, Cumberland Posey obliged any club that wanted to schedule his Homestead Grays in April. In the mid–1930s the Grays had competition from the Pittsburgh Crawfords, the best African-American team in the country, and, perhaps, the best team period. Most teams also tried to schedule the popular House of David team. Art Rooney's semi-pro team from Pittsburgh was a popular draw as well. In 1936, Charleroi scheduled teams as varied as the Pittsburgh Crawfords, House of David, St. Vincent College, Homestead Grays, Akron of the MAL, and the York team of the Class A New York-Penn League. York had become a highly sought-after opponent because the famous, or infamous, Alabama Pitts played for them. Pitts, a criminal who wanted to try his hand at pro baseball upon his release from jail, became a *cause celeb*. Many people believed his presence in Organized Baseball would tarnish the image of the sport. Pitts failed to impress Charleroi fans. *Charleroi Mail* sports editor Harry Barnett wrote, "He didn't look like much of a hitter." It quickly became clear that Barnett knew what he was talking about, and Pitts quietly left baseball before the season ended.[16]

Jeannette's Little Pirates won the first half of the 1936 campaign, while Greensburg's Red Wings took the second half. Lefty Ken Heintzelman, in his second year at Jeannette, dominated PSA batters. He won 20 games, the most in the league, while losing only eight times. He struck out 229 batters to lead in that category for the second straight year. Both his win and strikeout totals would stand as the all-time best for the PSA. He also worked the most innings (243) in the league. No one in the PSA was surprised when he began his big league career the following season.

Greensburg and Jeannette finished the season with the identical record of 66 wins and 44 losses. Greensburg did not have a pitcher as dominant as Heintzelman, but its ace, Frank "Rube" Melton (13–4), would spend time between 1941 and 1947 in the uniforms of the Phillies and Dodgers. Melton's 2.16 ERA was the lowest in the league. He did not get his nickname because he was an untutored farm boy, as fans thought, but as a diminutive of his full name Rueben Franklin Melton. In the playoffs, it was Heintzelman, not Melton, who dominated. He led Jeannette to the championship as the Jays won four games to two over Greensburg.

Monessen, despite a fourth-place finish, again was loaded with talent. Shortstop John Dudick captured the batting title with a .383 batting average. His double-play mate, Alex Clawson, finished right behind with a .370 average and led the circuit in hits. Outfielder Bill Fuchs clubbed 24 home runs to lead in that category. None of those three continued hitting long enough to make the majors, but several teammates did. George "Bingo" Binks, an outfielder, and pitchers Mike Palagyi and Jack "Tex" Kraus went on to play on baseball's biggest stage.

Another 1936 PSA player of note, Charleroi's Danny Litwhiler, got his first taste of professional ball and acquitted himself well, leading the Tigers with a .313 batting average. The Pennsylvania German youngster started the season late because he had to finish his sophomore year at Bloomsburg State Teachers College. Charleroi club president Steve Woodward signed the teenager to his first contract while Litwhiler was underage. After deciding he was a keeper, the Tigers had Danny and his father sign another contract, with a bonus of $200, better than his $75 a month contract. He remembered manager John McIlvaine as old, gangly, loud and deaf. The venerable manager did pitch in seven games, failing to win in three decisions. The Young Litwhiler went on to play 11 major league seasons for the Braves, Cardinals, Phillies and Reds, batting a solid .281 and playing in two World Series. After his playing days, he had an illustrious career as a college coach, first at Florida State (1955–1963) and then at Michigan State (1964–1982). He is credited with being the first player to lace the fingers of his glove together, as well as developing a prototype of the JUGS radar gun and creating a product today called Diamond Grit for drying wet dirt.[17]

Three league cities faced crises before the 1937 season. First, Charleroi lost its field when the local school board decided to construct a football stadium on the multipurpose Athletic Field site. Scheduled for completion by the fall football season, the site could not be used for baseball in the summer. Second, in McKeesport, Ryan left town to organize his own league, the Mountain State League, which operated in the coal fields of southern West Virginia from 1937 through 1942. Even worse, the owner of ancient Cycler Park died and his estate sold the park to Spritz Auto Wrecking Company for use as a junkyard. Third, the Pittsburgh Pirates decided to pull out of Jeannette, leaving that franchise in serious danger.[18]

As usual, Daily had made his January junket through small cities searching for potential backers of new franchises. His stops this time included Titusville, Oil City, New Castle, Beaver Falls, New Kensington, and West Newton. He found success in Beaver Falls where local businessmen were prepared to back a team to replace Charleroi. The Boston Bees agreed to stock the team with players. At the last minute, Jeannette managed to get a working agreement with the Buffalo Bisons of the International League, so it would open the season. In a surprise move, the Brooklyn Dodgers, a team Daily had courted unsuccessfully for several years, decided to purchase the Greensburg franchise itself. The Cleveland Indians, who had been affiliated with the PSA since its inception, decided to end its connection to Monessen, but the St. Louis Cardinals, who previously had a working agreement with Greensburg, shifted to Monessen.[19]

As opening day neared, the *Charleroi Mail* announced that Daily "has done the impossible again." He had five teams in the fold and had convinced the owners of Cycler Park to postpone their plans for a junkyard, but he still needed backers for the McKeesport franchise. Daily finally found an investor to take over the Tubers, a New Yorker named Bill O'Brien. He would have to operate the team in McKeesport without a major league affiliation. O'Brien set up and hired a manager who held a tryout and signed players. However, on opening day, O'Brien got cold feet and fled town. Rather than run the league with five teams, Daily agreed to operate the McKeesport club himself for the league.[20]

The 1937 Pennsylvania State Association season got underway on May 13 with six teams. When the carousel of moving franchises stopped, the Butler Yankees, Beaver Falls Bees, and Monessen Cardinals had working agreements with major league clubs. The Greensburg Green Sox were now owned by Brooklyn. Jeannette linked up with Buffalo, leaving the McKeesport Tubers to operate as an independent. As it had in the past, the league operated with a $1,000 per month maximum salary cap and a 130-game schedule. Brooklyn decided to install lights at the Greensburg High School field. Not to be outdone, early in the season the Yankees put in arc lights at Pullman Park in Butler. James Gold, mayor of Monessen and president of the ball club, pushed for funding in his town, but local powers shot down the idea.[21]

Rainy weather played havoc with early season games and flooded Tin Plate Field in Monessen, forcing players to join in the work on repairs. Leo "Muscle" Shoals remembered his introduction to professional baseball in Monessen. After a cold, rainy "spring" training in Portsmouth, and two nights sleeping in a car on the way to Monessen, he and his teammates went to work repairing the field and stands. Shoals helped install a chicken-wire backstop in front of the grandstand. The work was good practice because, when the season started, infielders had responsibility for raking their area of the infield dirt. He remembered his uniform with a red "R" on the cap (hand-me-downs from Rochester) and a pair of red wings sprouting from a baseball on the uniform shirt.[22]

3. A Minor League with Its Own Minor League 95

After the first month of the season, with Butler holding a seven-game lead, crisis struck. Jeannette had failed to post the league-mandated $1,500 guarantee. Twice, Jeannette president Harry W. Layh failed to provide the funds to the league, but claimed the money had been promised by Buffalo. Finally, on June 10, it became clear the money would not be forthcoming. The other owners felt they had little choice but to vote Jeannette out of the league even though the Bisons had a winning record (13–11) when they folded on June 6. With only five teams left, Daily decided it would be the better part of valor to give up his operation in McKeesport. The Tubers were losing games for their few fans, and money for the league and for Daily personally. The PSA would continue as a four-team circuit. At the time the two teams departed, Butler was making a run-away of the pennant race with a 19–4 record. Butler president Jack Dunlevy proposed to wash away the records and start over as a split-season; a new first half would begin on June 13. Butler's gift to the other teams mattered little in the first half as the Yankees coasted to the best record on July 20.[23]

Monessen finished at the bottom of the first-half standings after winning just one game in the shortened session. Mayor Gold faced the loss of its franchise. If one more team dropped out, the league would be finished as well. Monessen had averaged just 100 paying customers for weekday games in July. Business manager Andy French, whom the parent Cardinals sent to Monessen to operate the club, demanded lights for Tin Plate Park as a means of improving attendance. *Monessen Independent* sports editor Charles Kramer took up the call for lights. The 5:00 o'clock start for weekday games was the problem, Kramer maintained. The shift in the steel mills ended at 4:00 o'clock, leaving insufficient time for workers to get home, clean up, have dinner and get to the park by game time. Lights, he was certain, would solve the problem. Kramer linked his demand for lights with a call for St. Louis to send better players. Daily came to town to orchestrate a meeting between Gold, French and officials of the local Chamber of Commerce. They agreed to purchase a lighting system for $2,500 from an Akron, Ohio, company. According to Kramer, the club would put up $1,000 and the Chamber would contribute the remainder. After a phone conversation with Branch Rickey, French promised an influx of better players. Unfortunately, the businessmen of the Chamber of Commerce failed to come up with the funds and the Cardinals for their part failed to send any prospects. Somehow the Redbirds managed to finish the season, buried deep in last place.[24]

Not surprisingly, given their record, none of the Monessen players made it to St. Louis, but Andy French, during his season there, discovered the player who would become the Cardinals' greatest player of all-time, Stan "The Man"

Musial. French had heard about a kid who pitched and played first base for the American Legion team in nearby Donora, and invited him to a tryout camp at Monessen. French filed the first scouting report on Musial, calling him "raw," but possessing a "pretty fair curve ball" as a pitcher. French had the youngster work out with Red Wings manager Ollie Vanek. The more French saw, the more he appreciated the talent. French had to work very hard to overcome the objection of Stan's father, who wanted his son to go to work or to attend college, depending on which version of the story one accepts. French's work paid off. Young Musial signed a contract to play for Monessen. He never played there. The Cardinals thought it better for the youngster to wait until 1938 to begin his baseball career. The Cards sent him to Williamson, West Virginia, in Ryan's Mountain State League as a pitcher. Musial only lasted one season as a pitcher before he converted to a hitter.[25]

In August, the Butler Yankees went into a slump, allowing Beaver Falls to capture the second-half title, with Greensburg a close second. Even so, the Yankees compiled the best overall record. The parent Yankees again loaded Butler with talent. Second baseman John Russian hit a resounding .393, a mark that stood as the highest average ever achieved in PSA play. Outfielder Billy Johnson, who hit .356, would log in nine major league seasons. In an exciting seven-game playoff, Butler trimmed Beaver Falls by scoring three runs in the bottom of the ninth inning of the seventh game to gain the victory. Butler pitcher-manager Ernest "Lefty" Jenkins won three playoff games and shortstop Lloyd "Dinty" Moore was an RBI machine in the series, including three RBIs in game seven.[26]

Each of the four teams had a first baseman of note. Beaver Falls' 20-year-old Joe Zagami (.298) won all-star honors at the position. The left-handed hitter knocked around the low minors for ten years, never even making it to Class AA ball before retiring. Butler's Hank Sauer, Greenburg's Eddie Lopat and Monessen's Leo Shoals compiled more illustrious careers.

Sauer would eventually become the best hitter to come out of the 1937 PSA season. Playing in his first season of professional ball, the big (6-foot-4, 200 pound), raw, Pittsburgh native struggled at the plate. He managed to hit a weak .268 with only three home runs. Despite that slow start to his career, Sauer would go on to spend 15 seasons in the big-time, mostly with the Cincinnati Reds and Chicago Cubs, where he had his best seasons. On six different occasions he banged out 30 home runs or more. He led the National League in homers and RBIs in 1952. Those numbers garnered him the NL's Most Valuable Player Award.

At Greensburg, Eddie Lopat struggled even more than did Sauer. The New York native, still a teenager at the start of the season and away from home for the first time, batted a pathetic .229 without noticeable power. Muscle Shoals remembered Lopat moaning, "I can't pull the ball and I can't hit the curve." It was becoming clear that he might have a brighter future as a pitcher than as a first baseman. Once he shifted to the mound, as he did the following season, "Steady Eddie" was on his way to a 12-year big league career with the White Sox and Yankees, in which he enjoyed five World Series with New York.[27]

Unlike Sauer and Lopat, Shoals had no trouble hitting PSA pitching. Monessen fans, at least what few they had, fell in love with "Muscle" Shoals. Also known as "Lefty," the West Virginia native led the league in doubles and total bases, while finishing second in batting with a .366 average and crushing 18 dingers. These numbers clearly suggest that he should have been the all-star first baseman, but it foreshadowed Shoals' career. Shoals kept hitting year after year, becoming one of the great hitters of the low minor leagues, but he never got the opportunity to hit in the major leagues. When he retired in 1955 after 1,800 games, he had hit 362 minor league home runs and driven in 1,529 runs. On seven occasions he led his league in homers.

Each year Daily faced the task of rebuilding the league. The Yankees in Butler and the Dodgers in Greensburg gave him a solid base for 1938. Beyond those two Daily faced shifting sand. The PSA from its inception depended on major league teams for support. Upset by the condition of Tin Plate Field, the failure to install lights, and poor attendance, the St. Louis Cardinals pulled out of Monessen. The Boston Bees, after one year, left Beaver Falls. During the offseason Daily and Hockenbury once again visited Titusville and added stops in Ellwood City and Meadville, but nothing came of their canvas. Daily devoted the most time to Washington. Mayor E.G. Rowland was sympathetic, and a local organizer, Lewis Paul, put committees together to explore field sites, costs of lights and other matters. Dunlevy also visited Washington, adding his weight to the push to get Washington back into the league. The field issue, however, remained unresolved, so Washington went through another summer without a team.[28]

In McKeesport, the city parks department managed to get title to Cycler Field. Popular city councilman Ben Rosenberg stepped forward to organize support among merchants and other businessmen for a new team. He convinced enough backers that "this is just what the city needs." Rosenberg became the club president and began work on installing lights in the ballpark. He persuaded the Pittsburgh Pirates to back the team. Daily was delighted to accept McKeesport back into the league.[29]

The Pennsylvania State Association, again, went with only four teams for 1938. The St. Louis Browns agreed to affiliate with Beaver Falls, making

Operating out of the Penn-Eben Hotel, one of two hotels he owned in the mountain-top community of Ebensburg, Pennsylvania, Elmer Daily served as president of both the Middle Atlantic League and the Pennsylvania State Association (National Baseball Hall of Fame Library, Cooperstown, New York).

it possible for Claire Donnelly's club to continue. Butler, McKeesport and Greensburg rounded out the league. On a positive note, all four teams played under the lights and had agreements with major league clubs.[30]

The Butler Yankees fielded the strongest team in 1938, as they had done the previous year. McKeesport did manage to slip past Butler to take the second-half title and force a playoff. Hank Sauer, who had struggled in 1937, enjoyed a breakout season. Sauer was listed as a 19-year-old, but was really 21. He had spent time in the Civilian Conservation Corps, earning $22 month, before signing with Yankees scout Gene McCann in 1936. He led the PSA in 1938 in batting (.350), hits (135), runs (89), and doubles (29). Not surprisingly Sauer made the all-star team along with second baseman Dan Hayes (.291) and outfielder John Hyder (.340). Writers selected Ernest "Lefty" Jenkins as manager of the year. Third baseman Don Savage (.314), outfielder Jim Russell (.320), along with pitchers Herb "Lefty" Karpel (6–5) and Mel Queen, and, of course, Sauer, made the majors from that club.

McKeesport could not match Butler's firepower. Only outfielder Frank "Fats" Kalin (.346) and first baseman Harry Sweeney (.315) hit over .300. Pitcher Justin Fest was the league's best moundsman. His 16 wins and 1.87 ERA were league bests. He got one win in the playoffs, but that was the Tubers' only victory. Butler had little difficulty in disposing of the Tubers, winning four games to one.

Daily never quite achieved his goal of organizing the PSA in the desired fashion. He always hoped for an eight-team league, but he never achieved that objective. However, six teams were far better than the four teams his league had gone with in 1938. An original member of the Middle Atlantic League, Johnstown lost its franchise in that league when the St. Louis Browns, owners of the team, decided to move away from Johnstown because of poor attendance, mounting debt, and flood waters. Daily was delighted to accept Johnstown into the PSA. After the Browns pulled out, George "Chick" Cooper, sports editor of the *Johnstown Tribune*, began work to get a team in the PSA. He knew lots of people. In addition to his duties with the newspaper, he had chaired the city's Recreation Commission since 1936, a position that put him into contact with men interested in baseball. Cooper lined up people who wanted baseball to continue in the Flood City. They incorporated as The Johnnies, Inc. Cooper became the club president, a position he would hold for over a decade. The Philadelphia Phillies, who had not previously been involved with the league, agreed to a working agreement with Johnstown.[31]

The men trying to get a Washington franchise up and running finally succeeded. It took sheriff Matt Armstrong's and mayor E.G. Rowland's leadership to make it happen. Washington & Jefferson College refused to budge on the use of its field, but Armstrong and Rowland had more success in putting pressure on the school board, which finally agreed to allow the team to play at Washington High School Stadium. Armstrong agreed to stay on as team president. The St. Louis Cardinals jumped at the chance to affiliate with Washington. Both Washington and Johnstown would be solid members as long as the PSA operated.[32]

In another change, the Brooklyn Dodgers gave up on Greensburg. A syndicate headed by Howard Strange of Mansfield, Pennsylvania, and Howard Gee of Lansing, Michigan, purchased the Greensburg franchise from Brooklyn. Not surprisingly, the Dodgers refused to affiliate with the new owners. In order to get a major league affiliation, Strange and Gee had little choice but to arrange a working agreement with the Washington Senators, a team not known for a strong minor league system.[33]

Butler again dominated the 1939 regular season. Karl Drews led the Yankees and the league with 16 victories. Except for Drews, and rookie Joe Collins, whose .176 batting average attests to his struggles in his first year of professional ball, Butler was devoid of prospects who continued to progress to the majors. They did have a hustling team led by all-star catcher Ted Bosciak (.335), outfielder Charles Jamin, who posted the best batting average (.367), and another outfielder, Arnold Evans (.349), who led the league in stolen bases, hits, and runs.

The St. Louis Cardinals gave the managerial reins at Washington to Bob Scheffing, once a catching prospect, now a 25-year-old with a lame arm. His club finished a strong second. Scheffing had signed with the St. Louis Cardinals in 1935 as a strong-armed catching prospect, and reached Columbus, the top rung of the minors, before a sore arm apparently ended his catching career. Branch Rickey refused to give up on Scheffing, giving him instructions to play first base where he would have little need to throw. Scheffing batted .330, led the league in RBIs (96), and finished second in home runs. More importantly, toward the end of the season his arm came back to life. In 1940 he was back on track to becoming a big league catcher. After one season at Rochester he reached the majors in 1941. Washington also had a fine outfielder in 18-year-old Dick Sisler, son of Hall of Fame first baseman George Sisler. He batted .319 with the PSA-best 16 home runs. Sisler had his finest major league season in 1950 for the Phillies' Whiz Kids.

The PSA went to the Shaughnessy playoff system for the first time in 1939, shelving the awkward split-season format. Butler dispatched the Beaver Falls Browns, the third-place finisher, in the first round. Beaver Falls relied on ace left-hander Earl Jones (15–7, 3.52), the league strikeout leader, but he could not pitch every day. Washington just nipped Johnstown three games to two to reach the finals. Washington then surprised Butler, winning three straight games behind the strong pitching of Doyle Mills, whose 2.32 ERA led the league, and all-star selection Wilson Koewing (15–6), and the hitting of Scheffing and outfielder Lenny Frest (.336).

For the low minor leagues, maintaining membership always loomed as the paramount issue. The NAPBL's man to find leagues and teams had been Joe Carr until he died in May 1939. Carr's last project had been to help plan the gala celebration of baseball's centennial in 1939. Elmer Daily, already president of two leagues and owner of a hotel, succeeded Carr as promotion director for the minor leagues. The new job kept Daily on the road for much of the year. Centennial celebrations took much of his time in 1939 while old-timers games and other events at parks around the country kept Daily's calendar full. His new position, however, did not appreciably help in nailing down teams for the PSA. No matter how hard Daily tried, he failed to achieve his goal of an eight-team league. Before the 1940 season he again had to scurry to get even six teams lined up.[34]

Although no club but Johnstown reported a profit in 1939, all the teams except Greensburg were able to answer the bell in 1940. The Washington Senators gave up on Greensburg after one season. Without a major league team willing to help it, Greensburg relinquished its franchise. Men in several towns expressed interest in joining the league, including Meadville, Altoona, Charleroi and Canonsburg, Pennsylvania, and Alliance and Warren, Ohio. Interest, as usual, did not equate to investment dollars.

Only Warren, Ohio, came up with the needed financial support. For the first and only time in PSA history, Daily went outside Pennsylvania, if only by 15 miles, to Warren, a city of 42,837 in the Mahoning Valley not far from the Ohio River. The city had a bare-bones baseball park, but suitable for Class D ball. A resident named Tom Leffingwell took the leadership role in nailing down investors and raising money for lights. Moreover, the Cleveland Indians were willing to support the franchise, which would be dubbed the Redskins.[35]

The 1940 season opened to rainy, cold days, weather that kept fans away from the ballparks. McKeesport suffered the most. Crowds dwindled in May and the trend continued through June. In mid–June the team could not meet its payroll, leading the owners to sack their business manager. By July 4, Charles Howe, an accountant and majority stockholder, and his fellow investors, decided to cut their losses. On July 5 Daily shifted the franchise to Oil City, Pennsylvania. Daily had developed contacts in the northwestern Pennsylvania city of 37,328 during his annual visits. The editor of the *Oil City Blizzard*, Richard Amberg, wanted a team for his city and agreed to cover any losses. Oil City, however, lacked a field. Even so, for Daily, that was a no-brainer. The locals managed to quickly create a stock company to raise funds for the franchise and operate the team. They did, in fact, create a playing field named Ramage-Hasson Field, with a tiny covered grandstand and symmetrical dimensions (325–395–325). Members of the Oil City Baseball Club moved lights, bleachers and fences from McKeesport to Oil City. In two weeks the "Oilers" were ready to play in their new home. The move proved a good decision. For the remainder of the season the team averaged 1,500 fans.[36]

Throughout his tenure as league president, Daily often dealt with rhubarbs, usually between managers and his league umpires. As did most league presidents, Daily did his best to protect his umpires from abuse. In June 1939 he suspended McKeesport manager Leo Mackey indefinitely for an attack on an umpire. In 1940 he did not support his ump, and it led to him being chastised by the Commissioner Landis. In a June 6 game at Beaver Falls, where the home-standing Browns played Johnstown, a heated dispute broke out between Frank "Fez" Oceak, player-manager of the home team, and umpire Lenn Bugher over a foul ball. Cooler heads did not prevail. According to witnesses, Bugher was the aggressor in the argument, but it was Oceak who hit the umpire "a vicious blow," knocking him to the dirt. After the game W.E. Milliken, chairman of the board of the Beaver Falls club, and its business manager, R.J. Stoops, swore out a warrant and had Bugher arrested. Before the local police would release him, Bugher signed a confession of guilt for causing the fight. Subsequently, Daily held a hearing on the manner. Bugher failed to show. Witnesses, including a minister, testified in Oceak's favor. Daily fined Oceak $50 and suspended him for ten days. He suspended Bugher for 90 days "for being the aggressor." Bugher appealed Daily's decision to the Commissioner Landis, who held his own hearing. In February 1941 Landis handed down his decision. He rebuked Daily, ordered the PSA to pay Bugher's salary for 90 days, suspended Milliken and Stoops for five years, and Oceak for one year. Daily was livid. "He must have gone plum daffy," he said of Landis. It was "one of his smart-aleck decisions" and "wholly unwarranted and unjust." There was, however, little Daily could do. Oceak played the 1941 season for the semi-pro Cumberland Colts before returning to Organized Baseball.[37]

Butler and Johnstown finished the 1940 season in a tie for the top spot with a 65–44 record, the only teams above .500. Johnstown won a one-game playoff to settle the regular season title. The Johnnies' star pitcher, Bill Sample, won 20 games, compiled the league's best ERA (2.20), and logged in the most innings (219). Unfortunately, World War II ended his chance at a major league career. Infielders Vince Shupe (.313), Bill DeKoning (.283), and Bob Ramazotti (.306) made the majors. Outfielder Nick Orange led the PSA in batting with a .353 average, but his career languished after the War. Johnstown had drawn a PSA-record 61,000 fans to Point Stadium and showed a profit for the second straight year.

In the playoffs, however, the third-place Beaver Falls Browns upset Johnstown in their first-round series, winning two games to one. The Browns featured pitcher Ralph Ifft (14–4), whose 2.01 ERA was the league's best, and second baseman Oceak who garnered all-star recognition. In the other first-round playoff series, the Butler Yankees beat Oil City three games to one and went on to easily handle Beaver Falls, winning three straight games.

Butler featured two future Yankee stars, Joe Page and Joe Collins. First baseman Collins, born "Kollonige" in Scranton, Pennsylvania, rebounded from a terrible rookie year when as a 16-year-old he had been over matched by PSA pitching. In 1940 he became a league all-star after batting .320. It took Collins until 1948 to make it to New York, but then he logged in ten years with the Yankees, where he appeared in seven World Series.

Pitcher Joe Page, who would be dubbed "The Fireman," became the finest relief pitcher in baseball in the post war years. Still a starting pitcher in 1940, the big 6-foot-3, 200 pound left-hander compiled a tidy 11–3 record, which was the highest winning percentage in the league. Page grew up in the hard-scrabble coal camps of western Pennsylvania. He quit school to work two years in the coal mines and then he lost a year out of his life rehabbing from an automobile accident that nearly cost him his leg. After being away from the game for three years, he latched on with a local team in 1938. He signed a contract with McKeesport with instructions to report in 1939. A big 6-feet-3, 215 pound left hander with startling black hair and blue eyes he threw a blazing fastball. Wildness and his poor work ethic led McKeesport manager Leo Mackay to conclude Page would never be a pitcher, so he got a quick release. After another summer of town ball his manager recommended the lefty to Jack Dunlevy, who signed him to a Butler contract for $80 a month. So he was 22 years old when he joined Butler. He showed little regard for team rules, but he listened to manager Tom "Shakey" Kain, who taught him the finer points of pitching. After an appendectomy cost him a month, Page dominated the PSA with his fastball.[38]

Butler players were happy to wear Yankees pinstripes even if they were hand-me-downs with the "NY" logo removed. In addition to Collins and Page, they had several impressive minor leaguers. Outfielder Steve Greble combined power and speed, leading the PSA with 22 home runs, 40 stolen bases, 111 runs, and 237 total bases. Greble and third baseman Larry Hartman, who hit a strong .331, made the all-star team. Pitcher Bob Weyranch went 17–4. Neither Greble, Hartman nor Weyranch, despite the promise they showed, returned to baseball after World War II.

In 1941, for the first time, the PSA opened the season with the same six teams that had finished the previous season: Beaver Falls Bees, Butler Yankees, Johnstown Johnnies, Oil City Oilers, Warren Buckeyes, and Washington Red Birds. Before the season, however, Beaver Falls and Warren lost their major league affiliations. The St. Louis Browns, in what was announced as a retrenchment move, pulled out of Beaver Falls. Cleveland, after providing Warren with marginal players in 1940, left the eastern Ohio city in the lurch. The Warren club changed its name to Buckeyes. Both cities plunged ahead without any affiliation.[39]

Johnstown and Butler dominated on the field and at the box office. Johnstown finished the 1941 regular season with a comfortable lead. The Johnnies, under manager George Tredwell, won a PSA-record 70 games (70–39) for a .642 winning percentage, also a league record. The Johnnies boasted the league's best hitter in Howard Murdeski and the two best pitchers in Joe

Smolko and Vic Lombardi. Murdeski never made the majors, but he destroyed PSA pitching in 1941. During his electrifying season, he established the league records for home runs by banging 38 round-trippers, runs batted in with 139, 281 total bases, 129 runs scored, and 86 walks. Smolko compiled an eye-popping record of 20 wins with only three losses, while also posting a neat earned run average of 3.08, with 220 strikeouts in 210 innings. Unfortunately, he entered the service after 1942 and never regained the talent he showed in 1941. Lombardi, a 17-year-old portsider, would become a solid pitcher for the Brooklyn Dodgers after World War II. He won 12 games while losing only three, compiled a league-best 1.85 earned-run-average.

Despite Johnstown's firepower, the Johnnies faltered in the playoffs, allowing Butler to claim another league championship. The third-place Washington Red Birds managed to upset Johnstown by winning three straight games, as Smolko and Lombardi failed to notch a single win. Butler, the second-place finisher during the regular season, had to go five games to best Oil City in the other first-round series. It took first baseman Alex Hawke's game-winning RBI to give the Yankees the victory. The Oilers featured diminutive outfielder Al Gionfriddo (.334), famous for his catch to rob Joe DiMaggio of a home run in the 1947 World Series. Then Butler bested Washington three games to one. The Yankees walloped Washington in the final two games by scores of 14–0 and 10–2, leaving no doubt that they deserved the pennant. Hawke led the league with a .365 batting average. Future major league pitchers Mike Rossi (14–2), Dick Starr (14–7) and Canadian Ralph McCabe (8–1) led the Yankees during the season and in the playoffs.

Japan's attack on the U.S. fleet at Pearl Harbor changed everything. Soon after the attack, the two weakest franchises, Beaver Falls and Warren, announced they were dropping out of Organized Baseball. Both clubs had struggled through 1941 without major league affiliation. Not surprisingly, they finished with the two worst records. Already in debt and with the world in turmoil, quitting was an easy and logical enough decision.

In January 1942 Daily conferred with Butler's Dunlevy and Bob Rice, a Pirates scout and friend of Daily. They discussed the possibility of combining the Pennsylvania State Association and the Middle Atlantic League, with Butler, Johnstown, Washington and Oil City joining four MAL clubs. For the time being, Daily decided against that plan. The group did agree to try to play in 1942 even if the PSA had to go with only four teams. Daily had no success in attracting other cities to join the league. Nor were major league teams anxious to make new commitments given the uncertainty of World War II.[40]

In the four-team league of 1942, Butler won yet another championship.

Reverting to a split-season, Johnstown won the first half while Butler came on to take the second half, with Butler having the best overall record (69–41). The Yankees pitching staff included four future major leaguers: holdovers Dick Starr (18–5) and Roland "Tex" Hoyle (9–6), plus rookies Bob Alexander (1–1) and Joe Murray, whose 15–1 record set the PSA mark for highest winning percentage. Catcher-manager Dallas Warren led the league with a .359 batting average. Little Eddie Neville, who after the war became a fan favorite as a pitcher for the Durham Bulls, played outfield and batted .304 for the Yankees. He had fond memories of his days in Butler. He, especially, remembered eating chili and gravy on French fries, a local favorite, and Butler's economy jumping as the American Bantam Car Company turned out its famous jeeps, and other plants manufactured high-explosive shells and bombs.[41]

Oil City suffered at the gate because the local bus company, feeling the pressure of gas rationing, stopped running busses to the ballpark, and on the field because they had terrible pitching. After serving his one-year suspension, Oceak returned as player-manager of Oil City where he batted a resounding .343. Teammate Al Gionfriddo, who went on to play for the Dodgers, was even better, batting .348, second in the PSA. He also led the PSA in runs and triples. Fellow outfielder Bobby Ball, who hit .317 for the season, had the best day at the plate in PSA history. On July 6, in a game against Washington, Ball collected six hits in six at-bats, including two homers, as he drove in seven runs.

Despite the split-season format, all four teams entered the playoffs. The logic of the first-round pairings was hard to fathom; the two bottom teams, Washington and Oil City, squared off, while Butler and Johnstown played the other first-round series. Washington was led by Don Bollweg, who topped the league with 25 homers and batted in 105 runs. The Generals trounced Oil City in three straight games. Butler beat Johnstown three games to one. In the five-game championship series, Washington took a two-games-to-one lead, before succumbing to Butler, three games to two. The Yankees' win featured 19-year-old third baseman John Jerina, who hit .357 with 106 RBIs during the regular season. He also topped other hitters in hits, doubles, and total bases. Jerina entered the military service after the season and failed to make a comeback after the end of hostilities.

Initially, Daily took a wait-and-see attitude toward 1943. In December 1942, he said he would have to be a "Houdini" to predict what would happen in the coming months. By January, he urged waiting until March before making a decision. He did not have until March before the future arrived. Oil City's president, Bror A. Anderson, told Daily that because of restrictions on gas the local bus company would not run busses to the park. Without public transportation, he could not continue. Washington's Ray Dever just "lacked the heart" to continue. Butler and Johnstown had experienced a significant decline in attendance in 1942, but their leaders, Dunlevy and Cooper, wanted to continue playing. They urged a combined league, perhaps with Erie, Pennsylvania, and Zanesville, Ohio, the closest Middle Atlantic cities. Events were moving fast. Gas rationing was in place and travel restrictions were likely. Nevertheless, as late as mid–February, Daily remained hopeful the league could continue.[42]

In just a couple of weeks, by late–February, it was over. At the league meeting in Pittsburgh on February 21, 1943, the PSA voted to "suspend" operations for the duration of World War II. There was no shortage of reasons to stop playing. Gas rationing went into effect in May 1942. Most teams traveled by automobiles or busses, so the limit of four gallons per week for an "A" sticker would not get teams very far, and there was no way team cars would be issued "B" stickers as "essential" to the war effort. The rubber shortage struck first, in early 1942, so automobile tires were rationed. No new cars were being made for sale to civilians, so old cars had to stay on the road for the duration. A nationwide 35-mile-per-hour speed limit proved hard to enforce in rural areas, but public pressure to "keep it under forty" was real. With young men entering military service in ever growing numbers, owners really did believe they faced a shortage of players in the coming months.

Despite President Roosevelt's "green light" message to Commissioner Landis, owners of minor league teams found it difficult to argue that baseball contributed to the war effort. All minor league teams had experienced difficulty in generating investment during the Depression; with a war going on, it became impossible. Declining attendance could have been added to the list of particulars. With twelve million able-bodied men in military service, factories and mines running at full capacity, often three shifts, there was little time for baseball, even though people had money to spend. All in all, the uncertainties of the world at war were too great for men of limited financial means and talents to overcome. The PSA group was not alone, as only two class D leagues managed to operate in 1943.[43]

The PSA had operated for nine years, from 1934 through 1942. Each year brought new crises and new members. Eleven cities held franchises in the league, but none were members for the entire life of the circuit. The years of membership were as follows: Butler, eight seasons, 1935–1942; McKeesport, seven years, 1934–1940; Washington, six years, 1934–1935, 1939–1942; Greensburg, six years, 1934–1939; Beaver Falls, five years, 1937–1941; Johnstown, four years, 1939–1942; Monessen, four years, 1934–1937; Charleroi, three years, 1934–1936; Jeannette, three years, 1934, 1936–1937; Oil City, three years, 1940–1942; and Warren, Ohio, two years, 1940–1941.

3. A Minor League with Its Own Minor League

Daily's idea of two leagues interconnected through a major league team failed to take hold. The Yankees and Indians used the connection between their Class D and C leagues as Daily had anticipated. They shared tryout camps and spring training facilities, and shuttled players back and forth. They used the PSA as a developmental program for young players, keeping young prospects like Sauer, Collins, Henrick and McCormack in the PSA until they demonstrated their prodigious talent. By the third year of the PSA, most major league affiliates were simply looking to fill out rosters of their Class D farm team.

On the field, the Butler Yankees outclassed the rest of the league. The New York parent stocked the Butler club with good players. The Yankees took five PSA championships, winning in 1937, 1938, 1940, 1941, and 1942. In addition, they compiled the best regular season record in 1939, but failed to capture the championship flag. No other club came close to Butler's record. Greensburg (1934), Monessen (1935) and Jeannette (1936) each won one championship. Johnstown captured two regular-season titles, but could not bring home the championship flag.

Officially, the Pennsylvania State Association did not go out of business. It just notified the National Association that it was suspending operations for the duration of the war. Daily continued to pay the league's dues to the Association and to represent the league at the minor leagues' winter meetings. The league, however, did not resume operation after the end of World War II.

4

"Happy Days Are Here Again"
Glory Years, 1934–1939

As the country emerged from the bottom of the Great Depression, things began to turn around for the Middle Atlantic League in 1934, and for baseball in general. Attendance at both major and minor league games, which had bottomed out in 1933, began to grow and would continue to gradually increase for the remainder of the decade. The minors numbered just 14 leagues in 1933. Besides the MAL, only one Class C league had managed to operate that year. In 1934 the number of minor leagues jumped to 20. The increase in attendance and in the number of leagues, while real, were not enough for many people to recognize a new trend; nevertheless, things were changing for the better.

Baseball historians cite several factors for the improved condition of the minor leagues. The National Association of Professional Baseball Leagues' new president, "Judge" William Bramham, who took over in 1933, brought needed reforms. Increases in forfeit money for teams pretty much put an end to "July Fourth Leagues," i.e., leagues that just managed to make it through the lucrative Independence Day doubleheaders. It is noteworthy that no league folded in midseason for the remainder of the 1930s. Bramham created a promotion director in the person of Joe Carr, who doubled as president of the National Football League, to bring in new teams and leagues as well as to stabilize existing organizations. The Shaughnessy playoffs, popularized by Frank Shaughnessy in the International League, created a four-team playoff system at season's end. The new system kept players and fans involved during the tailend of the season, because more teams stood a change of making the playoffs, and, hence of winning the league championship. Night baseball, often cited as the savior of the minor leagues, had become almost universal by the mid–'30s. It gave working-men and women a chance to attend games. That had previously been difficult if not impossible when games were played in the afternoon. Before night baseball, minor league teams, just as major league clubs, aimed their product at businessmen, merchants, professionals and clerks, solid middle-class men who would come to games in their business attire. With the advent of night games, baseball began to attract a larger following from working-class people.[1]

The entire country found reason for renewed optimism in 1934. Franklin D. Roosevelt's election brought hope to a country which had been in the slough of despair since the Stock Market Crash of 1929. FDR's campaign song, "Happy Days Are Here Again," did inspire hope that things would be better. His pronouncement that "we have nothing to fear, but fear itself" may have been unsupportable by logic and evidence, but it engendered calm and confidence around the country. His fireside chats gave people the belief that the president, indeed the government, cared about their condition. The first hundred days of Roosevelt's New Deal had saved the banking and financial system, brought an end to Prohibition, put many men back to work, and provided relief for the unemployed. The National Recovery Administration failed to end the Depression as promised, but for the moment it gave Americans a sense that even if the Depression was not over, the beginning of the end was at hand.

The Middle Atlantic League entered its glory years. Long gone was the little league that started in 1925 where member towns were close enough together that teams could return home each evening after road games. Only Wheeling and Johnstown remained from the original league cities. The small western Pennsylvania cities of Scottdale, Charleroi, Jeannette, and Uniontown had been replaced by the booming Ohio industrial cities of Dayton, Zanesville and Springfield. The small cities of north-central West Virginia, Fairmont and Clarksburg, gave way to the state's two largest cities, Charleston and Huntington. In the remaining New Deal years, the MAL would develop its reputation as the strongest league in the low minors. It became a showcase for future big league players.

The league executives were so bullish on the future that they gave substantial raises to league president Daily and secretary-treasurer Hockenbury. Daily's salary went from $2,500 to $3,000, putting him solidly in the middle class. Hockenbury's salary rose from $1,000 to $1,200, which was not lavish, but he did not complain. For the time being, the league decided against adopting the Shaughnessy playoff format, preferring to stick with the traditional split-season arrangement it had used since the league's formation. For the 1934 season, the MAL operated with eight traveling umpires, two for each game, another sign of improved economic condition. The owners required franchises to post a $900 forfeit fee plus one-half of a month's payroll. They did require teams to carry six rookies, a policy designed to reduce teams' salary budgets. Daily's new Pennsylvania State Association would, he believed, allow MAL teams to have a backlog of prospects to shuttle between the two leagues. The league continued to use the Worth ball, which had produced inflated batting statistics, after the manufacturer gave assurance that the ball no longer jumped off bats like a rabbit.[2]

For the first time, the 126-game schedule included no doubleheaders except on the three major holidays, Memorial Day, Independence Day and Labor Day. The major leagues had restricted Sunday doubleheaders at their December 1933 meeting because they believed they were giving away an attractive admission. The MAL's decision stemmed from the optimistic assumption that teams would draw more for a single Sunday game and a weekday contest than they would from a Sunday doubleheader. As always in minor leagues, there would be a squabble over which teams played at home on July 4. Independence Day was the most attractive day on a team's calendar, traditionally drawing the largest crowd. Memorial Day could be cold and rainy, and by Labor Day fans had often lost interest if the home team was out of contention. After Fairmont left the MAL, Hockenbury took Doringer's job of drafting the schedule which he presented to the membership at a spring meeting. The decline in scheduling disputes over the years gave evidence that Hockenbury was good at the job.[3]

Daily could find plenty of reasons for optimism as he approached 1934. Pennsylvania finally ended its Sunday blue law that had prohibited professional baseball on the Christian Sabbath. The law had caused distorted scheduling to avoid Sunday games in Pennsylvania. It usually deprived Pennsylvania teams the opportunity for lucrative Sunday games. The lure of Sunday crowds had tempted teams to find ways around the law, often leading to the arrests of players (never management). Had the law been repealed earlier, some of the early Pennsylvania members of the MAL might have been saved from bankruptcy. By 1934, however, Johnstown was the sole Pennsylvania team remaining in the MAL.

All league teams understood the vital importance of a working agreement with a major league team. The nature of such agreements varied greatly. The New York Yankees owned the Wheeling Stogies outright. Yankees farm director George Weiss appointed Eugene "Gene" Martin as the general manager and Jack Sheehan as the field manager. Indeed, he staffed the Stogies roster entirely with Yankees farm hands. That arrangement had served Wheeling fans well in 1933, as *Wheeling Intelligencer* sports editor Tom Hopkins assured his readers that "fans need not fear being treated to ragged baseball." Hopkins reflected the belief that it was in the interest of the major league team to place quality players on its farm clubs. As it turned out, in 1934 Hopkins was wrong because the Yankees farm hands in Wheeling could not hold a candle to the previous year's squad. Moreover, the Yankees appeared exclusively concerned with player development, not with placing a winning team on the field. In other arrangements, the major league team did not directly own the MAL club, but they had a substantial economic investment so they staffed those teams with players capable of winning. This was the case with Cleveland in Zanesville and Brooklyn in Dayton. Unlike the Stogies, both the Ducks and Greys would add quality veterans who were non-prospects to the team roster in order to win. Holt "Cat" Milner and Jess "Shine" Cortazzo became key components in the success of Dayton and Zanesville. Commonly, working agreements gave the major league team first opportunity to purchase players from the minor league club, and to option however many players it chose to the minor league team. Detroit preferred this arrangement, but their farms seldom seemed to challenge for a championship.[4]

Huntington, Beckley, Charleston, and Johnstown were hustling for agreements as the 1934 season opening neared. When Detroit announced it would pull out of Huntington, team owner John Stuart decided he could not continue. With his Boosters $10,000 in debt, he put the team on the market. Initially he thought he had an agreement of sale to International Nickel Plate Company, but that fell through. Then local politician J. Pat Beacom, a member of the West Virginia House of Delegates, put together a group of local businessmen, headed by Henry H. Hutton, to purchase the team. Hutton served as president and Beacom as chairman of the board of directors. Fortunately, the St. Louis Cardinals signed on to a working agreement with the Boosters. Although the new owners had planned to keep Stuart on as business manager, the Cardinals insisted that Bill Walingham be appointed to that position. Walingham was the nephew of the Cardinals owner, Sam Breadon. Rickey's Cardinals were a better partner than Detroit, but the Boosters still lost upwards to $10,000 in 1934. The Tigers moved their affiliation up the Kanawha River to Charleston. No one should have been surprised that Huntington finished with a winning record and Charleston just managed to avoid the league cellar.[5]

Beckley and Johnstown had struggled to establish solid affiliations with major league teams. Unable to find a major league partner in 1933, Beckley had settled on a working agreement with another minor league team, the Memphis Chicks of the Southern Association. Now, Daily found a willing partner for Beckley in Larry McPhail, general manager of the Cincinnati Reds. To seal the deal with Beckley, the Reds agreed to play an exhibition game in Beckley against the Black Knights. The Reds sent scout Bobby Wallace to Beckley to conduct a tryout camp. Frank McCormick, a native of New

York City, remembered that McPhail sent him a bus ticket to Beckley, where he found 150 other hopefuls trying to impress Wallace. Johnstown was not as successful as Beckley in landing a working agreement. The Johnnies did get a loose agreement with Baltimore of the International League, but, basically, operated as the only independent team in the league.[6]

In Dayton, given his solid agreement with Brooklyn, Ducky Holmes undertook construction of a new park. He arranged a ten-year lease with an option to purchase agreement for Young Field at a discounted price. The field, where his club had played in 1933, was owned by the estate of William H. Young. Located on West Third Street between Kilmore and Ardmore Streets it was serviced by the Third Street trolley. For $75,000 Holmes built a new park on the site of the old field. For the 1934 season the new facility went by the name of West Side Park. After one year Holmes changed the name to Ducks Park. Unlike most other league parks, it boasted symmetrical dimensions, 360 feet to all fields, but had a high brick wall in right field. Holmes would be rewarded with an Opening Day attendance of over 5,000 fans and 115,000 paying customers for the season.[7]

The 1934 season was the MAL's best since its inception in 1925. No future Hall of Famers appeared in the 1934 edition of the MAL, but the league could boast of over 50 players who made the majors after donning MAL uniforms that year. The Middle Atlantic had never before enjoyed such depth of prospects. An additional 20 players who appeared on league rosters had prior major league experience. Alums of the 1934 season who went on to notable careers include first basemen Frank McCormick and Dick Siebert, the latter more famous as a coach at the University of Minnesota, infielders Eddie Miller and Eddie Mayo, outfielder Jimmy Outlaw, catcher Warren "Buddy" Rosar, and pitchers Claude Passeau, Atley Donald, Dykes Potter and knuckleballer Roger Wolfe. Tommy Henrich, the Yankees' "Old Reliable," came up from the Pennsylvania State Association for four games at the end of the season, so he does not count.

Frank McCormick enjoyed the best major league career of the lot. He began a 13-year career in the bigs at the end of the 1934 season when he got a brief call-up to the Reds. As the Cincinnati Reds first baseman, he played in eight all-star games, led the National League in hits three times, in RBIs once, and won the National League's Most Valuable Player Award in 1939. He played in three World Series, including the one that saw the Reds become the 1940 world championship team. Sabermatrician Bill James ranks him as the best fielding first baseman of the 1940s, calling McCormick "one of the best defensive first basemen ever to play the game."[8] McCormick "enjoyed" his year at Beckley despite having to eat hot dogs by the roadside, sleeping all night on the bus, "pushing the [bus] along a country road until you found a garage," and the clubhouses without showers.[9]

McCormick's problem of clubhouses without showers came at his home field. The Raleigh Manufacturing Institute (RMI) Park, a small traditional wooden structure, caught fire on June 14, destroying the grandstand and with it the clubhouse. Workers managed to cobble together new wooden stands by the July 10 exhibition game against Cincinnati, but did not complete the plumbing. Only a handful of intrepid fans found their way back to the park. Most Beckley residents stayed away in droves. Attendance proved so low that the *Raleigh Register* believed the final game of the season would be the last "for all time."[10]

Johnstown, as the only independent team in the league, continued to sign veteran players. The Johnnies' 32-year-old catcher, Vern Mackie, batted .365 and drove in 94 runs to lead the league in those categories. Outfielder Sam Thomas, in his seventh season as a Johnnie, hit .317 and led the loop in runs scored with 123. Nat Hickey, who now played the outfield, batted .330 and earned all-star honors. His first year at Johnstown had been 1925 when, as an already experienced pro, he was expected to help rookie Joe Cronin learn the ropes. The Johnnies also signed Shine Cortazzo, who had played in the MAL from 1925 through 1928 before going on to higher classifications. Cortazzo no longer hit for the average he had in earlier years, but he added spark and excitement wherever he played. His desire to win caused Johnstown to forfeit one game. After being ejected for arguing a call in an August game, he threw bats, balls, and other equipment from the dugout onto the field and refused to leave. After 15 minutes the umpire declared the game forfeited.[11]

The new ball manufactured by Worth did prove less lively than in past years, so batting averages stayed in normal range. Pitchers enjoyed the raised seams and lighter feel of the Worth ball, but they set few records. The MAL did see two pitchers hurl no-hitters in a season for the first time. Wheeling's Howard "Red" LaFlamme won only two games all year, but one of them was a no-hit game against Springfield on August 3. Two weeks later, veteran Bert Grimm of Zanesville held Charleston hitless. For the season, Charleston's Wayne LaMaster and Dayton's Roger Wolfe shared pitching honors. Both won a league-high 17 games, and LaMaster struck out 168 batters to lead the MAL.

Holmes and Wetzel, owners of Dayton and Zanesville, respectively, both wanted to win. Brooklyn and Cleveland provide them with young prospects, and, equally important, allowed them to acquire key veterans. Dayton, for example, had nine youngsters from the Brooklyn organization who eventually made the majors, but in addition the Ducks signed four players who had experienced the preverbal "cup of coffee" in the majors and were on the way back down the minor league ladder. Three of these veterans, Si Rosenthal (.324), Frank "Red" McDermott (.304), and Bill Steinecke (.371), batted over .300. The fourth was Cortazzo (.258), acquired from Johnstown during the season. Wetzel relied more on youngsters, but he signed Grimm before the season. The veteran pitcher gave Zanesville 13 wins and over 200 innings, and he briefly took over as manager in June. In July the Greys acquired Cat Milner, the experience hardened slugger who finished second in the MAL with a .353 batting average and garnered all-star honors.

Dayton and Zanesville split the seasonal crowns, with Dayton winning the first half and Zanesville taking the second half. The two clubs staged a hard-fought, take-no-prisoners, seven-game playoff series. The Greys entered the series with momentum. After finishing seventh in the first half, they went through three managers before Wetzel brought in Earl Wolgamot to catch and manage. He, with the help of those veterans, settled the youngsters and led an astounding turnaround. After the teams split the first two playoff games at Zanesville, a record 5,200 fans turned out at Dayton to see Wolff win a pitchers' duel from Grimm, 2–1. The Ducks needed only one more win after they took game four by a 4–2 score, thanks to Siebert's three hits.

The series turned on game five. With Dayton trailing, Holmes lost control. After arguing a call, as was his want, umpire Ed Osborne ejected Holmes from the game. Holmes then threw a tantrum, which concluded with him hitting the ump. Daily had little choice but to suspend Holmes. The penalty included the remainder of the playoff series and the first 90 days of the 1935 season. To increase Holmes' bitterness, his Ducks lost the game, 5–2. Even without their manager, Dayton appeared to have the series under control when they took a 5–2 lead into the bottom of the ninth inning of game six. Then the Greys broke Holmes' heart by scoring four runs to take the win. Milner, who had three hits for the day, drove in two of the four runs and scored the winning run. The series came down to game seven. Fans filled the grandstand in tiny Mark Park and stood behind a rope in front of the outfield fence. Dayton again took the lead, 3–1, only to see Zanesville score five runs in the eighth inning for a 6–3 victory. Tom "Red" Leonard's home run was the crucial hit for the winners. Zanesville had won back-to-back titles. Holmes had come close, but his temper had victimized his team.[12]

At the end of the 1934 campaign the MAL had several franchises on shaky ground. Huntington, Springfield, and Beckley had lost money due mainly to low attendance. In addition, Beckley had lost its grandstand in the June fire. In November Cincinnati announced it was withdrawing from the southern West Virginia city, citing the condition of RMI park. The future looked bleak for professional baseball in Beckley. Even after selling eight players to higher classifications, Beckley lost money.

Daily did not anticipate a serious problem in Wheeling, but that became the first trouble spot. George Weiss started shopping for a new location for his Class C farm team as early as November. He wanted to retain a team in the MAL, but he had soured on Wheeling and the city on him. Tom Hopkins, sports editor of the *Wheeling Intelligencer*, who claimed to speak for Wheeling baseball fans, placed the blame for low attendance squarely on the Yankees. Unlike the championship team of 1933, the Yankees stocked the 1934 Stogies with "green" players. There was truth in the charge; most players were in their first year of professional ball. Although nine of the Stogies would make it to the majors, only Rosar (.294) and Donald (11–10) posted even mediocre years at Wheeling. The level of play overwhelmed the young Stogies, who looked dreadful by finishing dead last, 33 games behind first-place Zanesville. Fans felt victimized, and they dropped away as fast as the team's pennant hopes.[13]

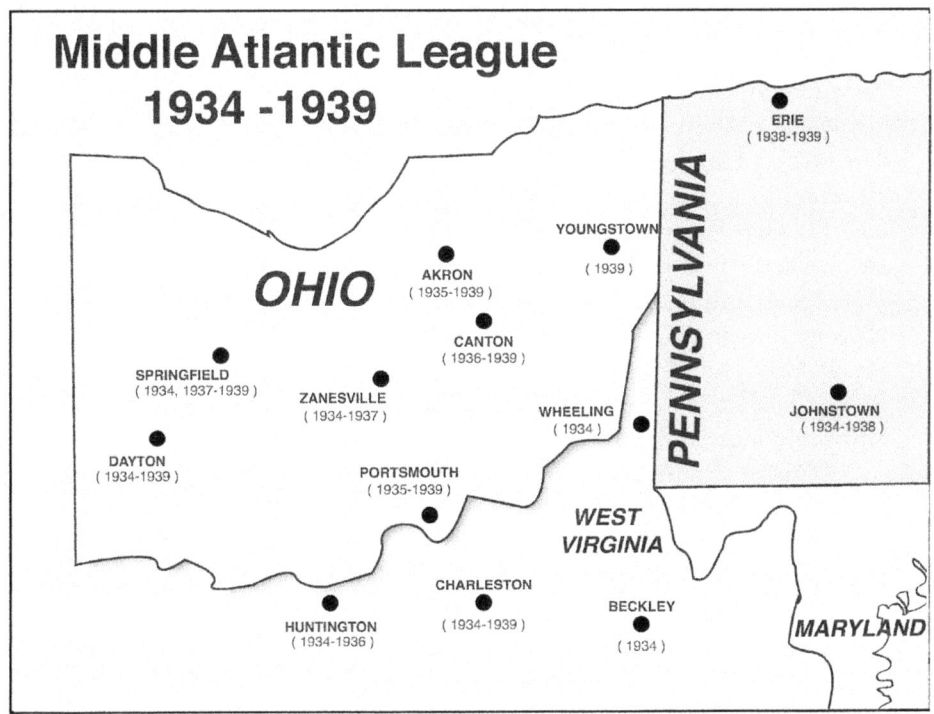

At its peak during the late 1930s, the Middle Atlantic League was an Ohio-centered league, with seven cities holding franchises (Michele Duncan).

If Wheeling gave up on the Yankees, Weiss obviously gave up on Wheeling. Daily, of course, wanted New York to retain an affiliate in his league. Daily tried to persuade Weiss to move to Beckley. Weiss had absolutely no interest in a town as small as Beckley, especially one without a decent park. Daily, Weiss, and Gene Martin, Wheeling's business manager, began openly canvassing cities. Daily next pushed Youngstown, Ohio, and Altoona, Pennsylvania, on the Yankees staff, but Weiss showed only slightly more interest in these cities than he had in Beckley. Then the Ohio cities of Portsmouth and Akron rose to the top of the Weiss list.[14]

Portsmouth had last seen professional baseball in 1905, but mayor Joseph L. Kounts and city manager Frank E. Sheehan believed baseball would benefit their city. Located on the Ohio River at the mouth of the Scioto River in southern Ohio, Portsmouth was a city of 40,000. It served as a hub for the Norfolk and Western Railroad, a local manufacturing center, and a county seat. The city's power-brokers understood they needed a ballpark in order to attract a franchise. Local boys played baseball at a place called Industrial Field, really nothing more than a sandlot without stands and a fence. Kounts and Sheehan first convinced the Chamber of Commerce to throw its weight behind the construction of a grandstand and a fence around the park. In early December Portsmouth's city council approved the construction of a 3,000-seat ballpark and approved a $40,000 bond issue for its construction. The Federal Emergency Relief Agency (FERA) agreed to undertake the construction project using relief workers. Without that assistance the project could not have been done for the money the city committed. Ten percent of each ticket would go toward paying off the bond issue. The locals placed their hopes on the county's favorite son, Branch Rickey, who was born and grew up in Scioto County. They envisioned him moving the St. Louis Cardinals farm club down the Ohio River from Huntington to Portsmouth. Rickey encouraged the city fathers to undertake construction of a stadium, but would make no promises.[15]

Without a commitment from Rickey and with Weiss still exploring other options, the Portsmouth leaders were receptive when Alex Pisula, owner of the Springfield club, showed interest in moving his franchise. Pisula had long since made it abundantly clear that his loyalty to community lasted only until the next chance came along. He learned this strategy from his mentor, Joe Cambria. Pisula claimed he took a licking in Springfield, and without question attendance there had proved disappointing. The Portsmouth Chamber of Commerce, believing a bird in the hand was better than waiting for the Cardinals to land, endorsed the transfer of Springfield to Portsmouth. The Pittsburgh Pirates agreed to follow Pisula to the Ohio River city.[16]

Being the hustler he was, Pisula continued to play Portsmouth and Springfield off against other offers. By mid–January he had yet to firmly commit to either city. Daily and Hockenbury once again floated Altoona, along with Steubenville and Canton, Ohio, Ashland, Kentucky, and Wheeling as options for Pisula. In this game of musical franchise locations, Weiss, for his part, hung on to the Wheeling franchise.

Daily announced that crunch time would be the Middle Atlantic League meeting in Zanesville on January 14, 1935. At that meeting, Pisula finally committed to Portsmouth. By that time, construction of the new park there had reached the point where a late April finish date looked firm. Weiss, for his part, made a tentative commitment to Akron, Ohio, contingent on sorting out problems with a playing field. Of the other league cities, Dayton and Zanesville were making as much money as possible in a Class C league. Johnstown and Charleston muddled along with weak teams, but there was no doubt of their return in 1935. Huntington lost money in 1934 and Rickey could not be counted on to pump money into the operation there. Beckley looked ready to fold its franchise.[17]

The city of Akron represented a highly prized territory. Akron's population of nearly 250,000 outdistanced that of Dayton, then the largest city in the MAL. Akron rightfully prided itself as the "Rubber Capital of the World." The big three of America's rubber industry, Firestone, Goodyear and Goodrich, were located in Akron. In addition, the city was home to Quaker Oats' cereal plant. The 28-story Central Tower Building, completed in 1931, advertised the city's prosperity even during the Depression. In the first few months of 1935, however, Akron faced turbulent times. Workers at the Goodyear plant protested a ten percent cut in pay by going on a sit-down strike. Local police refused to attack the strikers, which forced the company to settle the strike. Weiss looked beyond that disturbance; he saw a promising location for his team.[18]

Weiss, Martin and trusted scout Paul Krichell fell in love with the city's potential. A location for their team to play proved less than exciting. Professional baseball in Akron dated to 1881, but teams, leagues and playing fields had come and gone with dizzying regularity. Sportswriters Jim Schlemmer of the *Akron Beacon-Journal* and Ed Garman of the *Akron Times-Press* showed the Yankees delegation the options. League Park, built in 1928 at a cost of $35,000 for the Central League team named the Tyrites, seemed the most logical. A Negro National League team, also called the Tyrites, played there in 1933 until the team folded. The park, however, came with major problems and no shortages of idiosyncrasies. For the Yankees, the lease presented the major stumbling block. A woman named Edith Falor owned the first mortgage and controlled all the logical area for parking. The park itself was in receivership. The second park option was Firestone Stadium, a football facility that would require extensive renovation to make it playable for baseball. By February, Weiss said he was ready to give up and return to Wheeling. Bluff or not, the Weiss threat smoothed the way for a lease agreement on League Park and the parking lot.[19]

Problems with the park still remained, but many of them could be solved with the Yankees' money. Old Tyrites players from the Central League days claimed back salaries. They totaled $1,900, an easy figure for the Yankees to wipe out. The park required $2,500 in repairs and $5,000 to install lights for night games. Finally, on February 19, 1935, Weiss made the move from Wheeling to Akron official. Martin moved to Akron to run the operation as business manager. Weiss liked the fact that Akron lacked a long established nickname for its team, unlike the Wheeling Stogies, and thus could be called the Akron Yankees.[20]

Some Wheeling baseball fans believed they had found a reasonable alternative to the Middle Atlantic League. In March, the intrepid Dick Guy tried again to organize a new league. He planned a Class D league to be called the Bi-State League. He thought he had teams lined up in Wheeling, Clarksburg, Fairmont, and Grafton, West Virginia, to go with Pennsylvania towns of Charleroi, Waynesburg, Connellsville and Canonsburg. By April Wheeling had gathered 60 prospects for a tryout at Fulton Park. Then Clarksburg dropped out and quickly the whole plan came unraveled.[21]

Beckley remained Daily's biggest worry. On the final day of the 1934 season, local newspapers buried the Black Knights. Even though the team finished in the first division and boasted ten future big league players, local fans failed to return after the park fire. Principal owner Doff Daniels, a local physician, lacked the accumulated capital to continue pumping money into a debt-ridden operation. The park's hurriedly constructed stands built after the fire lacked a roof and any amenities. The club suffered from playing in the league's smallest city. Its location deep in the mountains of southern West Virginia required Beckley to travel the most miles of any league team. The Middle Atlantic team also faced stiff competition for fans and for space on the sports pages from West Virginia coal mine teams. Two mine leagues, each with eight teams, were centered in Beckley. To make matters worse for Beckley, Cincinnati withdrew its working agreement following the 1934 season, and no other major league club showed any interest in an affiliation.

It would have been understandable if Beckley had just mailed in its franchise. Instead, Beckley's wheeler-dealers and civic boosters stepped up to save professional baseball, at least for another year. Wealthy lawyer and operator of the Winding Gulf Coal Company, J. Lewis Bumgardner, was winding down his business interests, giving him time for other pursuits. As a "civic responsibility" he had just agreed to serve as the first president of the newly created West Virginia College, even though he lacked any experience in higher education. Nor did he have any experience in baseball, but he enticed theater owner C.D. Crawford to join him in organizing the Smokeless Coal Athletic Association with the aim of taking over the local pro club. They recruited other local businessmen to become stockholders in their venture. It proved easy to arrange the purchase of the MAL franchise from Daniels, which they did in February. Bumgardner served as president of the team and, initially, Crawford became business manager. Crawford hired on veteran minor league player Eli Harris to assist him and to manage the team. The 30-year-old Harris had covered shortstop for Beckley the previous four years, but he had bad legs and chose not play in 1935. Officially listed as field manager, Harris functioned as general manager as well. Bumgardner's group also changed the name of the team from Black Knights to Miners. That did not resolve the 300-mile trek the club would have to make to Dayton or the lack of a working agreement. Harris and Daily explored all available options, but in the end they failed to locate a major league team willing to join with Beckley. The newly christened Miners faced the difficult prospect of operating independent of major league affiliation.[22]

The league's new ballparks, in Akron and Portsmouth, offered sharp contrasts. Construction was finished on Portsmouth's shiny new ball yard in late April 1935, just in time for the opening of the season. Its location on the bank of the Ohio River at the foot of Boundary Street, just east of center city, gave fans easy access to the park on foot or by bus or car. The roofed grandstand constructed of steel, concrete and brick sat 3,000 people in twelve rows of seats. Clubhouses nestled below the stands. The main entrance, separate from the grandstand, contained a ticket window with offices on a second floor. A solid brick wall, nine feet high, surrounded the entire complex. The semi-circular brick wall made the distance from home plate to any field 349 feet. In honor of the city's favorite son, the city fathers named the new facility Branch Rickey Park.[23]

Akron's League Park sat 4,500 customers, more than Portsmouth, but the wooden stands on a steel frame appeared dilapidated several years before the Yankees arrived. Summit Beach Amusement Park and Summit Lake stood just a stone's throw to the east of the park. City streets surrounded the park on three sides, West Crosier to the north behind left field, Lakeside Avenue along the third base side on the west, Paris to the south, and Long Street down the right field line. A hill behind right-center field, dubbed "Poverty

Hill" during the 1935 season, allowed fans a free, if partially obstructed, view of the field. The general manager, Gene Martin, ended that by erecting a large canvas awning on top of the fence to obstruct the view from the hill. Trolley cars, which had run from center city to the amusement park, had ended in 1934, replaced by limited bus service, which never seemed to provide enough busses when games ended. A separate building housed the clubhouse. Typical of locker rooms of the day, it provided nails for players to hang their clothes on and not enough hot water for anyone to linger. In the outfield, a board fence, sixteen feet high, surrounded the playing field. Distances from home plate to the fence in right field and center were reasonable, 345 to right and 385 to center field, but the left field fence stood only 315 feet from home, making it an inviting porch for right-handed sluggers. The distance was only the beginning of left field's peculiarities. Almost no foul territory existed from third base to the left field fence. In left field the ground dropped sharply. There the fence leaned out from the park at a sharp angle. Batted balls driven to the fence, tended to bounce off the fence and out of the park. Such an occurrence was ruled a ground-rule double. The slant of the wall also made it possible for daredevil left fielders to run up the wall to catch a fly ball. Playing left field in League Park would remain an adventure.[24]

The Yankees fared well in their first season in Akron. On Opening Day, a parade through the city and a full house at the park could not have been more satisfying for GM Martin. Later in the season, an exhibition game against the New York Yankees on July 12 drew an overflow crowd of 6,000, which required fans to stand along the right-field fence. A late-season exhibition against the Cincinnati Reds drew only a disappointing 1,800 customers. Weiss did not duplicate the mistake he had made at Wheeling the previous year; he put quality players at Akron. The team finished in fourth place in the overall standings. Russell Brown, who did not make the majors, pitched a no-hitter against Beckley. Ten teammates did make it to the majors, including first baseman Johnny Neun (.323), outfielder Walt Judnick (.274), and pitchers Glenn Liebhartz (16-7) and Joe Beggs (15-14). Local fans got their money's worth.[25]

Whether a result of suggestions from the new minor league director of promotions or not, teams became more self-conscious about promoting the game. Opening Day parades, a staple before the Depression, had grown out of fashion in the darkest days of the Depression, but they returned in several cities in 1935. Akron and Portsmouth used parades to advertise the return of baseball to their cities. Holmes, in Dayton, always loved a parade. All teams sold beer in their concession stands, but now venders hustled popcorn and hot dogs in the stands. Most clubs organized Knothole Gang for kids, usually for eight- to 17-year-olds. Clubs normally allowed Knothole Gang members free admission to a limited number of games, but some clubs allowed them a free pass to all games if accompanied by an adult. Akron held special days where they gave free admission to members of the Scouts, YMCA, Jewish Community Center, and Catholic Youth Organization. Akron also sponsored an amateur team, the Junior Yankees. All teams had Ladies Days, typically once a week, where women were admitted free if accompanied by a male. In Zanesville the Greys held "girls" softball games before night games, with the women's teams coming from the local industrial league.[26]

Zanesville and Dayton again finished first and second in the overall standings, with Zanesville one game ahead. Despite posting the best record, the Greys were left out of the playoffs. Under the split-season format, Huntington, the first-half winner, and Dayton, triumphant in the second half, made the playoffs. Huntington had fallen to last in the second half, and fifth in the overall standings. No one thought it was fair that Huntington was in the playoffs rather than Zanesville, but nothing could be done at the time.

The Greys had treated Zanesville fans to some very good baseball and put outstanding players on display. All-star first baseman Jimmy Wasdell led the MAL in batting with a .357 average, in hits (182) and in doubles with a league-record 52. He would play 11 years in the majors. Outfielder Milt McIntyre, who never made the majors, slugged 24 home runs thanks to the short 304-feet distance down the left field line, and knocked in 110 runs. For the second time, sportswriters picked Earl Wolgamot as manager of the year. Eleven members of those Greys played in the majors.

Outfielder Tommy Henrich would become the best of the lot. He arrived in Akron after a strong year at Monessen, the Indians' farm in the Pennsylvania State Association. He made the MAL all-star team on the basis of a .337 batting average. Commissioner Landis would declare Henrich a free agent before the start of the 1937 season, claiming that Cleveland was "hiding" him, even though he had moved up to the Southern Association (then Class A1) after skipping class B and A along the way. Henrich signed with the New York Yankees, for whom he played 11 seasons, six of which saw the Yankees become American League champions. By the end of World War II scribes referred to Henrich, eventually a five-time American League all-star as "Old Reliable."

The Middle Atlantic was becoming a player development league, where major league clubs moved up farm hands after a year playing in class D, or starting stronger prospects on their career under the direction of organization managers. Nonetheless, there remained a goodly number of minor league veterans who had knocked around the league for a number of years. Cat Milner was gone, but others remained. Johnstown, being without a major league affiliation, needed such players. Sam Thomas, in his seventh season in the MAL, batted .329 and, again, was selected as an all-star. Grimm (Johnstown) and Roberts (Beckley) remained trusted arms. Bill Helmick, however, won only four games and closed out his career with a MAL record 108 victories. Infielders Hickey (Dayton), Cortazzo (Zanesville), Oceak (Akron), and all-star third baseman Noonan (Portsmouth) had been in the league since the 1920s.

Dayton got off to a slow start, in part because Holmes had to serve a 90-day suspension for his altercation with the umpire in the 1934 playoffs. He was, however, on hand at Opening Day to rededicate the park, called West Side Park in 1934, as Ducks Park. Daily, Hockenbury, and Carr attended, and Branch Rickey spoke at the dedication. Loren "Riley" Parker, veteran first baseman, replaced Holmes as manager at the start of the season, but the Ducks played poorly, finishing in the second division over the first half. For a change, Holmes took his punishment quietly. Daily ended Holmes suspension after the first half, and the Ducks turned around. Parker led the team with a .352 batting average. Young shortstop Rod Dedeaux and veteran second baseman Nat Hickey, who had played in the MAL's first season a decade earlier, made a slick double-play combination. Future major league pitchers Harry Eisenstat (18–8), Ed Hansen (15–7), and Roger Wolff (14–14) were inning eaters, as each threw over 200 frames. The race came down to the last day of the season with the Ducks playing a doubleheader against second-place Johnstown. The Ducks needed to win just one to take the second-half title. Johnstown won the first game, 5–3, but Holmes' club took the second game by a 4–3 score and with it the second-half crown.

The Huntington Red Birds were the least likely champions in league history. Only catcher Hugh Poland made the majors, and his career major league batting average was a pathetic .185. This was the fewest number of future major leaguers to come from any MAL team in years. They did have the league's best pitcher in Mike Martynik and the best shortstop in player-manager Benny Borgmann, but little else. In his first year of pro ball, Martynik had a career season. He won a league-best 21games, topped the MAL in innings pitched (246) and in strikeouts. He pounded the strike zone. His 299 strikeouts not only led the MAL, but they also were the most for any minor league pitcher. His strikeout record would stand as the most ever by a Middle Atlantic pitcher. Huntington, however, had no other pitcher with even a winning record.

Borgmann was a superb athlete. Like Hickey he was one of the greats of early professional basketball. Both Borgmann and Hickey are enshrined in the Basketball Hall of Fame in Springfield, Massachusetts. Basketball historian Robert Peterson simply termed Borgmann "the top offensive player of the era." A native of Haledon, New Jersey, he started playing professionally after graduation from high school in 1917. Even though he stood only 5-foot-8, by the 1921–22 season he led the Metropolitan Basketball League in scoring while playing for the Patterson Legionnaires. He duplicated that feat for the next three years. When the American Basketball League formed, he shifted to the Fort Wayne Hoosiers and led the ABL in scoring for five years until that league collapsed. Through the 1930s he continued playing on a variety of independent teams, including the Chicago Bruins, Newark Mules and Brooklyn Americans. After World War II he coached the Syracuse Nats of the National Basketball League for two seasons, and then coached at St. Michael's College and Muhlenberg College for the next decade. While playing pro basketball in winters, he began playing professional baseball in 1928 with Wilkes-Barre. He moved up the St. Louis Cardinals farm system as far as Columbus of the American Association, where he batted .340 in 1933 for one of the great minor league teams. After injuries cost him a down year at Rochester, the Cardinals gave him a chance to manage at Huntington. He hit .307 and led the MAL with 35 stolen bases.[27]

Usually, the team with momentum can be counted on to win a playoff series, but not in 1935. Huntington took the first game, 10–3, behind Martynik, supported by three RBIs each from Jack Lynch and Poland. Dayton took the second game, 2–1, as Eisenstat picked up the win in ten innings, thanks to outfielder Pat Patterson's game-winning hit. In the third game, outfielder Ray Zimmerman and first baseman Jim Grilk each collected four hits to lead Huntington to a 13–4 victory. The Red Wings took a commanding lead following a 7–1 win in game four. In game five, Joe Blackwell of Dayton and Martynik locked up in a pitchers' duel. The Ducks managed a 1–0 victory when Dedeaux drove in the only run. Then Huntington finished off the series, coming back from a 5–0 deficit in the seventh inning to take a 7–6 win before 4,000 unhappy fans in Dayton. Borgmann's two-run single proved the margin of victory. For the series, third baseman Jack Lynch, a journeyman minor leaguer who hit only .265 during the regular season, led the Red Birds with a .444 batting average.[28]

Before game three, Daily called a meeting of owners to hear a protest from Johnstown. The Johnnies, angered about losing the second half to Dayton on the last day, filed a protest charging Holmes with using an ineligible player for the last 18 games of the season. Logically, the protest would have been filed during the final game, but it was not. So the Dayton-Huntington series began as scheduled. Teams were prohibited from carrying more than six "class players," men with more than one year of experience above Class C. Daily determined that when Holmes added second baseman Orville Baker to the Ducks roster for the stretch run, they went over the limit of class players. Holmes maintained that he did not know Baker was a "class man," and then added the lame excuse that "everyone does it." That may have been, but Johnstown president Charles Reisser demanded that Holmes be suspended for the remainder of the playoffs and the Ducks' series share be distributed to the other clubs. Holmes then argued that the league bi-laws called for a $50 fine. Daily contended the fine was $50 for each game, hence he levied a fine of $900. The owners, meeting in Huntington, found Holmes guilty and upheld the $900 fine. For Holmes, his team's loss and the fine was doubly hard to take. Blaming Daily, he vowed that "you can bet this isn't the end of the matter."[29]

At the end of the 1935 season, everyone around the league understood that Beckley would not be back for another year. At the fall MAL meeting, Bumgardner allowed as how the Beckley owners wanted nothing to do with baseball next year. J.P. White and Dr. J.H. McCullough had taken over the principal ownership of the team in July 1935. They "took a rather sound financial beating during the closing months of the season and went ahead and paid off their debts without a whimper." They claimed to have lost $7,000. White, president of the Raleigh Coal Company, which owned the Miners' park, facing the prospect of strike by his coal miners, had other things to worry about. In September a local businessman, J.T. Lynch, organized an effort to save the team, but he found few willing to invest money in the Miners.[30] Business manager C.D. Crawford offered his analysis of the failure of the franchise. He blamed lack of parking and poor public transportation as causes for poor attendance. In reality, Beckley fans continued to support coal mine teams in the area. The city was far smaller than any other league town, it had the most miles to travel and the highest transportation costs, it had no major league affiliation, and its park was in poor shape. Those were more than three strikes. Officially, Beckley remained in the league until the January 1936 MAL meeting, when the Miners failed to even send a representative. The league officially dropped Beckley. Gene Martin of Akron threw salt on the wounds by proclaiming that Beckley had "no business in this league."[31] That was harsh, but true.

Holmes did not forgive Daily for the $900 fine, even though his fellow owners approved the levy. After the playoffs, he began to garner support to oust Daily. At the MAL's fall meeting he implied that Dayton would not be in the league the following year if Daily continued as president. At the World Series, he lobbied the *Charleston Gazette* sports editor about the fine, saying he would not pay. He tried to sell other owners on Jack McCallister, former Cleveland manager, as a candidate to replace Daily. The only ally he found was Portsmouth owner Alex Pisula. The fight came to a head at the January MAL meeting in Charleston. Holmes first asked to be reimbursed for expenses incurred in traveling to Canton, Middletown and Springfield, Ohio to drum up investors for the league. His request met with a vote of approval. When asked how much he was owed, Holmes answered, "Nine hundred dollars." The motion was quickly rescinded, with $250 approved for Holmes' expenses. Holmes then moved to replace Daily and Hockenbury. Only Pisula sided with him. Failing to find support for ousting the two, Pisula moved to reduce the salaries of the two executives. When that failed by the same vote, 5 to 2. Holmes and Pisula stormed out of the meeting to show their disgust with the proceedings. The owners approved $3,000 and $1,200 in respective salaries for Daily and Hockenbury. After Holmes and Pisula returned, Holmes threatened to withdraw from the league if his fine was not reduced; he moved to reduce his fine from $900 to $300. This motion failed by a 4 to 3 vote. Holmes and Pisula again left the meeting in a huff.[32]

Speculation about a replacement for Beckley focused on former MAL cities Wheeling, Youngstown, Springfield and Altoona, plus Canton and Middletown, Ohio, where Holmes had drummed up interest. Wheeling might have gotten the nod to return, but spring floods took the Ohio River into the ballpark, ending any discussion of reviving the Stogies. Emmett "Turk" Reilly of Zanesville, who had been instrumental in getting the franchise for his hometown, urged Daily to support Canton, but in the first months of 1936, no one from Canton stepped forward. Canton had been a member of the Central League from 1928 to 1932, but the city's sporting history had long been as a football town. The presence of the Pro Football Hall of Fame there attests to the importance of football in the city. The Canton Bulldogs, featuring Jim Thorpe, had taken over the baseball field, Meyers' Lakeside Park in the 1920s, but the football franchise had since shifted to Cleveland. By April, Daily considered the possibility of reducing the league to six teams. Johnstown, the last of the original MAL members, appeared the logical team to drop.[33]

Daily and Joe Carr essentially took up residence in Canton in March in their combined effort to find investors. They finally identified their men: local businessmen Oscar Barkey, Paul B. Belden and Julius S. "Judy" Hinchman. With Carr's assistance, the two organized the Canton Amusement Company with $25,000 capital. Barkey, manager of the Canton Pure Milk Company and a former high school football star, took over as president. Belden, who served as vice president, had operated Belden Brick Company since 1911 and turned the family business into a prosperous concern, with plants in Detroit and New York. Hinchman, a local sugar broker, held the posts of secretary-treasurer and, initially, business manager. Paul Vanderoort and Darwin Luntz filled out the board of directors. They decided on the name Terriers, a diminutive of Bulldogs, as the team nickname.[34]

Daily insisted that they have a working agreement with a major league club as a condition of joining the league. Carr talked to Cleveland on behalf of Canton. Barkey and Hinchman headed to Cleveland to meet with Billy Evans, the Indians farm director. Although the Indians would not drop their affiliation with Zanesville, it happened that Evans had just accepted the position of farm director for the Boston Red Sox. He gladly made Canton his first farm club.[35]

The Canton businessmen knew little about the operation of a baseball team. They, obviously, needed to hire a general/business manager and a field manager. Evans helped with the first. He recommended Bob Reilly, son of Evans' old friend Turk Reilly. Hinchman gladly turned the job over to the young man. Barkey looked to Daily for help finding a field manager. Daily recommended Floyd "Pat" Patterson, a veteran outfielder who had played for Dayton in 1935. A hard hitting, hard drinking Nebraska native who loved to bet the horses, Patterson was under contract to Holmes. It had to be difficult for Daily to ask Holmes for a favor, but he requested that Ducky release Patterson in order for him to take the managerial job. Holmes agreed, saying that a Dayton-Canton rivalry would be good for both clubs. It is not known if the disputed $900 fine was a *quid pro quo* or not, but there was no more public discussion of that issue.[36]

Canton's playing field, Lakeside Stadium, needed lots of work. The park, which had been home to the famed Canton Bulldogs football team, consisted of a covered wooden grandstand behind home plate and down the third base line. Bleachers down the left field line cost patrons just 25 cents. Much of the wood needed repair and all of it needed a coat of paint. The new owners ordered up a lighting system. It could not be installed by Opening Day, but was ready by May 19. The visitor's dressing room never got finished, requiring visiting teams to dress at their hotel. The playing field favored left-handed hitters. Down the left field line, the distance to the fence was 340 feet. It took a good clout to clear the center field fence 410 feet away. The short right field fence was topped with a 40-foot screen from the foul line to dead right field, at which point it dropped to 20 feet high out to right-center field.[37]

Before the season started, Portsmouth lost its major league affiliate when the Pirates pulled out, citing Pisula's management style. Pisula thought he could line up Cincinnati as a replacement, but the Reds were not interested.

The Boston Bees were known to be looking for a Class C farm team, but they too decided against Portsmouth. Pisula had little choice but to go as an independent in 1936. He did create a local "advisory council," which had no power but which was met with favor by Portsmouth business leaders. Knowing Pisula's failure to do much to promote the team, the new group proposed a Knothole Gang for kids under age 14, which Pisula adopted. With the Pirates gone he changed the team name to Panthers.[38]

On the field, 1936 proved to be a hitter's year. Turk Reilly, a salesman for the Worth Company, convinced the MAL to adopt his company's ball as a cost saving measure. Batting averages sored much higher than in previous seasons. The new ball proved to be lively; it had rabbit-like qualities, players said. Charleston's speedy, left-handed-hitting center fielder Barney McCosky batted an even .400. That made him the league's first .400 hitter since Joe Medwick in 1930. McCosky, who was born in Coal Run, Pennsylvania, but grew up in Detroit, went up to the Tigers in 1939 and stayed in the majors for 11 seasons, achieving a lifetime batting average over .300. Jeff Heath of Zanesville put up eye-popping numbers. The Canadian-born outfielder drove in a remarkable 187 runs, a league record. Heath also became the first MAL player to collect more than 200 hits in a season, finishing with 208. Finally, he led the circuit in doubles (47) and total bases (367). Walter Alston, Huntington's first baseman, slammed 35 homers, the most since Frank Welch's 38 in 1931.

Zanesville seemed to never stop hitting in bandbox Mark Park. As a team, the Greys hit for an astounding .327 batting average, the highest that any MAL team would ever achieve. They slugged 152 home runs; the next-best team hit just 98. That also set the MAL season record for homers. The Greys lineup saw future major leaguers at virtually every position. First baseman Oscar Grimes (.376) finished third in batting average and established the MAL record for runs scored with 150. Second baseman Jim Shilling (.350) was an all-star selection. Third baseman Don Gugler, fresh out of the University of Iowa, batted .359. Shortstop Frank "Skeeter" Scalzi, a University of Alabama product, hit .315. Heath (.382) held down left field. Center fielder Bill Sodd (.333) led the team in homers. Right fielder Frank DeManicor had little power, but batted .345. Even two reserve outfielders, Mike Buchoski (.317) and Carl Huffman (.304), hit over .300. The Greys pitching staff, led by Tom Reis' league-best 21 wins, contained seven future major league hurlers. In addition to Reis, the list included Ed Zuber, Charley Stancue, Charley Suche, Jack Kraus, Woody Davis, and Mike Palasy, not household names but good enough to make the show.

Not surprisingly, Zanesville led the league almost the entire season. The

Greys won the first half of the split-season by five games. Dayton made a charge at the end of the season, and the Greys managed to lose their last three games, to create a tie for the second-half title. Zanesville compiled the best overall record, finishing ten games better than second-best Charleston. Daily ruled that Zanesville and Dayton should play a three-game series to determine the second-half titlist. In the event Dayton won the series, the two teams would square off for a seven-game series for the league title.

Dayton lacked the power to really challenge Zanesville. Holmes continued to drive his players and berate umpires. In June, Daily had fined the rowdy manager $325 for a run-in with umpire Huston Milton. This time, Holmes quietly paid the fine. Holmes benefited from having the league's best second baseman in Don Paiement (.329) and all-star shortstop Woody Williams (.342). The Ducks managed one win in the playoffs, but Zanesville, after taking game two, won the rubber match behind Heath's home run and DeManicor's go-ahead hit. For the three-game series, Heath batted .390, followed by Grimes with a .374 average.

Howard "Ducky" Holmes, the colorful manager of the Dayton Ducks, fought with fans, opponents, umpires, the league president and his own players. He earned more ejections, suspensions and fines than any other manager. Around the MAL, fans loved to hate the Duck, as they turned out to jeer him (courtesy of Wright State University Library).

The Middle Atlantic League continued to churn out prospects at a prodigious rate. The 1936 group included over so who reached the major leagues, the most of any year to date. Notables included Huntington's tall, skinny shortstop Marty Marion, who played 13 years in the majors with the St. Louis Cardinals, won the National League Most Valuable Player Award in 1944, played in four World Series, and was selected for seven all-star games. The MAL's top hitter, Barney McCosky, still a teenager in

1936, went on to hit .312 over 11 big league seasons with Detroit, Philadelphia A's, Cincinnati and Cleveland. Heath would be a major league rookie with Cleveland in 1938. Two years removed from the MAL, he slugged 21 homers and hit .343. One of the finest Canadian-born players, his 14-year major league career merited his inclusion in the Canadian Baseball Hall of Fame. Before becoming a manager, Eddie "The Brat" Stanky (Portsmouth) played on three different teams that won World Series titles over 11 seasons. Leo Durocher described Stanky in the famous quote "all he does is win." Pete Suder (Akron) played his entire big league career, 13 seasons, with the Athletics, where he became a fan favorite. Two fine catchers, Clyde McCullough (Akron) and Bob Swift (Charleston), came out of the 1936 season. In the year of the hitter, few pitching prospects passed though the MAL. Ernie "Tiny" Bonham (Akron), a great control pitcher, worked ten years in the majors, won over 100 games, and appeared in three World Series and two All-Star Games, but there were no others of note.

Walter "Smokey" Alston of Huntington was the only one of the 1936 players to be enshrined in the Baseball Hall of Fame, but that resulted from his managerial, not his playing, record. After Huntington's season ended, the Cardinals called him up to St. Louis. The Cards already had two outstanding first basemen, Big John Mize and Rip Collins, but on the last day of the season Alston got to bat. In his only major league appearance, he struck out. Alston, of course, went on to become one of the most successful managers of all time. In his 23 years at the helm, his Dodgers won 2,040 games, including seven National League championships and four World Series titles. Alston was named National League manager of the year on six occasions, and in 1983 he entered the Baseball Hall of Fame.

The MAL fall meeting in November passed without fireworks. Pisula apparently had a deal to sell the Portsmouth franchise to the Pittsburgh Pirates. Around the league no tears would be shed over Pisula's departure. Financial reports encouraged Daily. Dayton, Charleston, and Huntington turned a profit in 1936. Akron and Canton posted a paper loss because of investments in park improvements. Zanesville, despite winning the league title with the heaviest hitting team in memory, lost a modest amount. Independent Johnstown also lost money, but not enough to give Daily pause. There was reason to expect all eight cities to be back in 1937. Owners decided to ditch the split-season format in favor of the Shaughnessy playoff system. Adopted in 1933 by the International League, the scheme had the virtue of making four, rather than two, teams eligible for postseason play. The league again awarded Turk Reilly the contract to supply the MAL with Worth baseballs, which the salesman promised would not be as lively as they had been in 1936. Finally, with no objection, owners renewed the contracts of Daily and Hockenbury at the same salaries as in 1936.[39]

Daily's optimistic expectation for a quiet offseason quickly proved to be unfounded. Pisula's deal to sell to Pittsburgh fell through when the Pirates determined the club's debt. Pisula had a history of burning bridges behind him; he had done so in Lima, Youngstown, and Springfield. Now he did so in Portsmouth. No one doubted that Pisula lost money in 1936, but newspapermen believed this "the result of mismanagement." Pisula dumped the problem in Daily's lap and walked away, leaving a $3,500 debt behind him. The general attitude toward Pisula was reflected in the *Charleston Gazette's* description of him as a "stooge and right timid man for Joe Cambria."[40]

No team had matched Zanesville's success on the field since the Greys entered the league. They had just won the league championship, their third in the last four years. Despite their success, attendance had sagged in 1936, causing the team to lose a modest $1,500. Far from staggering, the loss was less than that of Portsmouth, Dayton or Akron, but rather than absorb the loss, Buzz Wetzel pushed the panic button. Perhaps he was hurt or angered by some Zanesville fans who had voiced their belief that there was "skullduggery" involved in the Greys losing the final three games of the regular season to create a playoff series. Wetzel began to explore transferring the team to another city. He adopted a practice that would later become standard, playing one city against another. First he floated Youngstown as an option and then Springfield. At the same time he challenged the Zanesville business community to come up with money to cover the debt, threatening to move the team if the city refused to meet his demands. When he failed to get a quick response, Wetzel announced plans to move the team to Springfield. The Zanesville people mistakenly thought the Cleveland Indians had a love affair with their town and would continue to support the Greys with new owners. They were wrong. A Zanesville delegation went to Cleveland to meet with Cy Slapnicka, only to find out that he had approved the transfer of the Indians' affiliation to Springfield in advance of Wetzel's move.[41] As usual when a franchise moved to a new city that had been without baseball, the Springfield business and civic leaders greeted Wetzel with open arms. The city in west-central Ohio offered a population of 70,000, double that of Zanesville. The Crowell-Collier Publishing Company located there was one of the largest publishing houses in the world. A division of International Harvester employed 4,000 people. The new city-owned Municipal Stadium awaited Wetzel's team. A few years earlier, when Pisula owned the MAL franchise in Springfield, the team had a poor field and tiny stands. Now Wetzel had a park comparable to that of Portsmouth. Cleveland promised to continue sending

4. "Happy Days Are Here Again" 131

Wetzel the quality players that had made Zanesville the envy of the league. The Indians' ability to do so was somewhat compromised by Commissioner Landis' decision to free Henrich and others from the Indians farm system.⁴²

With Wetzel's move to Springfield, Zanesville and Portsmouth were left up in the air. In Portsmouth, Pisula's advisory council morphed into a fundraising and organizing group headed by Carl J. Phipps, manager of the Portsmouth Public Service Company and president of the Chamber of Commerce. The group aimed at paying off the debt that Pisula had left and finding a major league team to take over. Things moved fast in December. Nativeson Branch Rickey, in a strange move, told the Portsmouth people that he would have the Huntington Red Birds conduct their spring training in Portsmouth. Warren Giles, Cincinnati general manager, who had turned a cold shoulder to Pisula a year earlier, visited Portsmouth, and seemed interested in working with Phipps. Giles' move prompted Rickey to make a counteroffer to Portsmouth to move his franchise from Huntington, provided Portsmouth paid the debt. By New Year's Day, Phipps had the money. Two weeks later, city manager Frank E. Sheehan announced that Rickey had finally confirmed that he would move the franchise to Portsmouth.⁴³

Huntington soon received an even more staggering blow. This time it came from Mother Nature, or, more specifically, the Ohio River. In January 1937 Huntington experienced its worst flood in history. The waters washed over League Park, which was located on the riverbank. It did not appear that the park would be playable any time soon. At the Middle Atlantic League's winter meeting in February, John Stuart, who had returned as Huntington's business manager, appeared with forfeit money in hand. Huntington, he argued, was prepared to continue in the league. The club was debt free, and he had a pledge of $5,000 from the Chamber of Commerce to repair the park. League Park, Stuart maintained, would be in playing shape by May. Stuart's appeal fell on deaf ears. The league voted Huntington out because of flood damage. Only Watt Powell and Sam Politano of Portsmouth supported Huntington. Stuart called the vote "a blow below the belt." In fact, League Park had seen its last game. City fathers and the Army Corp of Engineers determined it should be demolished to make way for a new flood wall. Stuart went on to obtain a franchise for Huntington in the newly formed Mountain State League, a Class D loop, but his team had to play at tiny Long Park, up the hillside from the river.⁴⁴

With Huntington out and Zanesville vacant, a scramble began for the remaining franchise. Businessmen from Middletown, Ohio, expressed interest. Gene Martin, business manager of Akron, wanted a franchise for himself in Youngstown. Daily went to Youngstown and then to Zanesville to check out the lay of the land. In Zanesville, while the two newspapers moaned over the "slap in the face" from Wetzel and Cleveland, the Chamber of Commerce established a committee headed by Paul Perry to solicit investors. That impressed Daily, who went to work finding a major league affiliation for Zanesville. He ended up with the Boston Bees, who were willing to take on Zanesville as a Class C farm club. Boston general manager Bob Quinn sent his son John to Zanesville to watch over the operation. Quinn wanted the team to be called the Bees, rather than Zanesville's traditional Greys. The Zanesville men had little choice.[45]

In 1937, Akron became the first MAL team to broadcast all its games on radio. Canton allowed their Opening Day, all-star game and playoff games to be broadcast on station WHBC, but not regular-season games, fearing that fans would stay home and listen to games rather than come to the park. Akron contracted with radio station WJW to broadcast all Yankees games, home and away, except on Sundays. Announcer Bob Griffith recreated the away games from a glass studio in O'Neil's Department Store. A high school student named Al Ciraldo, only 16-years-old served as Griffith's sidekick. He went on to become the voice of Georgia Tech University football and basketball. Wheaties sponsored the games and gave boxes of their cereal to players for good plays. The players, in turn, passed boxes of Wheaties along to Ciraldo, who became very popular with neighborhood mothers.[46]

Ducky Holmes always wanted to own the land on which his park rested. In March 1937 he was ready to move, but he lacked the where-with-all. In order to raise the needed capital, he agreed to a reorganization of his club. He issued stock in the Ducks, and agreed to give up the title of president. The newly created board of directors elected Harry A. Mack the new president, Earl Reeder vice president, accountant Gene Haywood secretary, and Henry Ochs, vice president of Winters National Bank, treasurer. Holmes would continue to serve as field manager. The new owners arranged for Dayton to become a Chicago White Sox minor league affiliate.[47]

Johnstown had operated as an independent for several years, and usually struggled on the field. Local businessmen there finally tired of losing money and watching a losing team. When William O. DeWitt, general manger of the St. Louis Browns, offered the Johnstown investors a chance to sell, they jumped at the deal. So Johnstown moved from an independent team to a fully owned Browns farm club. DeWitt would serve as president. The Browns would fully stock the team, which would continue to be called the Johnnies.[48]

With all teams in the league serving as farm clubs, the MAL became even more of a player development league. The old standbys from the 1920s were finally gone. Cortazzo, Hickey, Noonan, Grimm, and Thomas, all picked up their pink slips. Sam Thomas and Jess "Shine" Cortazzo bowed out in 1936. Thomas, in his ninth year in the league, could only muster a .268 average for Johnstown. That brought his lifetime average in the MAL down to .327. Cortazzo, who had played in the MAL's first season, fared better, hitting .311 in 1936 by splitting time between Portsmouth and Canton. His .300 hitting did not matter, as the next year he was playing Class D ball. Only Frank Oceck at Johnstown remained from the group of lifetime minor league players, so popular with local fans.

Prospects now filled the rosters of MAL teams. Danny Litwhiler, still a student at Bloomsburg (Pennsylvania) State Teachers College, would go on to spend 11 years with the Phillies, Cardinals, Braves and Reds. In 1942 he became the first outfielder to go through a season without making an error. Following his playing career, he gained even more fame as a college coach at Florida State (1955–1963) and Michigan State (1964–1982). Johnny Berardino (later changed to Beradino for his acting carer), who batted .334 at Johnstown, logged in more time on the television program *General Hospital*, from 1963 to 1996, than he did on the St. Louis Browns, Cleveland Indians and Pittsburgh Pirates. Still, he had an 11-year major league career, beginning in 1939. His lasting memory of 1937 was the 35-cent daily meal money; even in the Depression that did not go far. Phil Masi, an outfielder for Springfield, had an 11-year career as a major league catcher, but is best remembered for a controversial play in the 1948 World Series. Picked off second base by Bob Feller, he was mistakenly ruled safe and then scored the only run of the game. Several dozen others who played in 1937 made it to the majors, including George "Bingo" Binks, Chuck Workman, Bob Katz, and Jack Graham.

Frank "Skeeter" Scalzi, the league's dominant hitter, and Wayman Kerksieck, the best pitcher, only managed to have a brief stint in the majors. Scalzi, Springfield's shortstop, stood just 5-foot-6, but somehow packed prodigious power into that frame. He led the league in batting (.377), home runs (34), hits (197) runs (147), stolen bases (32), and total bases (355). His 355 total bases stood up as the all-time high in the history of the MAL. He also became the league's first 30–30 player, with 30 or more home runs and 30 or more stolen bases. He spent 17 years in the minors, but appeared in just ten major league games with the New York Giants in 1939. Wayne Kerksieck won 24 games for the Canton Terriers. His win total tied the mark set in 1930 by Clarksburg's Red Proctor as the MAL's highest win total; the record would stand until the league folded. That outstanding season earned him a promotion to the Southern Association, where he spent five years. He showed promise, but only got to the big-time briefly in 1939 with the Philadelphia Phillies, where he lost two games without a win.

Canton and Springfield dominated the league in 1937. Springfield took the lead in June and led through June, July and August. Then, in late August, Pat Patterson's Canton club came on strong. Patterson himself led the way, batting .358 and driving in a league-leading 107 runs. Things looked bad for the Terriers when Kerksieck went down with a sore arm before the end of the season. Even without their best pitcher, the Terriers slipped past Springfield into second place on the Saturday before Labor Day. Canton then took a day-night doubleheader against Portsmouth before a packed house of 4,000 on Labor Day to grab the pennant from Springfield. Patterson's long home run in the bottom of the tenth inning of the second game gave the Terriers the pennant.

The MAL's initial Shaughnessy playoff followed Patterson's heroics. The Terriers again faced third-place Portsmouth in the first round of the playoffs. The Red Wings were without pitching ace Lee Sherrill, who led the MAL in strikeouts and innings pitched before going on the shelf with a sore arm. Portsmouth managed just one win against Canton. In the other first round series, Akron upset Springfield three games to one. First baseman Jack Graham, who banged out 28 homers during the season, put on a hitting display, hitting in the clutch and hitting with power.

Canton captured the league championship, but Akron put up a fight before falling in the five-game series, three games to two. Canton won the first game behind the pitching of lefty Bob Katz, whose 2.73 earned-run average was the lowest in the league. Akron then captured the next two games, which featured the hitting of Graham and outfielder Jim Browne. In the third game, after an argument broke out, Canton fans hurled bottles onto the field, one of which hit Browne. Canton fans got some satisfaction from the ejection of Akron manager Leo Mackey. Browne got his revenge by collecting four hits in a 9–4 Akron victory. Canton tied the series behind the pitching of Katz, who struck out 13 batters and won his third playoff game. In the final game, 6,300 fans overflowed Lakeside Park's grandstand with several hundred standing behind ropes in right field. They saw Canton overcome another Graham home run to take the championship with a 10–5 win. For their work, Canton players split $1,400. Akron and Springfield got $300 each to divvy up.[49]

In Dayton, Holmes did not find "just managing" worked so well. The White Sox gave him little talent and his club finished a disappointing fifth in the standings. His reputation as feisty, argumentative, and terribly tempered only increased. Holmes' relationship with the league president got worse when Daily upheld Canton's protest of a May 27 game. Dayton, again, used too many "class" players. This time Daily did not fine Holmes, but the loss stung. In June after being ejected from a game in Zanesville, Holmes refused to leave the field and had to be escorted off by police. He then went to a rooftop across the street and wagged signals to his team. This was not the first time Holmes had pulled this particular trick; he had been doing it since his first year in the league. In July he fought with his own catcher, Charley Schapp, and was fined $100 by his own team. On July 23 the league suspended him "indefinitely" for his actions in a game in Portsmouth; "indefinitely" in this case proved to be a week. In August, Holmes tussled with Akron manager Leo Mackey. When the umpires refused to eject Holmes, Mackey took his club off the field; however, umpires did convince Mackey to bring his team back to the field. Fans around the league loved to razz Holmes, who saw that as a badge of honor.[50]

Before the November 1937 league meeting, Holmes regained the title of general manager, which allowed him a voice in league affairs. Ducky announced his intention to stir the pot at the MAL's November meeting. First, he wanted the league to move to a higher classification. The MAL certainly had the population to justify a Class B designation. Daily, however, consistently opposed such a move, believing that higher salaries would strap clubs in smaller markets. Knowing Daily's attitude, Holmes prepared to oust the league president. He tried to sell the owners on the wisdom of making George Trautman, president of the American Association, head of the Middle Atlantic League as well. It was not unknown for a person to be presidents of two different leagues, and Trautman possessed strong administrative and interpersonal skills. On the other hand, Daily, with the assistance of Hockenbury, had run the MAL successfully for 12 years. Holmes found no support for his move to oust Daily, and the president prevailed on the classification issue. In addition to reelecting Daily president, and Hockenbury as secretary-treasurer, the owners boosted Hockenbury to vice president, replacing Gene Martin of Akron. The salary limit, now $1,800, would not include the manager for the first time; this made it easier for teams to employ non-playing managers.[51]

According to Daily, all teams except Zanesville turned a profit in 1937. Bill DeWitt objected to Daily's accounting, claiming that his St. Louis Browns lost money at Johnstown. Rumors surfaced that the Browns would move the franchise to Youngstown, but they stayed put for the time being. The Boston Bees, however, seemed intent on moving out of Zanesville. The marriage between the Bees and Zanesville never meshed. Zanesville fans were accustomed to a winning team after capturing three league championships in the previous four years. Boston's farm teams, on the other hand, did nothing but lose. In 1937 the Bees' farm clubs in Scranton (Class A), Columbia (Class B), Zanesville (Class C), Salisbury, North Carolina (Class D), and Salisbury,

Maryland (Class D) all finished in the second division of their leagues. Only Beaver Falls of the Pennsylvania State Association (Class D) enjoyed a first-division finish. Zanesville fans felt betrayed and avoided Marks Park all summer. Bob Howard, *Zanesville Signal* writer, summarized the local attitude: "Last year followers of baseball merely yawned and looked around for something else to do when the Bees were scheduled to play at home." Howard estimated the club's losses at a whopping $35,000, although that figure seemed high. In January, the Quinns began making the rounds. They appealed to the Zanesville Chamber of Commerce to make up all losses over $2,500; they later claimed the Chamber had agreed, but that seems unlikely. They moved on to Huntington, Wheeling, Youngstown, and Erie. Daily gave them until the early–February league meeting to decide where the Bees would land, but extended the deadline when Boston continued to dicker.[52]

In late March Boston finally decided to move its franchise from Zanesville to Erie, Pennsylvania. Erie, with a population of 115,000, lay on a plain above Lake Erie. A major port on the Great Lakes' shipping system, Erie's waterfront received heavy cargoes of coal, grain, iron ore and fish. In summer months the sandy beaches nearby attracted tourists, but when ice locked the lake and winds blew off the lake, the city can be a harsh place. The ballpark, called Athletic Field until the name was changed in the 1940s to Ainsworth Field, was owned by the school district and had a school behind the right field fence. The park dated from 1923, and was undergoing major renovation from wooden stands to steel and concrete. That project would remain incomplete during the 1938 season. There was seating for 3,000 under the roof in the semi-circular grandstand. Bleachers extending down both baselines took the seating capacity to 5,000. Lights had not yet been installed, and a ditch ran from right field to center field, endangering fielders if they were not careful. The right field fence was officially listed as 300 feet, but really measured just 286 feet from home plate. Dead center field, however, was 420 feet from home; no one ever hit a ball out in that direction. Ruts in the infield made fielding ground balls an adventure. When completed it would be a classy looking facility, but in 1938, according to baseball historian David Pietrusza, the park "boasted what many considered the worst playing surface in baseball."[53]

Holmes disliked not controlling what he thought of as his Ducks. In the previous offseason he had given up control of the Ducks in order to raise capital to purchase the land his park sat on. By February 1938 he had gone into debt, but he managed to buy back enough stock to regain controlling interest in the club. He proceeded to make himself club president, vice president, secretary, treasurer and general manager. With all these offices, he decided to forego the duties of managing. He selected Russell "Red" Rollings, a 34-year-old with 12 years of minor league experience, as field manager.[54]

By the time the league's winter meeting rolled around, Holmes seemed pleased with himself and kept a low profile. At the major-league meetings in December 1937, the National League had adopted a new, slower ball after several years of offensive explosions. The MAL followed suit by adopting a new ball, in the MAL's case, the "white" ball, white leather, with white stitches and silver lettering. The owners expected the ball would be harder to hit because batters would be unable to pick up the ball's rotation. The meeting did not tinker with the playoffs, but, following the example of the majors, the owners introduced an all-star game to perk up interest around the league. The team leading the league on July 20 would host the game and play an all-star aggregation selected by baseball writers. The $1,800 monthly salary limit remained and still did not include the salary of managers.[55]

As it turned out, the white ball did nothing to rebalance hitting and pitching. Lower seams on the ball, which made it difficult for pitchers to throw breaking balls, apparently more than balanced the difficulty of batters to pick up the ball's rotation. Three teams compiled batting averages over .300 for the only time in league history. Portsmouth as a team hit .310, while Springfield batted .307 and Canton finished with a .305 average. Portsmouth also led in home runs and scored the most runs.

Despite Portsmouth's hitting prowess, the 1938 regular-season pennant came down to the wire. Canton took over first place with a 3–2 victory over Portsmouth just in time to win the right to host the all-star game, and kept the lead through August. With five games to play, Canton led by three and a half games, a seemingly commanding lead as the Terriers rolled into Portsmouth for a four-game series. Canton took the first game of a September 2 doubleheader, but the Red Wings came back to take the next three games. Canton left Portsmouth clinging to a game and a half lead. On Labor Day, Charleston, with a losing record, swept a double bill from Canton. Portsmouth took both games from fourth-place Akron to take the lead. On the final day of the season, Canton did beat Charleston, but it was too late as Portsmouth again topped Akron.

The Portsmouth roster contained a nice mixture of outstanding prospects and veteran minor leaguers put together by business manager Sam Polatani and field manager Benny Borgmann. All the starters except the catcher batted better than .300. Third baseman George "Whitey" Kurowski put together one of the greatest seasons the MAL would see. His .386 average bested all other hitters. He became the second MAL player to reach 200 hits in a season, finishing with a league record of 209. He also led the league with 133 runs. Alston returned to man first base and put up his usual numbers: 28 homers, 103 RBIs, and a .311 batting average. Borgmann held down second base and batted .313. Shortstop Bill Hart, who made the majors, hit .342. In the outfield, 18-year-old Darin Clay, David Danaher and Chet Wiezorek hit .335, .314 and .366, respectively. Wiezorek also led the league with 130 RBIs, 46 doubles, and 333 total bases. Pitcher Warren "Moose" Fralick won 18 games, but it would be Fred Martin (16–9) and Ernie White (15–6) who would find a place with the parent Cardinals.

Portsmouth charged through Springfield in the first round of the playoffs, but had to go the full seven games to beat Akron for the league title. Third-place Springfield won one game against Portsmouth, thanks to Chuck Workman's grand-slam homer, but could only score four runs in the other three games. Akron got to the finals by sweeping Canton. The Terriers' end-of-season collapse continued into the playoffs. Not even Cecil "Tex" Hughson, the league's best pitcher (22–7), could stop Canton's free-fall. Akron featured second baseman Frank Silvanic, the MAL's most valuable player. Still a teenager, Silvanic clobbered a league-high 35 home runs, thanks to the friendly left field fence in Akron's League Park, drove in 112 runs, and batted .363. The Yankees won two of three games at Akron. In Portsmouth, Akron captured game four when all-star catcher Herb White drove in the winning run in the thirteenth inning. A cold snap brought temperatures in the thirties with drizzling rain that kept attendance to 500 at game five and 800 shivering fans to game six. Portsmouth won both by one run, thanks to homers from Alston, Hart and Wiezorek. When good weather returned, 4,000 saw the Red Wings take a 7–6 win in the final game. Home runs by Wiezorek, Hart, Alston and Clay accounted for all of Portsmouth's scoring.

Despite Canton's late-season collapse, they had the consolation of winning the first MAL all-star game. Over 4,000 fans turned out to see the August 5, 1938, game at Lakeside Park in Canton. The host's shortstop, Joe Kelly, homered, and catcher Bob Finley hit a key double in the seventh inning to give the Terriers the lead they held. Kelly collected three hits, and Frank Genovese also homered for the winners. Hughson got the win thanks to four double plays.[56]

No one around the league should have been surprised that Ducky Holmes could not sit quietly through a whole season without getting into trouble. When the Ducks got off to a terrible start, Holmes could not resist taking over the managerial role himself. As the team's performance failed to turn around, Holmes became more volatile. The explosion came on July 22. Ducky lost control during an argument with umpire Charles Whittle after the ump called one of Holmes' players out on a close play at second base.

Whittle had the reputation of disliking managers as much as Holmes disliked umpires. In fact, the *Portsmouth Times* labeled Whittle the "best hated umpire in the Mid-Atlantic." As Holmes explained, "Whittle just stuck that big chin out at me once too often and I socked it." For that action, Daily suspended Holmes for 120 games. Portsmouth protested the game because Holmes continued "directing" from the stands, but Daily did not allow the protest.[57]

Whittle was not the only umpire to face brutality during the 1938 season. In late July at Akron, umpire Dave "Red" Parker took verbal abuse from a female fan and her male companion as he was leaving the field after the first game of a doubleheader. According to Parker, "When a woman calls any man what I was called ... that's too much." Parker instinctively gave her the finger. The man then followed Parker into the dressing room and cracked the umpire on the back of his head with a rock. Parker spent the night in City Hospital, but refused to file charges. After Daily heard the case, he decided that Parker was the instigator and levied a $25 fine and five-day suspension on the umpire. In addition Daily required Parker to write an apology. That was a hard penalty for a man who had been cracked on the head with a rock.[58]

The country and the world were changing rapidly in the fall of 1938. In the November elections, Republicans made gains in the House of Representatives, the Senate and governorships. The Democrats retained control of both houses of Congress, but President Roosevelt had failed in his effort to purge conservative Democrats in key elections. The combination of Republican gains and FDR's failure to control his own party brought an end to the New Deal. The President's attention shifted to the world stage where dangers loomed wherever he looked. Germany absorbed Austria in 1938 and then demanded the Sudetenland. Britain and France gave in at the famous Munich conference; appeasement triumphed war. Americans had little heart for another war, especially in the isolationist heartland of Ohio. Attacks on Jews across Germany in November 1938, and the beginning of Nazi concentration camps, did little to alter American attitudes.

In such troubling times, baseball proved a reassuring tonic; things may be bad around the world, and people still lived in hard times in the U.S., but baseball was a constant. The number of minor league teams continued to increase, as did attendance in both the major and minor leagues. Of course, things hardly ever remained constant in the Middle Atlantic League. Daily knew there were problems in Charleston, Akron, Erie, Johnstown, and Dayton.

In Charleston, Watt Powell wanted a new major league affiliation, one that would finally give him players to win with. The National League Boston Bees, after having an unhappy experience owning the Erie club, gladly put the Erie franchise on the market and prepared to move to a lesser role in Charleston. Leo Thomas Miller stepped forward to take the Erie franchise. Miller, a native of Erie, a former insurance adjuster, had owned the Erie club in 1932, its final year in the Central League. He had moved on to Indianapolis where he owned that city's American Association team. Miller's return to town brought excitement to Erie fans, who gave him a huge reception at the Civic Center. Miller brought with him a working agreement with the Cincinnati Reds, and young Norman A. Perry, Jr., son of the former Indianapolis president, to run the team as secretary and business manager. With slicked down hair parted in the middle, a cigar in his mouth, and shirt sleeves rolled up, Perry looked every inch a confident local booster. He had energy and ideas. At the same time Miller rehired popular and rotund Julius "Jocko" Munch as manager.[59]

The New York Yankees continued to be unhappy about the condition of Akron's League Park and the uncertainty of its lease. Akron, however, seemed a good location. The economy hummed as the city's rubber plants returned to full production. Symbolic of the return to prosperity, Summit Beach Park, next door to League Park, which had demolished its rollercoaster in 1934, opened a new coaster, the "Sky Rocket." Although Weiss grumbled, the Yankees signed a three-year lease on the park. The New York club also brought in Ray Brandenberger from San Antonio as the new business manager. The Texan placed high hopes on the Knothole Gang and Junior Yankees. The Knothole Gang enlisted kids aged nine to seventeen in a program with the Yankees, supported jointly by the city recreation department, the YMCA, the Boy Scouts and Girl Scouts, the Jewish Community Center, Catholic Youth Organization and the Association for Colored Community Work. The kids received a pin, admission to special Knothole games, and encouragement to bring their parents to games. The Junior Yankees fielded a team of teenaged boys who had aspirations of professional careers. The amateur team got good publicity and it produced a few minor league players whose careers the local papers followed with great care. Brandenberger also introduced annual contests between city and suburban all-star amateur teams prior to the Yankees' games.[60]

Dayton offered more serious problems. After declines in attendance and wins in 1938, Holmes found himself in serious financial trouble. Holmes lined up a post season exhibition game against Brooklyn in September. He hoped it would make up some of the attendance shortage, but, alas, the sheriff attached the gate receipts because of Holmes' debts. In order to pay Brooklyn its guarantee, Holmes was forced to give outfield prospect Oris Hockett (.341) to the Dodgers. In January 1939 Holmes' club went into receivership. The court appointed Carl Storck as receiver. Roly-poly and affable, Storck was to Dayton football what Holmes was to baseball. A star player at Saint Mary's College (University of Dayton), he had run the Dayton Triangles in the National Football League from 1921 until he sold them in the early 1930s. He had served the NFL as its secretary-treasurer since the league's inception. When NFL head man Joe Carr died later in 1939, Storck would assume the presidency. He established a new organization, the Baseball Club of Dayton, and convinced Brooklyn Dodgers general manager Larry McPhail to invest $10,000 and acquire controlling interest in the organization. Storck became the president of the club, with state senator Don Thomas the treasurer and Mickey McConnell as secretary and business manager. The real power in the organization, however, would be Branch Rickey, Jr., whom McPhail sent to Dayton to operate the club. Young Rickey took the title vice president and then decided to officially become business manager as well. So everyone would know that Ducky Holmes no longer controlled the operation, the new owners jettisoned the name "Ducks." The club would be the "Wings." McPhail gave Holmes a job as a scout for the Dodgers.[61]

Daily looked forward to a settled and prosperous season without the headache of Holmes, with an economy beginning to show signs of life after the recession of 1938. The league meeting went smoothly. The league replaced the "jackrabbit" white ball with the traditional Worth ball. The league leaders felt optimistic enough to guarantee payments of $700 to the regular-season winner and to the playoff winner, and $300 each to the runners-ups. In late January Hockenbury issued the 1939 league schedule, the earliest it had been published, a further sign of stability.[62]

After 13 years as league head, Daily should have known a minor league seldom stays the same from season to season. To his surprise, the St. Louis Browns decided in early March to move their franchise from Johnstown to Youngstown, Ohio. When Donald Barnes bought the St. Louis club in 1937, he believed he could change the losing culture by shaking up the organization from top to bottom. His team in Johnstown was losing money, variously reported at $25,000 to $30,000 over the 1937 and 1938 seasons. General Manager DeWitt blamed the losses on poor attendance. True, Johnstown drew only 30,000 fans in 1938, a far cry from the over 100,000 the Johnnies had drawn in 1935. On the other hand, the teams the Browns gave Johnstown fans were terrible, winning 52 games in 1937 and finishing dead last with only 50 victories in 1938. DeWitt should not have been surprised at the poor attendance given the bad teams he offered Johnstown.[63]

Daily expressed astonishment and surprise at the decision, but St. Louis owned the franchise, so there was little he could do. Personally, Daily felt saddened at the move, both because Johnstown was the closest city in the league to his home in Ebensburg, and also because it was the last of the original Middle Atlantic League cities. Daily knew Johnstown had been a good baseball town and believed it would be again. He did offer Johnstown a spot in the Class D Pennsylvania State Association. Johnstown proved Daily right; the Johnnies immediately became the best-drawing team in their new league. The loss of Johnstown, however, did make scheduling easier for the Ohio-centered Middle Atlantic League.

With the move to Youngstown, the Middle Atlantic League took on the look of the old Central League. Six of the eight members now represented Ohio cities that had been members of the Central League when it went bottom up in 1932. Erie and Charleston did remain as representatives of the original league states. The MAL no longer looked like a Class C league. Its membership included two cities with populations over 200,000 (Akron and Dayton), three over 100,000 (Youngstown, Erie, and Canton), two between 60,000 and 70,000 (Charleston and Springfield), plus Portsmouth with 40,474.

The Browns needed to move quickly in Youngstown. DeWitt brought in William L. Osley from San Antonio to run the operation. He formed the Youngstown Browns Baseball Company and issued 250 shares of stock, the majority owned by the Browns. DeWitt became president and Osley business manager. Youngstown, a steel city in the Mahoning Valley just 65 miles from Pittsburgh, boasted a population of nearly 170,000. Little steel companies, Bethlehem and Republic, who employed 9,000 workers, and Youngstown Sheet and Tube with 7,500 employees, defined the city. Strikes of Little Steel workers in May and June of 1937 brought brutality, riots, violence, and the Ohio National Guard to the city. The steelworkers were recent immigrants, not surprising considering that over half the city population was foreign born. Slovaks and Slovenians headed the list of home countries, with Poland and Italy close behind. The Browns set up shop in Idora Park, a streetcar amusement park southwest of downtown. The park, termed "Youngstown's Million Dollar Playground" in the 1920s, included a dance hall, salt-water swimming pool, theater, animals, rides, and a ballpark. The ballpark in the shadow of the roller coaster, needed lots of work, especially the lighting system, deemed so weak the Browns would have to play home games during the day for the first half of the season.[64]

Youngstown got off to a fast start in 1939. The Browns led the league at the beginning of June and clung to third on July 4. They drew well. After seven years without baseball, Youngstown took to the Browns. The first night game on May 15 had to be delayed because ticket sellers could not handle the overflow crowd. Umpires quickly established ground rules to cover balls hit into the crowd lining the outfield fences. Fans loved the double-play combo of shortstop Floyd Baker and second baseman Len Schulte, both of whom later enjoyed solid major league careers. Baker married a local girl and made his home in Youngstown. Predictably, the Browns kept falling in the standings, finally finishing seventh, a place the team had regularly occupied in Johnstown. Nonetheless, the early popularity of the team assured the Browns an attendance of 94,000 for the season.[65]

The last year before war broke out in Europe belonged to the Canton Terriers. In late June, the Red Sox send hustling first baseman Kerby Farrell to Canton. He energized the Terriers who won ten of the next eleven games to take over first place. They never looked back as they went on to top Charleston by seven and a half games. Manager Pat Patterson's lineup card included a bevy of future major leaguers. Farrell held down first base. Al Mazer manned second and teamed with shortstop Eddie Pellagrini, a league all-star, to make a slick double-play combo. Outfielders John Lazor and Frank "Chick" Genovese both batted over .300 and hit double-digit home runs. Lazor drove in a league-best 103 runs, and collected a team-record 171 hits. Genovese topped the MAL with 113 runs scored, and drew a league record 133 base on balls. Bob Finley handled the catching. Pitcher Ralph Waite never duplicated his fine 19–5 record and was out of baseball in two years. Other pitchers, Al "Eli" Hodkey, an MAL all-star lefty, Bill Voiselle who did not yet wear the number 96 he later made famous, Hugh Kirkman, and Norm Brown, did make the big leagues. Canton fans responded with enthusiasm. Nearly 97,000 paid the admission fee, and another 15,000 attended free.[66]

Canton kept winning throughout the playoffs. After third-place Akron took game one behind Hank Sauer's home run, the Terriers reeled off three straight to take the first-round series. The fourth-place Springfield Indians upended second-place Charleston three games to one. Springfield took the crucial third game on Chuck Workman's home run, and won the final game thanks to Charleston errors. In the deciding series, Canton lost game one to Springfield, who rode Charles "Red" Embree's pitching and Workman's four RBIs. That was all Springfield would win as Canton reeled off four straight victories. In the series Lazor, Farrell and Mazer pounded the ball. Mazer's three doubles and three RBIs highlighted the 5–2 win in the final game.

Some 43 players who played in the MAL in 1939 advanced to the majors. Of that group, Springfield's Bob Lemon and Portsmouth's Alston made the Baseball Hall of Fame. Neither gained fame for the position they played in 1939. Alston, of course, gained fame as the long-time manager of the Dodgers. Lemon, still a teenager, played shortstop for Springfield, showed a strong arm, and batted a respectable .293. He continued to play the infield through

Bob Lemon played parts of two seasons for the Springfield Indians. As the regular shortstop in 1939, he batted a solid .293 and displayed a strong arm. After World War II he switched to the pitching mound, making his way to the Cleveland Indians and, in 1976, to the Hall of Fame (National Baseball Hall of Fame Library, Cooperstown, New York).

1942, even appearing in a few games at third base for Cleveland. After World War II he took his strong arm to the pitcher's mound, and posted 207 career wins for the Indians. He entered the Hall of Fame in Cooperstown in 1976. In 1939, Lemon did not get a chance to pitch to Jim Hegan, the Springfield catcher, but he did in Cleveland where the sturdy catcher played for 17 seasons.

Springfield teammate, pitcher Allie "Super Chief" Reynolds, compiled an 11–8 record. He had signed out of Oklahoma A&M University (now Oklahoma State) for a $1,000 signing bonus. He went on to win the Hickok Belt in 1951 as the best professional athlete of the year, after starring for the World Champion New York Yankees. He won 182 major league games in 13 seasons, and went 7–2 in six World Series, but he fell short of the Hall of Fame. He was always a fierce competitor. Whitey Ford remembered, "Everybody looked up to Reynolds. We were all afraid of him. I was and Mantle was and I think even Martin was."[67]

Akron's Hank Sauer would be named National League MVP in 1951 after leading the National League in homers and RBIs, but in 1939 he hit only 13 homers while batting .301. Sauer's teammate, catcher Aaron Robinson, won Akron's most popular player contest for which he received a watch, a pair of shoes, gloves, ten dollars, and a tire. Such was life in the low minors. Robinson, who batted .353, became a solid catcher for the Yankees until being replaced by Yogi Berra.

Following the 1939 season, Daily allowed as how that season was his "happiest in baseball." He experienced a "minimum of trouble." Perhaps, that remark came from his not having to deal with Holmes all summer. Daily had another reason to be pleased. In late May, Joe Carr, who held the title of promotion director of the National Association, died of a heart attack. Daily already served on the executive committee of the Association as representative of the Class A, B, C, and D leagues. NAPBL president William Bramham appointed Daily to replace Carr. In doing so, Bramham called Daily "the dean of minor league presidents." With his 14 years as league president, Daily's tenure exceeded that of any other sitting league president. He did have to relinquish his position as representative of the low minors, but, of course, he sat on the NAPBL's executive committee in his new role. Nor did Daily have to give up his jobs as president of two leagues. Bramham saw the job as part-time. Carr, after all, had doubled as president of the National Football League.[68]

Daily had reason to be pleased at the conclusion of the 1939 season. The MAL stood head and shoulders above all other Class C leagues. Forty-three players from the MAL in the 1939 season would advance to the major leagues.

No other Class C league produced half as many future big-leaguers. The East Texas League came closest with 20, while the Western Association and Cotton States League had 18, the Pioneer League produced 12, the Canadian-American League had eight, the Interstate League had only four, and the Cape Breton League brought up the rear with one. Nor did any other league command the population base of the Middle Atlantic, whose cities had a population of over one million (1,017,435). The major leagues recognized the quality of the league. It was the only league in its classification with every member affiliated with a major league club. Personally, Daily had to be pleased with his appointment as promotion director of the minor leagues, and with the recognition of his seniority as the longest-serving league president.

5

"We intend to keep things going"
War Years, 1940–1945

Even before the 1939 season ended, the Germans, on September 1, launched a *blitzkrieg* attack on Poland. France and Britain immediately declared war on Germany. Like a black cloud, the threat of war had hovered over Europe since the mid–1930s. Now, it was a reality. Most Americans still wanted their country to stay out of this war, but agreed with President Roosevelt that America should be "the arsenal of democracy." In October Congress agreed to allow belligerents to purchase U.S. goods on a "cash and carry" basis. The economy, which had improved in the first half of the year, began to purr as American industries geared up for military production. People were beginning to find jobs and with those came money. Since nothing much happened in Western Europe in the first months after the declaration of war, the so-called "phony war," Americans seemed free to go on with their lives as if there were no war. That changed in the spring of 1940 when the Soviet Union invaded Finland and Germany moved against the Western European democracies. The baseball season was just starting when Germany overran Denmark and Norway.

All that seemed a long way away to the leaders of the MAL, who faced problems throughout his league even before the end of 1939. The Yankees continued their litany of complaints about the condition of the field and the lease of Akron's League Park. They had paid $3,000 to lease the park and were responsible for maintenance. Now, in November, Edith Falor put the park up for sale. George Weiss threatened to move the club. He let it be known that the Yankees were considering sites in Springfield, Steubenville, Zanesville and Lima in Ohio, as well as Fort Wayne, Indiana, and New Castle, Pennsylvania. Weiss went to Akron himself and Daily joined him there. Akron business manager Ray Brandenberger demanded "a suitable playing field." He contacted Goodyear and Firestone about leasing their fields, but neither company offered acceptable terms. Brandenberger also complained about poor bus service to the park. He got the attention of Mayor Lee D. Schroy, who pressured the bus company into accommodating the concern of the Yankees. Only after Weiss and Bradenberger visited Erie in March did a new lease get done. Falor reduced the price on the lease and made the lease renewable through 1942.[1]

Some issues around the league were less taxing, but troublesome nonetheless. Portsmouth, with the smallest population in the league (40,474), had not drawn well in 1939. The St. Louis Cardinals expressed unhappiness, but as long as Branch Rickey called the shots, chances were good that Portsmouth would continue as a Cardinals farm team. In Charleston, Watt Powell's club had gone through hard times, forcing him to take on a partner, Chester Lewis, a wealthy dairyman who owned Valley Bell Dairy. Although Charleston still needed help, Powell would do whatever he needed to do to keep his team alive.[2]

More serious problems existed in Erie and Springfield. The Springfield Indians had lost money in 1938 and 1939. In early December, Buzz Wetzel told Dick Hudson, the sports editor of the *Charleston Daily Mail* that he did not "intend to stick around here, scratching to make dollar bills meet." That comment seemed more than a little strange, since "scratching to make dollar bills meet" could have been the definition of any owner's life in the low minors, but it made clear Wetzel's intention to get out of Springfield. He wanted to sell, and found a buyer in the person of wealthy Bob Ireland, president of Ilanna Coal, who purchased the club on December 8, 1939. Wetzel had told Ireland that Cleveland would not continue to affiliate with Springfield, but Ireland failed to fully appreciate the implications of that comment. After talks with the Cleveland people, Ireland understood that the Indians were not coming back to Springfield. Ireland, with Daily's assistance, began looking for a major league tie-in. Detroit seemed the most promising candidate.[3]

Wetzel moved quickly, transferring the Cleveland farm club from Springfield to Charleston. The deal gave Wetzel an option to purchase Lewis' half-interest in the Charleston franchise following the 1940 season. Wetzel and Powell had both begun their managerial careers in Charleston before World War I, so they had known each other a long time, and there was a level of trust between the two. Since the Indians had a record of stocking their MAL farm with quality players, there was no complaint from Charleston sportswriters and fans. Indeed, the *Daily Mail* reported that Charleston fans were more "keyed up" than at any time since 1931, when Charleston got its MAL franchise. Powell was ecstatic. "Boy, oh boy," he exclaimed, "this is the best hook up Charleston has had in the Middle Atlantic League." The next three years proved Powell right.[4]

The problems in Erie began when the Cincinnati Reds decided to pull out of the city. Leo Miller still had the tie-in with Indianapolis of the American Association, but minor league affiliations never worked well. The Sailors had played all day games at home and drew only 40,000 fans in 1939. The Erie school board owned Ainsworth/Athletic Field and refused to make the improvements that Miller demanded. He, especially, wanted the board to install lights. The greater problem was that Miller was tapped out; he wanted to sell. In the spring when the Yankees were threatening to abandon Akron, he had hopes that New York would take the franchise off his hands. In mid-March, Weiss and others of the Yankees brass actually visited Erie to inspect the facilities. It is likely that Weiss merely wanted to put pressure on people back in Akron to help him with the field problems. When a big March snowstorm greeted the Yankees brass, they beat a hasty retreat. Miller gave up. With no buyers, he returned the franchise to the league.[5]

The biggest bomb to fall on the MAL, and all of minor league baseball, in the offseason came from Commissioner Landis, who always disliked the farm system concept and detested Branch Rickey who created, defended, and personified the system. Rickey's St. Louis Cardinals operated the largest farm system, either owning or having working agreements with 32 farm clubs. All other teams lagged far behind the Cardinals. The Dodgers and Detroit ranked next with 12 farm clubs, followed by the Yankees with 11 and Red Sox with nine. In 1938, Landis had taken on Rickey when he freed 74 Cardinals farm hands from their contracts. Now, in 1940, when Landis moved to blow up the farm system, it was not Rickey he took on, but rather the Detroit Tigers. On its 12 farm clubs Detroit owned the rights to some 165 players. The consistent failures of Detroit-backed MAL teams attested to poor scouting rather than lack of investment in the farm system. Staff members in the commissioner's office had uncovered irregularities, rules violations, and "secret agreements" made by the Tigers, especially by farm director/general manager Jack Zeller. On January 16, 1940, Landis ordered 91 Detroit players, including five on the Tigers roster, freed from their contracts. He also ordered Detroit to pay $47,250 to 15 players who had been sold by Detroit. The Tigers calculated the losses at "close to half a million dollars," but that may have been a conservative estimate.[6]

Landis' ruling went well beyond dealing with the irregularities found in the Detroit farm system to be an attack on the farm system in general. The system, the commissioner argued, was inherently "evil" because of its effect on both minor league players and clubs. In his view, the reason major league teams operated farm clubs was in order "to control great numbers of players, imperiling their essential rights." The farm system, he stated, restricted players to "grooved advancement." Of course, Landis refused to go to the heart of the matter, the reserve clause that bound players in perpetuity to the club holding their contract. The farm system, he also added, "reduces minor clubs to subservience."[7] The details came in "point 5" of Landis' dictum. It read: "Working agreements must be executed by the club actually making same and must not be executed in the name of affiliated or subsidiary clubs to whom the major or other higher classification club supplies the necessary funds." If Landis had his way, signing players to contracts of minor league affiliates but keeping them under the control of the major league team would now become a thing of the past. On the face of it, *The Sporting News* opined this would seem to end working agreements, but allow major league teams to own outright minor league clubs.[8]

Landis proposed a bold new plan of his own to replace the farm system. Announced on January 26, 1940, in a 3,000-word letter to major league club owners, Landis plan contained three components. First, he would entirely eliminate the practice of optioning players. Since 1932, teams had been allowed to option a player three times. Second, recognizing the player development value of farms, he proposed to create centralized developmental schools financed by all major league clubs. Third, in order to sustain the lower minors, major league teams would grant subsidies to Class B, C, and D leagues.[9]

Reaction came quickly. The exodus from working agreements began immediately. The Cardinals cancelled ten working agreements and the Yankees ended seven, including the agreements with Akron and with Butler of the PSA. Detroit had the most reason to be spooked. Newspapers carrying the AP story headlined it "Chains Doomed." Brooklyn president Larry McPhail attacked the proposal, predicting the plan, if implemented, would kill ten to fifteen minor leagues. Landis' proposals would, of course, require action by the major and minor leagues. The revolutionary changes never had a chance to be approved by either the major leagues or the minor leagues.[10]

The "usually amiable" Daily "made no secret of his dislike of the Landis decision." He vowed to fight for the minors. "We intend to keep things going no matter what," he said. The phone call he received from Leo Miller saying that, because of the Landis decision, Indianapolis would withdraw its working agreement with the Erie Sailors and Miller would return the Erie franchise to the league, contributed to Daily being upset. "He [Landis] doesn't realize our plight," Daily moaned.[11]

In a month, voices calmed down. Landis seemed satisfied with the reaction and decided not to push the issue. For the Middle Atlantic League, the impact of the Landis decision remained clear. Despite the success that Ireland had in raising money in Springfield, Detroit was not about to challenge Landis, nor was any other major league club willing to confront the commissioner directly. Neither Springfield nor Erie could find a major league affiliate for 1940.

When the MAL met in Youngstown in mid–February and in Canton in late March, Erie and Springfield announced their withdrawal. Neither dared to go without a working agreement with a major league club. Daily admitted he had no hope of finding replacement cities; even if he could, it would not have been possible to find a major league club willing to help with a working agreement. The league had no choice but to go with six teams in 1940—the Akron Yankees, Canton Terriers, Charleston Senators, Dayton Wings, Portsmouth Red Birds and Youngstown Browns. Akron and Youngstown were owned outright by the major league club. The other four teams had solid agreements: Canton with the Red Sox, Charleston with Cleveland, Dayton with Brooklyn, and Portsmouth with the St. Louis Cardinals.[12]

During 1940, the world became more dangerous and a scarier place for Americans. German troops, after conquering Denmark and Norway in April and May, rolled through Belgium into France by mid–May. Splitting the French and British armies in a lightening move, the Germans isolated the British in a defenseless position. The British were forced to ferry 300,000 troops off the European continent at Dunkirk between May 26 and June 4. German troops entered Paris on June 14 and France signed an armistice on June 22, giving Hitler control of all of continental Western Europe. The Battle of Britain began in July 1940. Despite the efforts of the America First Movement, Americans cheered Prime Minister Winston Churchill and the brave RAF pilots who defended Britain. America's military buildup, called "preparedness," began in the summer of 1940. The first peace-time draft, officially the Selective Service Training and Service Act, went into effect in September. President Roosevelt called on the United States to be the "arsenal of democracy." In November, given the dangers to the country, President Roosevelt was elected for an unprecedented third term.

The 1940 season got off to a dreary start. Rain in May played havoc with the baseball schedule, causing postponement of 35 games in that first month. At Portsmouth rain washed out eight games in a row. Attendance around the league never really recovered from the soggy start. The Portsmouth team struggled, finishing in last place on the field and at the box office. Only 20,000 fans came to the ballpark. That was the lowest attendance in memory for any

MAL city, although back in the 1920s there had been lower numbers. In Akron, the Yankees took over first place from Canton on July 16 and stayed there for the remainder of the season. Attendance at Akron, however, estimated at 40,000, lagged far behind the 1939 levels. A strike at General Tire contributed to the low attendance. A mid–June exhibition game against the parent Yankees provided Akron's only sellout of the year. Only in Charleston did attendance rise. The Cleveland Indians provided a strong cast of players, giving the Senators excitement and a second-place finish. The Senators drew a league-high 69,000 fans.

The Akron Yankees not only captured the regular-season flag, but also rolled through the playoffs to take the official championship as well. Akron wore hand-me-down uniforms recognizable by the traditional New York pinstripes but with the "NY" logo removed. Their blue caps with a white block "A" were new. Fans labeled the hustling club "The Gas House Gang of Akron." The Yankees batted a collective .275, well below the high team average for the past few years, but the league's highest in 1940.

First baseman Steve "Bud" Souchock provided the heaviest lumber. Souchock, son of a Pennsylvania coal miner, had signed with Greensburg of the Pennsylvania State Association in 1939 after impressing at a tryout camp. Financially strapped Greensburg sold him to the Yankees organization after two months. With Akron, he clubbed 24 homers, drove in 105 runs, and hit .310. His average dropped dramatically in the second half of the season and he complained of eye problems, especially during day games. After the season he checked into Johns Hopkins Hospital and learned he had "photophobia," a problem that was cured with medication. After the war he would spend eight years in the majors with the Yankees, White Sox and Tigers.

In addition to Souchock, two career minor leaguers, second baseman Tony Sams and outfielder Ed Tighe, contributed mightily to the Yankees' attack. Sams, an enormously popular player with Akron fans, topped the MAL in hits (163), runs (109), and total bases (277) while hitting 19 homers and batting .318. The left-handed-hitting Tighe compiled a .325 batting average, the highest in the league, and he collected the most triples, 16, as well. Mel Queen led the pitching staff with 18 wins, a 2.70 ERA, and a league-best 202 strikeouts.

In the playoffs, the Yankees struggled to get past third-place Youngstown before taking out Dayton. Youngstown's Fred Sanford (14–12) and Queen locked up in two pitchers' duels in the first series, each winning one game. Queen, however, won the decisive game, giving him two of Akron's three wins over Youngstown. After fourth-place Dayton upset second-place Charleston three games to one, the Yankees had little trouble beating the

Wings. The Yankees knocked out the Wings in six games, as Queen picked up another victory in the championship series.

Even though the league operated with just six teams, it managed to produce almost as many future major league players as it had done in 1939. Even though none became superstars, the MAL sent 37 players to the majors. Youngstown's all-star third baseman, Bob Dillinger, broke the league record by swiping 67 bases; he would continue stealing bases for the St. Louis Browns, leading the American League in 1947, 1948 and 1949. The bespectacled Dillinger also tied for the league lead in hits with 163 and runs with 109. Teammate Clarence "Hooks" Iott, a flame-throwing left-handed pitcher with little control, set a more dubious record by walking 195 batters. It was an unmatched record. Iott also led the MAL in losses (16) and runs allowed (136). Iott actually pitched in two games for the Cardinals in 1941 and put in a season in the big leagues after the war. He pitched in the minors until 1957, winning 175 games. A third Youngstown Brownie, first baseman Jerry White, topped the circuit in RBIs with 124.

During the season, on June 24, the last-place Portsmouth Red Birds fired Fred Dorman as manager and replaced him with first baseman Walter Alston. It marked the beginning of a Hall of Fame managing career. No one knew that at the time, and the change at the helm made little difference; the Red Birds still finished in last place. As a player, Alston again led the league with 28 home runs.

That Charleston led the league in attendance was amazing, because early in the season the team lost its grandstand in a fire. The late-night fire on May 14 took part of the grandstand, bleachers, concession stand, clubhouse, and office, all part of the original park which was built in 1916. The *Charleston Daily Mail* estimated the damage at $5,000. Somehow, two weeks later, with new wooden stands, but without a roof, office or clubhouse, the Senators resumed play in Kanawha Park. Club secretary Bill Martin scheduled lots of promotions and special events to boost attendance—*Daily Mail* Night, Ed Hall Night to honor the popular team manager, the Elks' drum and bugle corps and drill team, and a Jesse Owens Night where the 1936 Olympic star raced a horse around the bases. Following the season, the team stayed in town to play exhibition games against two Negro League teams, the Toledo Crawfords and the Brooklyn Royal Giants.[13]

Elsewhere around the MAL, results proved uneven. Youngstown pleased the parent Browns when it attracted 58,000 fans. Portsmouth, on the other hand, smelled doom given its low attendance and rumors that the Cardinals would pull out of Portsmouth. There was also danger that the Dodgers might pull out of Dayton, which lost money and had drawn only 37,000 paid customers.[14]

The rumors in Portsmouth proved to be true. Branch Rickey would pull out of his hometown. Losses had continued to mount in the river city. Even in the championship year of 1938, the club had lost over $5,000. The next year attendance dropped to 40,000 and financial losses continued to mount. In the rain-soaked season of 1940, the Red Birds' losses mounted to over $15,000, perhaps as much as $22,000. Rickey could no longer justify the bottom line to his boss, Sam Breadon. The Cardinals had begun selling off minor league clubs in 1940; Portsmouth was next in line. Rickey paid a visit to Portsmouth in early February and city manager Ross E. Windon led a Portsmouth delegation to St. Louis a couple of weeks later. Rickey made it clear that the Cardinals had made the decision to relinquish its ownership of the team, but indicated his willingness to enter into a working agreement if local ownership took over the club. Local men who had the money to invest knew the bottom line, so not enough investors could be found to raise the necessary capital. Windon gave up the ghost by the end of February.[15]

In Springfield, Ireland still wanted a ball club. He had been left holding the bag in 1940 when Wetzel pulled out for Charleston. He showed up at the November MAL meeting with an application for membership. So did men from Zanesville, Erie and Wheeling, a clear sign that the economy was turning around. Ireland's coal business provided him plenty of money. Nevertheless, upon returning to Springfield he went to work to create broad-based support for a franchise. By the end of February, he had enlisted 4,000 people who pledged to put money into his enterprise. Ireland's enthusiasm appealed to Rickey, who decided to cast his lot with Springfield. With the working agreement a reality, Springfield returned to the MAL for 1941 as the Springfield Cardinals.[16]

The Brooklyn Dodgers, like the Cardinals, looked to cut their losses. Branch Rickey, Jr., claimed that the Dodgers had lost $37,000 in the two seasons as owners of the Dayton Wings. He put the franchise up for sale. Three different suitors lined up, but none wanted to spend much money. In late February, Ducky Holmes announced he was repurchasing the team. He got busy selling tickets, raising over $5,000 in advanced box seat sales. Although Holmes had been selling tickets for six weeks, it was not until April 13, 1941, that Rickey, Jr., made the formal announcement that the Dodgers were relinquishing the Dayton franchise to Holmes. Both Brooklyn and the Cincinnati Reds promised to help Holmes with players, but he would have to manage without a formal working agreement. Brooklyn invited Holmes' club to join the Dodgers' minor leaguers in Wilson, North Carolina, for spring training. Holmes was just happy to be back in business after spending 1940 managing the Fayetteville Angels in the Arkansas-Missouri League.[17]

5. "We intend to keep things going"   155

Sportswriters around the league loved having Holmes back; he gave them plenty to write about. Ducky told Dick Hudson of the *Charleston Daily Mail*: "Tell 'em in Charleston that the Duck is back." Hudson opined that the Charleston faithful "liked the snarling, clowning, Holmes." He attracted fans to the park, if only to boo him. Joe Hootey of the *Zanesville Signal* noted that fans have "affection for their villains as for their heroes."[18]

Zanesville mayor Tom V. Moorehead got assurance from Daily at the league meeting in November 1940 that his city had a lock on a franchise, except for two obstacles. First, a major league club needed to affiliate with Zanesville, and, second, an eighth team needed to enter the league. The reason for Zanesville's confidence was a new ballpark. Brand new Municipal Stadium stood on Main Street (U.S. route 40) at Townsend Street, ready to go. A multi-purpose facility, the park had been built with Works Progress Administration money. The baseball grandstand, a steel and concrete structure with a roof covering seating for 3,800, went up first. It contained fourteen rows of board

Gant Municipal Stadium in Zanesville, Ohio, opened in 1941 to rave reviews. Built on Main Street by the Works Progress Administration, it sat 3,800 for baseball. It represented an early effort at a multi-purpose facility with a separate football grandstand down the left field foul line (courtesy BallparkReviews.com).

seats, a press box at the top of the stands directly behind home plate, and dugouts cut into the stands. Down the third base line, separate football grandstands had gone up before autumn of 1940. It was a sparkling facility. In December 1940 George Trautman, president of the American Association, came over from Columbus to help the local baseball enthusiasts create an organizing committee. Daily sent Ken Shriver, an ambitious young Akron native, from the MAL office to serve as business manager of the club. He also located William S. "Bill" Simpson, an Akron grocer, who was willing to invest his own money in Zanesville. Daily made sure the MAL granted the franchise to Simpson. Daily then went shopping for major league sponsors at the baseball winter meeting in Atlanta. After striking out with Washington and the Chicago White Sox, Daily got the Chicago Cubs to agree to align with the new franchise. At the league meeting, held in Zanesville, Daily welcomed Zanesville back into the league as the Zanesville Cubs.[19]

Daily found an ex-scout living in Nashville, Tennessee, named Jimmy Hamilton, who was interested in operating a franchise in Erie. Into March, hope for Erie rested on Hamilton, but his interest and Daily's in him began to fade with the spring thaw. In mid–March Daily visited Erie and urged Mayor Charles Barber to become active if he wanted a team. With the help of Ray Peebles, sportswriter for the *Erie Dispatch-Herald*, a local group began to organize. They incorporated as the Baseball Club of Erie, Inc., with former Erie manager Julius "Jocko" Munch as president. The rotund Munch was enormously popular in Erie baseball circles. He began playing professionally in 1912, and, after coming to Erie in 1930 as manager of the Central League club, made his home in the lake city. When his playing days were behind him, Munch seemed content to run the sporting goods department at the Sears Roebuck store. Peebles agreed to act as business manager until a professional could be hired. From then on, Daily worked with the Munch/Peebles group to the exclusion of Hamilton, who eventually dropped out of the running. If that group had pulled out, Daily had a fallback plan. A Rochester businessman was interested in running a team in Portsmouth, but the Erie group was ready to operate and willing to try to make a go of it as an independent club. The Braves and Reds promised to option players to the Sailors.[20]

With the addition of Erie and Zanesville, the Middle Atlantic League was back to an eight-team circuit for 1941. Daily looked forward to a 136-game schedule and a "banner season.." He had to be pleased that the MAL owners extended his contract and that of his sidekick Russ Hockenbury for three years. Daily, of course, did have to deal with Holmes again. At the first owners' meeting after his return, "the Duck" proposed that after August 1 teams in the first division be allowed to purchase home games from second-division teams for $150 per game. This, he argued, would increase overall league attendance. Holmes did think outside the box. The league, of course, voted down the idea.[21]

By March 1941, Congress approved the Lend-Lease program to make Roosevelt's "arsenal of democracy" pledge a reality. FDR began supplying war material to Britain, and after Hitler invaded the USSR in June, to the Soviets as well. In order to protect the Atlantic shipping lanes from the East Coast to Britain, the United States sent troops to Greenland in April, followed by the occupation of Iceland in July. While the Battle of Britain troubled Americans, most people were only vaguely aware of events in Asia where Japanese aggression threatened the entire region. On the plus side, unemployment rapidly disappeared and wages began to rise. By the opening of the baseball season, most Americans had coins in their pockets to rub together.

With his league back to eight teams for 1941 and the economy humming, Daily had reason for his confidence. Erie fans welcomed baseball back by coming to the ballpark in throngs. The Sailors drew over 110,000 fans for the season, nearly twice as many paid admissions as any other team in the MAL. That assured the team turned a tidy profit. In Zanesville, the Cubs finished the season dead last in the standings, but brand spanking new Municipal Stadium drew a respectable 57,000 fans. At Dayton, Holmes just seemed happy to be back in the league with his own team. Although Charleston finished in the second division, fans were spending money to see the Senators. Their attendance ranked second in the league. Canton continued to draw decent crowds. Other cities did not benefit from the country's return to prosperity, though. Youngstown continued to disappoint its owners both on the field and at the box office. In the biggest surprise, Akron did not draw well, even though it had a first place team. Al Schacht, the "clown prince of baseball," sold out League Park on June 24, but that was Akron's only sellout of the year. For the season, only 40,000 fans turned out, about the same as in 1940. The club lost $8,000, and at season's end it was a foregone conclusion that the franchise would be up for sale.

The drop in attendance at Akron was difficult to fathom, because for the second year in a row the Akron Yankees took the regular-season crown. The Yankees took over first place in late May, won 28 of 33 games by Independence Day, and managed to stay ahead of Erie and Canton as the race went down to the wire. The 77–48 record was the best Akron achieved in the MAL. In reality though, the 1941 club lacked the talent of previous Akron teams. Their team batting average of .243, seventh in the league, attests to the team's weakness. Infielders Joe Collins, Joe Lutz, and Al Buzas would make the majors, but were overwhelmed by MAL pitching; none hit higher than .248. The team lacked power; outfielder Ed Sauer, Hank's younger brother, topped the club with a mere six home runs. Only catcher Gus Niarhos, with a .304 batting average, managed to bat over .300. On the other hand, the Yankees did have solid fielding and outstanding pitching. Nineteen-year-old Willis "Bill" Baker, the best left-hander in the league, posted a tidy 14–7 record with an ERA of 1.98. Unfortunately, injuries and the war curtailed Baker's development; he never again enjoyed a year like 1941. Walt "Monk" Dubiel also won 14 games, with a 2.44 ERA. Three other pitchers posted double-digit wins.

Ralph "Buzz" Boyle, in his first year of managing, somehow got the Yankees to win with hustle, scrap, and plenty of fight. Their historian described the 1941 Yankees as "a jabbering, talkative, fighting ball club." Boyle set the tone in May when he went after a Youngstown bench jockey, touching off a free-for-all. Niarhos and Boyle got into a more serious brawl in a game at archrival Canton. After Akron's George Verbeck and Canton second baseman Lee Mohr got into an argument, Niarhos stuck his nose in and soon he and Mohr were slugging each other. Boyle entered the fray and "KOed" Canton's Francis "Red" Walsh. Pandemonium ensued, requiring four policemen to intervene before order could be restored.[22]

In the first round of the playoffs, the Yankees' limitations caught up with them. Against Canton, Akron eked out a 3–2 win in 14 innings in game one, beating Lou Lucier (23–5), the league's best pitcher. Baker's two-hit shutout in the second game gave Akron a two games to none lead; it provided the highlight of the series for Akron. Then Canton took over. They won game three, 7–6, in ten innings, behind the pitching of starter Harry "Fritz" Dorish and superb relief work of Joe Ostrowski. Canton bats pounded out a 9–4 win in game four to even the series. In that game, Lucier was beaned and sent to the hospital, increasing the animosity between the two clubs and their fans. In the deciding game at League Park, a bench-clearing brawl delayed the game, before Canton's weak hitting first baseman, Malone "Bones" Sanders, who hit just .236 on the season, knocked in the go-ahead run in the top of the ninth inning to give Canton the lead. Then Niarhos and Mohr came to blows, touching off a wild melee that required four policemen and three umpires to restore order. Ostrowski, in relief of Lucier, set down the Yankees in the ninth.[23]

The Canton team that beat the Yankees in the playoff semi-finals possessed the hitting that Akron lacked. The Terriers led the MAL in team batting average with a respectable .271 and in home runs with 60. Elmer "Butch" Nieman led the attack with ten homers and a .321 batting average. The Red Sox kept sending Canton kids who could hit: Hollis "Bud" Sheely batted a solid .278, Denny Doyle chipped in with a .336 average, George

"Pinky" Woods hit .362, and shortstop Ben Steiner batted .296. All made the majors. Canton also boasted the league's best pitcher in Lucier, and backed him up with pitching depth in Bill Voiselle, Dorich, Woods, and Ostrowski. Lucier dominated the MAL hitters. He led the circuit in wins (23), earned-run average (1.51), strikeouts (199), winning percentage (.821), and innings pitched (247).

Erie's patchwork team finished a close second to Akron in the regular season. Erie's president, Jocko Munch, manager Kerby Farrell, and business manager Milt Woodward, scrapped, begged, and scouted far and wide for players. Nearly half the roster had played in the Class D Pennsylvania State Association in 1940, but Munch still found several players at tryout camps. The Cincinnati Reds sent a few players to Erie, as did the Boston Braves. The Yankees shipped Monk Dubiel to the Sailors late in the season. Woodward's big coup was acquiring all-stars Cosmo Cotelle, from Dayton, and Bill Mongiello, from Canton, during the season. Cotelle, a diminutive 36-year-old outfielder went to Erie in late July and proceeded to pace the MAL in batting (.367) and hits (170). Cotelle was not afraid to sacrifice his body for the club; he led the league in times hit by the pitcher (10). He played in the minors for 20 years without reaching the majors. Canton management felt the club had such strength that it could sell Mongiello, a MAL all-star third baseman, but not a major league prospect, to Erie. Mongiello had played in Canton the year before and would continue to play in the MAL until the league closed its doors, giving him the record longevity in league history. He batted a respectable .288, solidified the infield, and led the league in walks.

The playoffs belonged to the Sailors. In the first round, Erie swept the fourth-place Springfield Cardinals three straight games in their best-of-five series. For Springfield, player-manager Walt Alston put up his usual numbers leading the league in home runs (25), RBIs (102), total bases (240), runs (88), and walks (85). Gil Dobbs (14–9) had pitched a no-hitter against Youngstown in an 18–0 Cardinal win, but he was helpless against Erie. The Cards had little else.

Their sweep of Springfield left Erie well rested for the finals against Canton. The Sailors rolled over Canton, four games to one, in the best-of-seven series. After Erie took game one behind lefty Ted Mallet (11–4), Lucier collected the win in game two as Canton tied the series. The Terriers had lost their best hitter, Butch Nieman, when he broke a collarbone in the Akron series. After the second game, a "physically and emotionally exhausted" Terrier club "turned out to be easy prey" as the Sailors won three straight. In the final series Mallet won two games, while pitching ace Horatio Bartleson (19–8) and Monk Dubiel (14–8) each picked up a win.[24]

Zanesville, Youngstown, Dayton, and Charleston made up the second division. At Dayton, Holmes turned the managing over to shortstop Bill McWilliams for much of the season, but the Ducks finished sixth, nearly 20 games from fourth place. At Youngstown, young infielders Joe Lutz (.155), Len Schulte (.257) and Dick Kimble (.201), and pitchers Earl "Lefty" Jones (7–11) and Jim Bilbrey (1–3) were overmatched by the level of MAL play, but they would eventually make the majors. The Browns could crow about outfielder Bob Jones, their only all-star and the team's only .300 hitter (,303). Jones was hands down the best fielding outfielder in the league; his .995 fielding average was the highest ever recorded in the MAL. Charleston came within one win of a .500 season, plus they put some nice prospects on the field. Pitcher Ed Klieman won 16 games with a 2.22 ERA. Second baseman John Blatnik (.246), catcher Ralph Weigel (.222), and outfielders Gene Woodling (.217) and Clint Connatser (.248) struggled with Class C pitching in 1941; still they became more than just wartime players in the majors. Zanesville ran through more players than any other team. Only Ed Sauer (.296) gave their fans something to cheer about.

During the season, the war machines of Germany and Japan continued to roll. On June 22, Germany invaded the Soviet Union and in July Japan struck French Indo-China. The U.S. responded by freezing Japanese assets and placing an embargo on aviation fuel. Japan needed rubber and oil and looked to Southeast Asia to acquire it. In the fall, the United States and Germany began an undeclared naval war as American merchant ships ferried goods to Britain and Russia across the North Atlantic where German U-boats lurked under the waters. On October 30, German submarines sunk the American ship *Reuben James*. President Roosevelt had every reason to ask Congress for a declaration of war, but he did not.

The world changed forever for America when the Japanese bombed Pearl Harbor on December 7, 1941. "The day which will live in infamy," President Roosevelt said. All Americans agreed. Everyone would remember exactly where they were when they heard the news of Pearl Harbor. It meant the United States was in the war. Men and boys went in droves to recruiting stations to join the fight. Others waited for the draft to call their number. None expected to avoid the effects of the war.

Daily believed "the beneficial effects of baseball on the morale of our people is [sic] more widely recognized today than it was during the first World War." President Roosevelt proved Daily right when he gave the green light for the sport to continue. Organized baseball gave a collective sigh of relief. The uncertainty as to whether baseball could go on was lifted. Still, some people thought it the patriotic duty of baseball to close down for the duration.

Others predicted a shortage of players as young men swarmed to the armed forces.²⁵

Given all the uncertainties, the MAL faced a difficult time in lining up for the 1942 season. Erie and Charleston had attracted the most fans and proven the most profitable in 1941, but they were geographical outliers in the Ohio-centered league. Rationing of gas and tires, both of which were anticipated, would make travel to those cities difficult, if not impossible, for the other teams. Akron and Youngstown were the most troubled franchises. The New York Yankees had until February 15, 1942, to renew the lease on League Park in Akron. Negotiations with the mortgage holders had been acrimonious from the beginning. Now the owners put the park up for sale. Even though prospects for a sale before the 1942 season seemed slim, the Yankees had made the decision to pull out of Akron before the final game of the 1941 season. Disappointing attendance, in spite of consecutive pennant-winning teams, soured George Weiss on Akron. Following the attack on Pearl Harbor, but before the Yankees officially announced they were leaving Akron, respected sportswriter Jim Schlemmer made it clear to his readers: "This [the Yankees' pull out] is a move that cannot be blamed on the war." In his view, the park lease, the deteriorating condition of the park, and low attendance made the decision to leave Akron a logical one for New York. In previous years when New York threatened to leave Akron, an alternative location appeared on the horizon, but not this time. The Yankees let it be known that they would not return to Akron, and that the franchise could be had for $3,000. Even at this cut-rate price, investors could not be found in Akron or elsewhere. Daily continued to hold out hope for Akron long after reason dictated otherwise.²⁶

Back-biting quickly set in among the remaining MAL members. All understood that seven was not a workable number of teams, so, if a replacement for Akron could not be found, one franchise would have to go. Attention focused on Erie and Charleston, the only teams outside Ohio. In Charleston, Watt Powell was troubled by his own poor health as well as by the long hauls to Erie and Dayton. He considered jumping to the West-Virginia-based Class D Mountain State League. Holmes, never one to mince words, came to Charleston's defense, threatening to pull Dayton out of the league if the MAL voted out Charleston. In Erie the park needed repairs after winter storms destroyed the fence and damaged the stands, but the school board, owners of the park, refused to approve money for the park's upkeep.²⁷

Despite the distances involved, neither Erie nor Charleston left the MAL in 1942. William DeWitt, vice president and general manager of the St. Louis Browns, resolved the MAL's dilemma by giving up on Youngstown. He returned the franchise to the league at the March 8 MAL meeting in Springfield. DeWitt said the Browns' decision resulted from an "acute shortage of players. The Browns may have been the poorest team in the American League, but DeWitt had developed an extensive farm system; only the Cardinals, Dodgers, and Yankees had fielded more farm clubs in 1941. DeWitt, however, cut the system in half for 1942. Youngstown became a victim of DeWitt's chopping block.[28]

Daily had a short window of opportunity to find a replacement. Lima, Ohio, seemed a possibility. Lima had fielded a team in the Class D Ohio State League in 1941, but that circuit failed to reorganize for 1942. Even so, Daily could not find backers in Lima for a Middle Atlantic League team. Then, M.A. Rinder, who headed the Warren, Ohio, team in the Pennsylvania State Association, told Daily that his city was ready to join the MAL. Rinder likely would have gotten a franchise if it had been just necessary to replace Akron, but Daily lacked another city to pair with Warren.

There was some thought that Daily was "losing some of his wizardry" because he failed to find teams to fill out the league roster. With some grumbling, the owners decided to go with just six teams in 1942. Holmes was not among the unhappy owners. Rather, he predicted a baseball boom in Dayton. In Erie the team received good news when the school board finally agreed to the Sailors' demands for new lights, a new fence, and repairs to the grandstand. The Sailors would continue to operate as the only independent team. In Zanesville, absentee owner Bill Simpson claimed he had lost $10,000 with a last-place club in 1941. The *Zanesville Signal* doubted that figure because the Cubs had drawn reasonably well; nevertheless, there was agreement that Simpson had "lost heavily." Simpson gladly agreed to sell to a local group headed by Charles Wynn, operator of the Zane Hotel. The locals incorporated as the Zanesville Baseball Club, with Wynn as president. Once the season got underway, Wynn turned over the operation of the club to secretary and business manager George Archer, a sound and creative baseball man.[29]

The league made efforts to accommodate the demands of war. Teams would make four trips to each city, playing three games on three trips and four on the other. Hockenbury calculated that the schedule involved 6,000 miles of collective travel. Night games would now all start at 7:30 instead of 8:00 to save on electricity. Each team was required to donate the proceeds of one home game to the USO, and to designate one game as a War Fund game, with proceeds going to the Army-Navy Relief Fund. Most teams held scrap metal nights where fans were urged to bring scrap metal to the game. If they brought enough metal, they received free admission.[30]

The league hinged on pitching more than in any season since the 1920s.

Hockenbury thought the Spalding ball, which the MAL adopted, seemed dead. Whether it was the result of a dead ball or the quality of the pitching, the 1942 season was a bad year for hitters. Charleston led the league in team batting average with a weak .258 mark. That average represented a significant drop from Canton's .271 batting average which was the highest in 1941. It was a long way from some seasons in the 1930s when the league used the Worth ball and several teams hit over .300. Zanesville's .327 being the high mark. The ball carried so poorly that the Charleston Senators' entire team could only muster a total of ten homers.

Alston, who was the Middle Atlantic League's greatest slugger, again captured the home run title in 1942. Highlighting the hitting difficulties, he managed to hit just a dozen homers. It was the third straight year and fourth time overall that Alston topped the league in home runs, having previously led in 1936, 1940, and 1941. No one surpassed Alston's career total of 128 MAL round-trippers. In addition, Smokey led the circuit in runs-batted-in for the second straight season. If Alston could only manage to hit 12 home runs, then 1942 was an inauspicious year for hitters.

Even without power, Charleston enjoyed its most successful season in 1942. The Senators nosed out Dayton for their first title in a decade. Sparkplug Johnny Blatnik hit .314 before being drafted in August. Catcher Ralph "Wigs" Weigel batted .306, and Joe Tipton, who split time between catcher, outfield and third base, chipped in at a .313 rate. Shortstop Frank Yankovich, a teenager in his first year of professional baseball, man-

Walter Alston did not get to the Hall of Fame because of his hitting, but he stood out as the premier slugger of the Middle Atlantic League. The big first baseman led the league in home runs four times and his total of 128 MAL career homers stands as the league's highest (National Baseball Hall of Fame Library, Cooperstown, New York).

aged to hit .319, led the Senators in RBIs, and was named the league's best shortstop. In a pitcher's season, Senators manager Jack Knight trotted out three of the best. Bob Kuzava posted the league's only 20-win season, going 21–6, a record that was also the MAL's best winning percentage. He allowed only 1.73 earned runs per game. Lefty Don Bayliss recorded an even lower ERA with a league best 1.52 to go with a 17–11 record. Kuzava, Bayliss and Chuck Byers (17–8, 2.48) all pitched over 200 innings. The Charleston staff threw a total of 20 shutouts during the season.

The Senators got hot in May and led the league for all except five days. Charleston had some big days at the gate. Merchants chipped in lots of giveaways for fans at *Charleston Daily Mail* night. The Charleston high school band played at the Army-Navy Relief Fund game. On Appreciation Night, fans were treated to giveaways donated by local merchants and the chance to say goodbye to popular Johnnie Blatnik who left for the service after the game. No game was larger than the War Fund game against the Norfolk Naval Training Station on July 29. The grandstand filled and another 2,000 fans stood in the outfield to see the Senators tackle Bob Feller and his teammates. The ceremonies included former heavyweight boxing champion Gene Tunney inducting 150 recruits into the navy. By season's end, the Senators had drawn 110,000 fans to Kanawha Park.[31]

Dayton's Holmes deserved to be manager of the year for 1942. Ducky intended to stay away from the dugout, so he appointed former major league catcher Paul Cherunko as his manager. Unfortunately, the Ducks got off to a horrible start. On May 28, with his team in last place, Holmes took over as manager. Even though he lacked a .300 hitter, Holmes drove his charges to win. After Holmes took the reins, first baseman Marv Rackley, who batted .293, began to hit and drive in runs. He molded a solid pitching staff headed by Roland Marquart (17–9, 2.10), Jack Franklin (12–8, 2.60), and Arnold Reichert (11–6, 1.50). Reichert's ERA was the lowest in the league. Gradually the Ducks moved up the standings, reaching the first division by August 6 and second place on August 13, after winning three games at Erie. Holmes had never been more popular around the league. Charleston sportswriter George Holbrook called Ducky "the league's best drawing card." Just when Holmes got his team within striking distance of the Senators, his fiery temper got the better of him. In an August 17 game against Canton, Holmes lost control. His confrontation with umpire Bob "Boots" Crouch led the ump to eject Holmes from the game. When Ducky refused to leave the field, Crouch forfeited the game to Canton. Daily then suspended Holmes indefinitely and fined him $150. The suspension turned out to be a week. The Ducks got to one and a half games behind Charleston, but could not catch the Senators.[32]

5. *"We intend to keep things going"* 165

The Boston Red Sox loaded Canton with prospects, but the youngsters slipped in August, falling to third. Terriers manager Pat Patterson could field a team composed entirely of future major league players. That lineup would look like this: first baseman Vance Dinges, second baseman Bill Sommers, third baseman Fred Hatfield, shortstop Virgil Stallcup, outfielders George Wilson, Sam Gentile, and Stan Wetzel, catcher Matt Batts, and pitchers Mel Parnell, Al Widmar, Bob Katz, and Stan Partenheimer. By the end of the season the Selective Service draft played havoc with the Terriers; they lost hard hitting outfielder Cal Barnes (.314), first baseman Joe DiCeasare, outfielder Bill Stevens, infielder Sam DiBlasi, and Stallcup to the military. Parnell, the classy left-hander who became the ace of the Boston Red Sox staff after the war, led the Terriers' pitchers with a 16–9 won-loss record and a 1.59 ERA. He pitched in a league-high 294 innings.

Third-place Canton did manage to knock off Charleston in the first round of the playoffs. Kuzava, the ace of the Senators pitching staff, came down with an appendicitis before the playoffs, and Blatnik and outfielder Del Leslie answered the draft call, depriving Charleston of three of their best players. Canton, behind the pitching of Katz and Chuck Dykes (8–2, 2.62) and the hitting of Gentile, swept the Senators in three games. Gentile had led the MAL in hits and runs scored.[33]

In the other semi-final series, underdog Erie took on Holmes' Ducks. The Tars had a losing record (63–65), but their fourth-place finish qualified them for the playoffs. Erie had continued to operate independent of a major league affiliation. For the past decade, that had been a prescription for disaster; independent teams more often than not were at a competitive disadvantage. Able management accounts for Erie's success at using the system to its advantage. Not being a farm club allowed Erie to keep key players under contract, which meant they did not to have to worry about their top players being promoted by the parent club. From the championship 1941 club, the 1942 Sailors returned manager-first baseman-turned-pitcher Kirby Farrell, all-star outfielders Cotelle and Ed Henrich, pitching ace Horatio Bartleson, and third baseman Mongiello. While the other returnees played out the season, Mongiello entered the Coast Guard after only 39 games. These veterans contributed mightily to the Sailors' success. Cotelle, a wisp of an outfielder, won his second straight batting title with a .327 batting average. Henrich, voted the most popular Sailor by Erie fans, hit a solid .317. Farrell played every game, batting .276 and going 7–1 as a pitcher. Bartleson remained the ace of the pitching staff, winning 13 games.

Erie managed to win a nip-and-tuck series from Dayton. After Dayton took game one, Erie stole the second game when Cotelle doubled in the sixteenth inning to bring Farrell home for a 3–2 win. Dayton came back to win game three, but Erie evened the series when an outfielder named Ray Waters, a .197 hitter, knocked in the winning run. In the finale, Cotelle picked up four hits and Bartleson allowed just four hits by Dayton.

Erie claimed a baseball first when Betty Brookhouser started writing a baseball column for the *Erie Dispatch-Herald*. Erie has since championed her as the first woman in the country to write a baseball column. In her father's barber shop, she met and befriended players. Years later she remembered, "My friends and I had many great times meeting players.... We would mostly get together and play (board) games at night." She soon developed a keen knowledge of baseball. In the summer of 1942 she approached sportswriter Ray Peebles about writing a regular column called "Woman's Angle on the Erie Sailors." Peebles liked the idea and installed Betty's column in the sports section. Apparently, Peebles liked Betty as well; after World War II they were married. She continued writing about baseball. In the 1950s she had a feature in *Baseball Magazine* for several years. During those years, Ray served as general manager of a series of minor league teams. She eventually became editor of the women's section of the *Erie Daily Times,* a job she retired from in 1983.[34]

The Tars closed out the exciting 1942 season by sweeping Canton in four games to become the first team with a losing record to win the league championship. The key moment in the series came in the eighth inning of game one when Canton, trailing 8–7 after blowing a 7–2 lead, loaded the bases with none out. Bartleson entered the game in relief and managed to close the door. Erie then beat Parnell, 5–1, in game two. Erie lefty Paul LaPalme (12–11) threw a five-hit shutout in the third game to win a 1–0 pitchers' duel. Bartleson then pitched a four-hit shutout and Farrell collected three hits in Erie's 2–0 win to nail down the Sailors' second straight league championship.

At the bottom of the standings, Springfield and Zanesville played out the string with little talent or enthusiasm. At Springfield, manager and first baseman Walt Alston, the undisputed home run champion of the MAL, collected his third consecutive home run title and led the MAL in runs batted in with 90 and in total bases with 201. The parent Cardinals provided Alston little talent to support his efforts. Zanesville had returned to the league with a new ballpark and high hopes as a Chicago Cubs' affiliate. The parent Cubs let the city down, supplying Zanesville with players who were mediocre at best. The team started the season in unusual fashion. On Opening Day, during the raising of the American flag, fans recited the Pledge of Allegiance. The playing of the "Star-Spangled Banner" had not yet become a universal event prior to games.[35]

Wartime features abounded during the season. All teams held war bond nights. At Canton, for those games, even players and umpires paid for admission to the game. Scrap metal and paper drives were common; fans usually got discounted or free tickets for bringing scrap metal or old newspapers. Charleston and others staged induction nights where numbers of young men were inducted into military service. In Charleston on *Charleston Daily Mail* night, the local high school band played the National Anthem before the game. Throughout the league, servicemen in uniform were admitted free.[36]

By the end of the 1942 season, teams were losing a sizeable number of players to the military, either due to the draft or as volunteers. The federal government had restricted the use of chartered busses even before the 1942 season. That ruling affected only Zanesville, which had contracted with a local bus company to transport players to and from away games. The ruling forced the club to purchase its own bus. Most teams still traveled by car, but gasoline rationing, which began on the East Coast in May 1942, threatened that practice.

Erie sportswriter Ed Bierbauer offered a solution to the travel problem. If Charleston transferred to Youngstown, it would be possible for all clubs to travel by railroad, thereby avoiding the coming gas rationing. Powell in Charleston could be expected to yell at the idea, but it died for lack of support. The military already clogged the trains and few people expected rail travel not to be restricted, but the high minors did manage to use the trains during the war years.[37]

By the winter of 1942–1943 the civilian population began tightening its collective belt. The nation's shortage of rubber and gas led the government to place restrictions on automobile travel. The Roosevelt urged Americans to stop pleasure driving. On December 1, 1942, gas rationing began in earnest, President Roosevelt ordered a 35-mile-per-hour speed limit across the country. Under the rationing system, holders of an "A" sticker could receive a mere four gallons of gas a week. Since ballplayers could not seriously maintain that their travel was essential to the war effort, the A sticker was the only choice. As to the speed limit, Americans generally disregarded the letter of the law, but instead set their own limit defined by the slogan "remember the 40."[38]

Daily understood the new regulations painted a "dark picture for us," but in November he urged league members to "wait and see." He believed that the picture would become clearer in the next two months. Milt Woodward, Erie's business manager, voted with his feet by taking a defense industry job in Meadville, Pennsylvania. Holmes got a job in a defense industry in Dayton. Powell concluded in February that all minor leagues should shut down for the duration of the war. To complicate matters even more, it appeared that the government would ban night games, which by 1942 were the life blood of minor league baseball. Tire rationing started in January and food in April 1942.[39]

By February Daily knew that the Middle Atlantic League, as then constituted, could not operate in 1943, unless, as he said, "present restrictions on gasoline and pleasure driving are relaxed." Erie had drawn well at the box office in the 1942 season, and still had money in the bank. Ray Peeples, who took Woodward's place as business manager, said the Sailors were ready to go. George Archer of Zanesville was anxious to play, but uncomfortable about how to manage the travel in the MAL. No other MAL owners believed it would be possible to play. Oscar Barkey, Canton's president, did not "see how we can possibly operate this year." His park, Lakeside Park, located outside the city, served by only one bus line, depended on fans coming by car, which would not be possible if the pleasure-driving restriction was enforced. Other clubs faced similar problems, which they could not imagine overcoming.[40]

Daily then looked to merge the MAL and the Pennsylvania State Association into a geographically tighter circuit, thereby making travel between cities conceivable. He put out a press release stating that he considered it "a patriotic duty to keep going." George E. Cooper, president of Johnstown of the PSA, gave enthusiastic endorsement for the plan. Johnstown still had cash reserves in the bank. Daily believed that Butler, where owner Jack Dunlevy had been a loyal supporter, could be counted on to continue playing. Oil City had wiped out its deficit in 1942, and seemed in shape to continue. He, also, had contacts in Youngstown that might be willing to operate a team. He still counted on Erie and Zanesville.[41]

Despite the fact that no other Class C league was prepared to operate in 1943, Daily called a joint meeting of the MAL and the PSA in Pittsburgh. He urged the owners to agree to combine the two leagues. To his disappointment, only Johnstown, Erie and Youngstown would commit to playing in 1943. Powell, citing the transportation problems and the difficulty of getting players, did not think it "advisable." Holmes could not see how he would be able to combine baseball and his defense industry job. H.E. Garst, who represented Springfield, said the St. Louis Cardinals were no longer interested in having a team in Ohio, now that Branch Rickey had moved to Brooklyn. The club representatives concluded that they had no choice but to close up for the duration of the war. Both leagues voted to discontinue operations. Daily dutifully sent a letter to Judge Bramham, president of the National Association, stating, "The action of suspension of operations becomes effective as of February 25, 1943. This was deemed necessary because of the World War emergency, and its attendant circumstances such as transportation difficulties, lack of manpower, and local conditions in our league cities."[42]

Daily made one last ditch effort to operate a league for 1943. In early March, he approached James I. Bearinger, president of the Michigan State League, a Class C league that had suspended operation prior to the 1942 season. Daily wanted to combine Michigan State League cities of Saginaw, Flint, Grand Rapids, and Fort Wayne with Akron, Dayton, Canton, and Youngstown. This combination would merit a Class A designation. Bearinger allowed as how the proposal was interesting, but it came too late to implement in 1943. He proposed that they revisit the possibility in 1944 or at the end of the war. As it happened, the idea was never revisited and the Michigan State League never restarted.[43]

Daily had little to do until the baseball winter meetings in December except run his hotels in Ebensburg. He had no leagues to run and no promoting of minor leagues. The minor leagues had shrunk to nine active leagues. His position as Promotional Director of the minors had been suspended as a cost-cutting measure. At the minor leagues' gathering on December 1 and 2, the high minors initiated a fight to unseat the National Association president, Judge Bramham, and replace him with International League President Frank Shaughnessy. Bramham had brought a degree of order to the minors, cracked down on rowdiness, and presided over steady growth of leagues from 14 in 1933 to 44 in 1940. By the war, though, he had become something of a dictatorial leader.

Daily's sympathies, however, lay with Bramham, who had appointed him first to the NAPBL's executive committee and then made him promotion director for all the minor leagues. Shaughnessy had the support of five of the nine active leagues, including the three highest leagues: the American Association, the International League and the Pacific Coast League. The high minor leagues were determined to replace Bramham with a man more sympathetic with their concerns. Besides, no one doubted Shaughnessy's administrative abilities. In September, prior to the meetings, Bramham had ruled that only active leagues could vote, a decision which appeared to cost Bramham his job. Daily apparently discovered Rule 25 of the minor league rules, which made clear that suspended leagues, who were still paying dues, were, indeed, members and entitled to vote. What followed became known as "the battle of the proxies." According to respected sportswriter Hugh Fullerton, Jr., Daily "looked after the detail of preserving the Bramham regime" by collecting enough proxy votes to assure Bramham's reelection. When the outcome became apparent, Shaughnessy's supporters had the grace to make the vote for Bramham unanimous. The losers, however, appealed to Commissioner Landis, who supported Daily and Bramham, labeling the insurgents' action "conduct detrimental to baseball." Fullerton concluded, "Elmer apparently proved the theory that it takes a country boy to out slick the city slickers."[44]

Other activity at the minor leagues' winter meeting impacted the MAL. Former left-handed pitching great Carl Hubbell, recently named farm director of the New York Giants, began to build a farm system from the bottom up. He offered to bear a portion of the costs if Erie entered the Class D Pennsylvania-Ontario-New York League (PONY). Munch and Peebles had been ready to play in 1943, so they jumped at the opportunity. Joe Donnelly of Columbus was moving rapidly to organize a new Ohio State League, a Class D operation. Archer at Zanesville and Ireland of Springfield were anxious to get back to playing baseball. Donnelly apparently approached Holmes of Dayton and Barkey of Canton, but they declined, citing ballpark problems. Hubbell then approached Ireland, offering an affiliation with the Giants, thus cementing the deal for Springfield. Erie, Zanesville and Springfield technically remained inactive members of the MAL. Donnelly set February 13 as the date for the Ohio State League to formally organize. This necessitated Archer and Ireland to pressure the MAL to decide if it would play in 1944 prior to the Ohio State League meeting. Daily called both the MAL and PSA to meet in Pittsburgh on January 31. Powell, who kept busy as the president of the greater Charleston War Industrial League, understood that travel restrictions made it impossible for his club to manage the distances required to operate in the MAL. Before the MAL meeting, Pittsburgh concessionaire Myron O'Brisky purchased controlling interest in the Erie Sailors. He remained committed to the tight little PONY League. Neither Powell, Holmes nor Barkey felt they could play in 1944. Clearly the MAL lacked enough clubs to operate in 1944. The owners granted permission for Erie, Springfield, and Zanesville to join other leagues for that one year.[45]

Daily attempted to put the best face on the decision not to play: "In view of transportation and other big problems.... I feel it would be unpatriotic to try to operate." Unpatriotic or not, Daily had no choice but to keep his leagues parked. Perhaps he could have denied permission for the three clubs to join other leagues, but the leagues in question were Class D leagues, so Daily fully expected Erie, Springfield and Zanesville to return to the Middle Atlantic at the first opportunity.[46]

The following winter, 1944–1945, Daily made little or no effort to organize either the MAL or the PSA. Among other minor leagues there was no rush to return to play, but the Carolina League and the North Carolina State League did resume operations. In 1945, the MAL would not play for the third straight season. Erie, Springfield and Zanesville continued to field teams in their Class D leagues and to draw well. Erie, despite a second-division finish in the PONY League, drew 62,000 fans in 1945. The Springfield Giants finished in the second division of the Ohio State League, but drew 43,583 paying customers, well above their 1942 level. The Zanesville Dodgers captured the Ohio State League crown and pulled in 55,308 fans. Both Springfield and Zanesville enjoyed a positive experience in its new league.

World War II, of course, came to an end before the conclusion of the 1945 baseball season. Germany surrendered in May and Japan gave up after the U.S. unleashed two atomic bombs in August. Servicemen were coming home and the baseball players among them began to return to their old clubs. Everyone looked forward to peace, a rapid demobilization, the return of players from the war, and the return of baseball as it had been before the war.

6

"The muddle gets muddier"
Postwar Years, 1946–1952

With the end of the war in 1945, America moved rapidly to convert from a military to a peacetime economy, to get the troops home and to return to normal. That included the revival of minor league baseball. Daily had been reluctant to reorganize until the war ended. Perhaps, in retrospect, that was a mistake. He had made the rounds of his league's cities in 1944 to begin postwar planning, but had not been as diligent in the first seven months of 1945. By fall it was time to begin planning for 1946. Daily and Hockenbury expected to return to baseball as they had left it in 1942.

Daily called a meeting of his two leagues in Pittsburgh for the last day of September 1945. He already knew his little Class D Pennsylvania State Association faced serious obstacles; only Johnstown, Butler and Oil City were prepared to operate in 1946, and George Cooper of Johnstown had already lobbied Daily to return the Johnnies to the Middle Atlantic League. On the other hand, it looked as if the MAL would be good to go.

Zanesville, Springfield and Erie had operated Class D teams the past two years, but remained members of the MAL. Those cities already had solid organizations in place and functioning. The other three teams that had closed down after the 1942 season were Charleston, Canton, and Dayton. Watt Powell notified Daily that Kanawha Park remained out of commission due to its fire several years before, deferred maintenance during the war, and on-going decay. So, Powell made clear, Charleston would be unable to operate in 1946. Despite Powell's pessimism, Daily felt confident that Powell would have the park back in playing condition by May 1946. If Charleston were not ready, Daily had men willing to operate a franchise in Youngstown, which had been a league member as recently as 1941. In addition, Johnstown wanted to rejoin the league, and Akron, which had left following the 1941 season, still remained a possibility in Daily's mind despite the deplorable condition of its park. Dayton and Canton officially retained their league membership from 1942. An eight-team league seemed a strong possibility.[1]

At the September meeting it became clear that Daily's initial optimism was misplaced. Charleston's mayor, Daniel Boone Dawson, confirmed Powell's assessment that the city-owned park there really would not be ready for 1946. Powell, laid up with serious health problems, had received a political sinecure as director of the state parks, so he had neither time nor energy to devote to rebuilding his old club. Oscar Barkey of Canton informed the other owners that ancient Lakeside Park was so dilapidated it was not possible to play there. Unwilling to invest the money necessary to level and rebuild the park, Barkey explained that he was withdrawing Canton from the league. The most serious problem arose when the leaders of Springfield and Zanesville indicated they were wavering; they might prefer to remain in the little Class D Ohio State League rather than return to the Class C Middle Atlantic. Bob Ireland, owner of Springfield, had not been a fan of Daily since he purchased the franchise from Buzz Wetzel, who, with Daily's blessing, had moved the Cleveland affiliation to Charleston, leaving Ireland empty-handed without a major league affiliate. During his two years in the Ohio State League, Ireland's Springfield club had established a satisfactory working agreement with the New York Giants. Meanwhile, Zanesville had new leadership with no ties to the MAL. George Archer, former business manager of the MAL Greys and who had been "Mr. Baseball" in Zanesville for a decade, retired at the conclusion of the 1945 season. Frank Worstall, the new president of the Zanesville club, had no connection with the MAL.

When the MAL met again in mid–October, both Ireland and Worstall asked to be released from the Middle Atlantic. The Giants also had a farm club in Erie, so they would be unable to keep both Erie and Springfield as affiliates in the MAL. When the Giants let it be known that they liked Springfield as a Class-D-league farm club, Ireland, who remembered his inability to find an affiliat3e back before the war, decided he needed to stay put. Worstall had found a comfortable home in the Ohio State League, so he felt no pressure to return to the MAL or to Class C baseball. All Daily could do was to ask for a couple of weeks.[2]

Daily scheduled the next meeting in Zanesville in the hope of influencing the Greys to stay in the MAL. The issue came to a head at the October 28 meeting. After a "stormy" three-hour meeting, the MAL officially released Springfield and Zanesville to the Ohio State League. The league then added Johnstown and Youngstown. Johnstown was technically a member of the Pennsylvania State Association, but since Daily was president of that league, it proved a formality to get the franchise released from the PSA. Johnstown president George "Chick" Cooper, a local sports editor and long-time head of the Johnnies, was well known to most of the MAL representatives. Youngstown had been out of baseball since 1941, when the St. Louis Browns owned the MAL franchise. When the Browns expressed little interest in reengaging with the MAL, the franchise was awarded to man named Tom Murra, Jr.[3]

The decision to release Zanesville and Springfield was undoubtedly the MAL's and Daily's worst hour. It destroyed the Ohio-based league of midsized industrial cities that had existed in the 1930s. At the conclusion of the Zanesville meeting, the MAL consisted of Erie, Johnstown, Youngstown and Dayton. Daily was determined to line up at least two more members by the December minor league meetings in Columbus. He thought Akron would be one and still hoped that Charleston would be the other.[4]

Things continued to get worse for the MAL. Bill DeWitt, vice president of the St. Louis Browns, unleashed a vicious attack on Daily for giving the Youngstown territory away. He claimed the Browns held territorial rights on the basis of having held the MAL franchise in 1941. St. Louis, he said, wanted the franchise back. He vowed to appeal to Judge Bramham and, if necessary, he would take his case to the commissioner. Confident he would win his case, DeWitt vowed that once the Browns were back in the league he would unseat Daily as league president.[5]

More trouble came from within the league. Ducky Holmes had been a thorn in Daily's side since Holmes obtained a franchise for Dayton in 1934, but, on the other hand, there had been no more loyal supporter of the MAL than Holmes. Daily and the MAL suffered a major loss when Holmes, after two strokes, died on September 18, 1945. Baseball would miss Holmes. In a kind of eulogy, Dick Hudson of the *Charleston Daily Mail* penned a piece titled "Fans Will Miss Ducky." He wrote: "Around the Mid-Atlantic, the fans went out to see Ducky parade around the coaching lines, mock the umpires and stick his extra-long nose into their faces with a sarcastic snarl. He argued with the fans in the bleachers because they liked it, and he liked it too." Daily hoped that Holmes's widow would continue to operate the franchise, but she was anxious to get away from Ducky's debts. Instead, a man named Dr. Warren G. Bradford, a 41-year-old osteopathic physician, who had been the Duck's physician in Holmes' last year as owner, took control of the Dayton operation.[6]

The Middle Atlantic received a devastating blow in December when Bradford informed Daily of his desire to leave the MAL in order for Dayton to hook up with the Ohio State League. Bradford explained that with Springfield and Zanesville out of the MAL, the nearest league city to Dayton would be Youngstown, over 250 miles away. The distances seemed just too great. No doubt if Holmes was still running the show in Dayton, he would have seen things differently, but Ducky was gone.[7]

Daily, rightly, came in for criticism from other quarters for losing Ohio. In December, after Dayton's defection, Hudson summed up the charges: "the MAL muddle gets muddier." The Zanesville decision, he opined, made no sense. It made one "wonder how in the name of anything logical that Daily ever 'gave' Springfield and Zanesville away." Hudson was at a loss, unable to comprehend why "the M-A directors let this happen." The decisions continued to be "another mystery" to him. Hudson expressed confidence that, by 1947, Charleston, Akron and Canton would be ready to rejoin the league. So it seemed to him that a league of Akron, Canton, Charleston, Dayton, Erie, Springfield, Youngstown, and Zanesville could be recreated. As it stood, however, "Daily continues his mad undirected dash for a Mid-Atlantic set up."[8]

Daily's "dash" did continue, but in a circuitous route. He faced the reality that his Pennsylvania State Association could not be revived. When he called the PSA organizing meeting, only Oil City and Butler answered his call. Both teams had enjoyed stable organizations when the league suspended operations after the 1942 season. Jack Dunlevy, president of Butler, had a strong connection with the New York Yankees going back to 1936. Dunlevy and Daily worked well together and had developed a close friendship. The Oil City Athletic Association, which had operated the PSA franchise, remained intact with over 200 members. Ray Anderson, wealthy owner of two local trucking companies, along with sheriff John E. "Jack" Cunningham, headed the Oil City group. They believed they enjoyed a good relationship with the Pittsburgh Pirates, who been their major league affiliate in the PSA years. With Johnstown now in the MAL, Daily would need at least two, preferably four, teams in order to operate the PSA in 1946. He had little or no hope of finding those cities. By early November 1945 Daily admitted the PSA was dead.[9]

In the course of all this, Daily received a personal blow from outside the MAL. Since 1939 he had held the position of promotion director of minor league baseball. Daily had two leagues and two hotels to look after, so the job had been very part-time. When minor league czar Judge Bramham began planning for the postwar years, he decided the position should become a full-time job. With his PSA dead and the MAL on life-support, a full-time position must have been tempting for Daily, but he dutifully stepped aside so that Bramham could appoint a full-time promotion director.[10]

All hope of recreating the powerful MAL of the prewar years had become unlikely by New Year's Day 1946. Any MAL at all appeared doubtful. Jocko Munch, president of Erie, was tired of waiting for Daily to find a full slate of teams. In early January he made noises about returning Erie to the PONY League. In Youngstown, the city's only newspaper, *The Vindicator,* not only supported Bill DeWitt, it opposed the city hooking up with the MAL at all. Only Cooper in Johnstown remained solidly behind the MAL. All Daily could do was cobble together a collection of franchises that could answer the bell when the 1946 season opened in May. He turned to Butler and Oil City, where the leaders still hoped to find a league in which to play. Dunleavy of Butler and Anderson of Oil City jumped at Daily's invitation to join the MAL. Daily called an organizing meeting in Erie for January 21, 1946. Munch was ready to ante up the $3,200 franchise fee and keep Erie in the MAL. Daily's man in Youngstown, Tom Murray, however, had developed cold feet. That left only four franchises, Erie, Johnstown, Butler and Oil City.[11]

Two others soon joined to make a six-team league. Daily found men willing to take on the Youngstown newspaper and the St. Louis Browns. Businessman Bill Koval, a Pennsylvania native, headed a local group in Youngstown

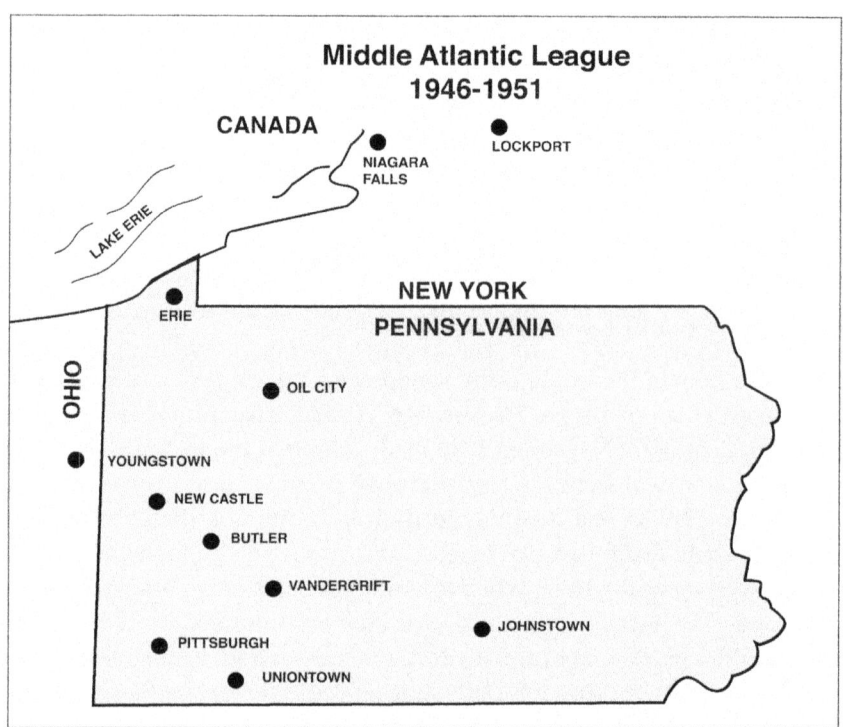

Following World War II the Middle Atlantic League all but left Ohio and West Virginia, retreating back to its Pennsylvania roots. It ventured only slightly outside the Keystone State during its postwar years (Michele Duncan).

who took the franchise. Koval enticed Charles A. "Brute" Kramer, a former local high school football star and more recently a sports editor in Monessen, Pennsylvania, who was currently the public relations director for Saint Vincent College, to run the Youngstown club as business manager. DeWitt decided to drop his opposition. Finally, an odd group of Rochester businessmen, who also owned the Sherbrooke, Quebec, team in the Border League, stepped forward with a proposal to operate a franchise in Niagara Falls, New York. William J. Burns put up most of the money. His partners were John Gabri, a Massena, New York, tavernkeeper and Hyman Lazerson, a Rochester junk dealer. Burns designated his son Bill Burns, Jr., as general manager to operate the club.[12]

The Middle Atlantic League of 1946 limped to the starting line with six teams: the Butler Yankees, Erie Sailors, Johnstown Johnnies, Niagara Falls Frontiers, Oil City Oilers, and Youngstown Gremlins. The postwar MAL hardly compared with the powerhouse league of the late-'30s. Only Youngstown and Erie remained from the prewar years. Niagara Falls, Johnstown, Butler and Oil City hardly compared with Akron, Dayton, Springfield and Canton. The relative strength of the league shows in the populations of the member cities in the following table:

1939		*1946*	
Youngstown	167,426	Youngstown	167,426
Erie	116,955	Erie	116,955
Akron	243,130	Niagara Falls	78,020
Dayton	211,456	Johnstown	66,668
Canton	107,862	Butler	24,477
Springfield	70,712	Oil City	20,378
Charleston	60,408		
Portsmouth	40,408		
Total	**1,018,423**	**Total**	**473,924**

The average population of the 1946 members was 78,987, compared to the 1939 average of 127,302. The prewar league resembled a Class B league or higher in population; there would not be that confusion in 1946. Except for Erie and Youngstown, the circuit looked more like the prewar Pennsylvania State Association, a Class D league, than like the old Mid-Atlantic.

Teams scurried to line up affiliations and get set for Opening Day. The New York Yankees had supported Butler during the Pennsylvania State Association years and continued to do so. Before the start of the season, the club invested $20,000 in new lights for Pullman Park, and added 1,300 more bleacher seats down the foul lines past the free-standing dugouts. During Erie's two years in the PONY league, it affiliated with the New York Giants, who continued the Erie connection even though the Sailors moved up from Class D to C. Erie's park, now named Ainsworth Field, no longer had the worst playing surface in the league, but its right field wall still stood a woefully short 286 feet from home plate. Johnstown's prewar connection with Brooklyn continued in 1946. The Johnnies had drawn fans to Point Stadium before the war, and it remained the largest stadium in the league. Niagara Falls started the season with the smallest park in the league, 2,500-seat Hyde Park. When the season began, the Falls club was without a major league affiliation, but Cincinnati signed a working agreement in July. Oil City also installed lights at Ramage-Hasson Park, but the grandstand still lacked a roof. The Oilers felt fortunate to be a Pittsburgh farm club. That left Youngstown as the only independent team, a difficult, but not impossible condition as Erie had proved before the war. Part of the problem the MAL faced in finding affiliates was that by the time the league got organized for 1946, the traditional big league sponsors—Red Sox, Braves, Cardinals, Tigers, and Indians—had already lined up their Class C affiliates, most of them with more than one.[13]

The first Opening Day after the war proved to be a mixed bag. Everyone had lived with wartime shortages for four years, but no one expected the conversion to peacetime to present problems for baseball. Yet it did. Teams, especially, faced equipment shortages. Johnstown's road uniforms failed to arrive by the start of the season. In fact, they failed to arrive for the entire season, forcing the Johnnies to wear home whites for away games. Youngstown's uniforms arrived on time, but where a "Y" should have adorned the uniform cap, a "4" appeared instead; the best that could be done was to remove the number and go with a plain cap. At Erie the team stockings failed to arrive. Most players possessed some stockings, but for the first month of the season the Sailors were a motley bunch. In Oil City, when business manager Bob Holden opened the new uniforms, instead of "Oilers" across the front, the lettering read "Pirates." The team directors solved the problem by quickly changing the name of the team to Pirates.[14]

Johnstown won Daily's award for drawing the most fans to Opening Day, but all clubs expressed satisfaction with their turnout. The Johnnies' spacious Point Stadium pulled in 5,100 for the first postwar game, with plenty of room to spare. Erie, which had drawn well in the PONY League the past two years, had a crowd of 3,291. Youngstown announced an attendance at Idora Park of 3,100. The Oil City Oilers/Pirates expected 5,000, but only 2,614 fans paid admission. Butler (1,450) and Niagara Falls (1,200) drew the fewest spectators. Since the rule of thumb was that a team should break even with an average of 1,000 spectators for 65 games, no one was complaining.[15]

Manager Steve Mizerak's Erie Sailors jumped out to a fast start, winning

13 of their first 15 games. Seven of the 13 victories were shutouts. A former army sergeant named John Uber threw shutouts in his first three professional games, two of which were two-hitters. Uber went on to become the league's best pitcher, compiling a record of 18 wins against four losses and a 1.72 earned run average with a MAL-high 192 strikeouts. Uber jumped to Class A in 1947, winning 14 games at Sioux City. He went as high as AAA ball, but could not win consistently at that level. Erie was loaded with pitchers beside Uber. Sam "Red" Webb (18–6, 2.18) tied Uber for most victories while George Bamberger (13–3) posted a league-best 1.35 ERA, and first-year pro George Sabine notched 16 victories. Lefty Steve Rushmock (11–3, 2.75), who pitched a no-hitter against Youngstown on May 21, rounded out the rotation. This stable of pitchers allowed the Sailors to withstand an impossible schedule, which required them to play eight consecutive doubleheaders between June 8 and 15. The Sailors did have some hitting. All-star outfielder Jerry Scala led the club with a .339 batting average. The Tars topped the league in home runs, but with a mere 36 round-trippers. Not a single Erie player reached double-digits in homers. It was not a year for power hitters.

Erie coasted to the pennant, 13 games ahead of second-place Butler, the largest margin of victory in MAL history. The Sailors kept winning right through the playoffs. They knocked off third-place Youngstown with ease, three games to one. Then they had their hands full with fourth-place Niagara Falls, after the Frontiers' surprising three-games-to-one win over Butler. Erie required the full seven games before taking the championship from Niagara Falls. The turning point came in game six when Webb and Niagara Fall's Frank Wagner (11–13) locked up in a pitchers' duel that lasted 14 innings before Erie prevailed to even the series. Then Erie won a 12–11 slugfest in game seven. The players, bus driver and clubhouse attendant all got $60 and a watch for their effort.[16]

The clearest sign that the postwar MAL lacked the firepower of the prewar years came in the number of players that went on to the major leagues. The 1946 MAL sent only six players to the big-time. That represented quite a decline from over 40 that characterized the antebellum years. The 1946 class consisted of Erie pitchers Webb and Bamberger, Sailors' outfielder Scala, Johnstown first baseman Herb Gorman (.286) and Brooklyn-born catcher Steve Lembo (.200), and John Kucab who pitched for Youngstown. Kucab's 1946 record of 12–1 was the highest winning percentage in MAL history. None of the six players experienced much more than a "cup of coffee" in the major leagues. Bamberger, however, gained fame as pitching coach of the Baltimore Orioles (1968–1977), and as manager of the Milwaukee Brewers (1978–1980, 1985–1986) and the New York Mets (1982–1983).

After the season, Daily made an effort to pull the old MAL cities back into the league. Ray Ryan, prewar president of the Mountain State League and the Virginia League, was trying to create a new league to include Charleston, Huntington, Fairmont, Logan, Williamson and Beckley in West Virginia, along with Lexington, Kentucky, and Portsmouth, Ohio. Daily moved to forestall Charleston's joining with Ryan by lobbying Watt Powell to return to the MAL. His efforts were to no avail. Despite promises by mayor Boone Dawson, Charleston still had no park suitable for Organized Baseball. Dayton technically remained a member of the MAL, which had given Dayton permission to play in the Ohio State League only for one year. The Dayton people, however, made it clear they wanted to stay in the Ohio State circuit.[17]

Although both Charleston and Dayton rebuffed Daily's lobbying efforts, other cities wanted admission to the league. Unfortunately, they all were small cities. J. Preston Flaherty, president of Johnson Bronze Company, presented a strong case for New Castle, Pennsylvania, except for the fact that he lacked a park. John K. Brieter, an insurance man from Vandergrift, Pennsylvania, urged the MAL to grant a franchise to his city. Uniontown and Sharon, Pennsylvania, also wanted admission. All sent representatives to the league meeting in Butler in November 1946.[18]

The MAL made what appeared to be an odd choice in awarding a seventh franchise to Vandergrift. The town's population of 11,470 was half that of the next smallest league city. Built in 1895 as a model industrial town by the Apollo Iron and Steel Company, Vandergrift had been designed by renowned landscape architect Frederick Law Olmsted. Located on a bend of the Kiskiminetas River 40 miles northeast of Pittsburgh, the town's tree-lined streets of worker-owned homes curved around the steel mill and foundry which employed 3,700 people. The Vandergrift Athletic Association, formed by John K. Brieter, James E. Gibson, Clair N. Kelly, Clair Thomas and Walker Adams, was well capitalized. Brieter, an insurance agent, served as president. It had a park, Davis Field, with lights and a covered grandstand seating 3,000 plus additional seating in bleachers behind first and third bases. Built on a city block, its dimensions were 298 feet to the fence down the left field line and 256 feet to dead right field, but a whopping 494 feet to center field. Breiter enticed Charles Kramer to leave Youngstown, where he had been business manager, to become general manager of Vandergrift. The dapper Kramer put the organization on sound footing.[19]

The final spot in the league went to Uniontown, making the MAL an eight-team league again. If Vandergrift was a model steel town, Uniontown consisted of sprawling, haphazard, dirty streets, dating its settlement to before the Revolutionary War. The livelihood of its 21,819 inhabitants depended mainly on the bituminous coal industry. Uniontown had previously boasted a franchise in the MAL for the 1926 season. It had been undercapitalized and had not drawn well because the Hopwood Speedway Park on the National Road, where the team played, was several miles outside town with no public transportation. The new ownership group, headed by Harry C. Isabel, manager of Pittsburgh Brewing Company, Joe Petko, and Lloyd Humbert brought organizational skills and sound financial backing to the 1947 enterprise. Isabel served as president, Petko as vice president and secretary, with Humbert as treasurer. They had no choice but to play at Hopwood Park. The facility, which had once been a grand wooded track, by 1946 had disintegrated to a half-mile dirt track. It needed lights and a diamond, but its 7,000-seat grandstand, plenty of parking, and three-year lease made it attractive. Banking on these alterations being completed by the opening of the baseball season, the league admitted Uniontown in early February. Isabel's group did, in fact, make the Speedway ready for baseball in time for the Uniontown Coal Barons opening game. The owners also persuaded the Pittsburgh Pirates to transfer their farm from Oil City to Uniontown.[20]

Pittsburgh's shift to Uniontown was the first of several changes in major league affiliations. Oil City changed its name from Oilers/Pirates to Refiners, and hooked up with the Chicago White Sox. The Niagara Falls Frontiers lost its connection to Cincinnati, but found a promising new one in the Philadelphia Athletics. At Vandergrift, Kramer happily inked a working agreement with the Philadelphia Phillies. The Phillies, under wealthy new owner Bob Carpenter, were signing tons of prospects and spending money on its farm system after decades of neglect. Butler, Erie, and Johnstown retained their affiliation with the New York teams, Yankees, Giants, and Dodgers, respectively. Youngstown changed its name from Gremlins to Colts, but continued to operate as an independent club, without any major league affiliation. Around the league, the owners and Daily were saddened by the loss of longtime Butler president Jack Dunlevy who, along with his wife, was killed in an automobile accident on the Pennsylvania Turnpike during spring training.

Minor league baseball reached the zenith of its popularity in the postwar years of 1947, 1948 and 1949. The MAL enjoyed its most successful postwar season in 1947. Erie and Johnstown led the league in attendance as they had done in 1946. The third-place Sailors pulled in 107,000 fans to Ainsworth Field. Johnstown, with a population of 66,000, drew 101,000 to see a last-place club. Obviously, having a winning team did not always determine attendance level. While the Johnnies drew over 100,000 with a last-place club, Niagara Falls with a second-place team attracted the fewest fans, only 48,000. Kramer, the Vandergrift general manager, blamed the failure of Niagara Falls on Bill Burns' poor management. Uniontown finished a distant seventh in the standings, but attracted a surprising 75,000 fans. Isabel attributed the Uniontown success to the newness of professional baseball in the town.[21]

The MAL's most surprising operation had to be Vandergrift. With a population of only 10,500 the Pioneers had an attendance of 87,000. They also won the pennant and the postseason playoffs. Kramer brought in Floyd "Pat" Patterson to manage the Pioneers. Patterson, the long-time and highly successful manager of the Canton Terriers for eight prewar years, 1936 to 1943, had managed the Durham Bulls for the 1945 and 1946 seasons. The Kansas native, who married a Canton girl, had already won two MAL championships and 502 games. The Phillies stocked Vandergrift with good Class-C-level players. Shortstop Alex Grabowski led the league with a .396 batting average and in triples with 15. Mike Goliat, who would become a key figure with the Phillies' Whiz Kids of 1950, batted .370. Goliat, a former coal miner from nearby Yatesboro, had just been released from the army when he showed up at a preseason try-out camp in Vandergrift. Phillies scouts quickly signed him to his first pro contract. Jackie Mayo, also a Whiz Kid, hit .355. After winning the pennant, the Pioneers swept Erie in three straight games, and then knocked off Butler in four straight, winning the Butler series by resounding scores of 12–2, 10–6, 8–0 and 5–0.

The Butler left-hander, soon to be known as Whitey Ford, could not claim to be the best pitcher in the league in 1947, but he went on to become the best pitcher to ever come out of the MAL. No other MAL pitcher, with the possible exception of Chief Bender, could touch his Hall of Fame career. Born Edward Charles Ford on October 1, 1928, in New York City, Ford was only 18 when he arrived in Butler. He grew up in the Astoria section of Queens and attended Aviation High School, where he played first base and did a little pitching. In the summer of 1946 he pitched his Queens team to the New York sandlot championship. That feat brought him to the attention of the Red Sox, Giants and Yankees. The famous Yankees scout Paul Kitchell signed the little lefty for a $7,000 bonus. That bonus and his lofty Butler salary of $250 a month assured that he would move quickly up the Yankees chain. Ford stood 5-foot-8 and weighed 150 pounds in Butler, but he continued to grow to 5-foot-10 and 178 pounds by the time he reported to the Yankees three years later. He possessed a sharp-breaking curve, good control, and a decent fastball. Although Lefty Gomez had pinned the nickname "Whitey" on Ford in spring training, most people still called him Eddie until he became a member of the New York Yankees. He enjoyed playing at Butler, but was less enthusiastic about the 10- to 12-hour, all-night trips on an old school bus. While there, he did make a lifelong friend in second baseman Frank Verdi, a Brooklyn lad.[22]

6. "The muddle gets muddier" 183

Eddie Ford established himself as the best pitching prospect in New York City at the age of 17. Soon after, in 1947, he joined the MAL's Butler Yankees and won 13 games while losing only four. Within a few years he was in the majors, where as Whitey Ford he became a household name and a Hall of Famer (National Baseball Hall of Fame Library, Cooperstown, New York).

At Butler, Ford compiled good but not eye-popping numbers. Ford did have the best winning percentage (.765) among pitchers, based on his 13–4 record. Far from being a dominant pitcher, he struck out 114 in 157 innings while walking 58 batters. He compiled a decent, but far from remarkable, 3.84 ERA. Those were not numbers that light up the scouting reports. Hitters, however, batted just .244 against Ford.

Ford's record at Butler earned him a promotion to Norfolk (Class B) in 1948. After stops in Norfolk (1948), Binghamton (1949) and Newark (1950), he got the midseason call to report to the Yankees. He responded with a 9–1 record in 1950 and won New York's final World Series victory over the Phillies. In his 16-year major league career, he won 236 games and lost 106 with a 2.75 earned run average. He led the American League in wins three times (1955, 1961, 1963), winning percentage three times (1956, 1961, 1963), and ERA twice (1956, 1958). He holds the record for most World Series appearances (11), wins (10), strikeouts (94), and consecutive scoreless innings (32). He retired in 1967 because of elbow problems. Sportswriters elected "the Chairman of the Board" to the National Baseball Hall of Fame in 1974.[23]

Ford's numbers hardly compared to Erie's Egon Feuker, who put up the best among MAL pitchers, leading the league in wins (18) and ERA (2.81). Feuker distinguished himself by pitching the longest game in MAL history. On May 28, Erie and Vandergrift went 18 innings before Erie scratched out a run to prevail, 5–4. Feuker, lanky right-hander, pitched the entire game despite giving up 19 hits and walking seven batters.

In the 1947 playoffs, Vandergrift dominated as the Pioneers had during the season. They dispatched Erie three games to none, then knocked off Butler in four straight by convincing scores of 12–2, 10–5, 8–0 and 5–0. In the final game it was Eddie Ford who absorbed the loss.

The MAL's final playoff game of 1947 had hardly ended before the Niagara Falls franchise came unglued. Despite a second-place finish, attendance had withered to a league low of 48,000. Business manager Bill Burns, Jr., and his father sold their share of the team to their minor partners John Gabri and Hyman "Hy" Lazerson. The new co-owners then decided to shift the franchise to New Castle, Pennsylvania. The absentee owners appointed Mike Cannavino as president and George "Pappy" Smith as business manager. Cannavino was himself an absentee, officially residing in Erie where he had been elected to the Erie city council in 1944. Smith signed a working agreement with the lowly Washington Senators. A year earlier, the MAL had rejected an application from New Castle because the city lacked a suitable playing field. In the intervening year, New Castle had erected P.J. Flaherty Field on property owned by the Johnson Bronze Company at the reported cost of $100,000. The spacious field measured 375 feet to left, 350 feet to center and 350 feet to right, and sat 7,000. The New Castle Chiefs opened Flaherty Field on April 30 with an exhibition game against the Homestead Grays. To no one's surprise the Chiefs fared no better than the parent club, finishing seventh with a dismal 43–83 record, and drew poorly although new teams generally drew well their first year, no matter how well or poorly they played.[24]

The league made no significant changes for 1948. Because of the death of Dunlevy, George Cooper of Johnstown was elected vice president of the MAL. The maximum monthly salary went from $3,200 to $3,400. The number of roster spots was lowered from 18 to 17, but included the three required spots for war veterans established in 1946. That raised the average salary to $200 a month, the highest MAL players would enjoy.[25]

The Vandergrift Pioneers experienced a topsy-turvy season in 1948. Manager Pat Patterson started the season with high hopes of adding a fourth MAL pennant to his resume. His Pioneers got off to a fast start, taking the early lead and holding it through mid–July. Then they went into a slump. At Uniontown on July 15 they lost the first game of a doubleheader and for the first time that year fell out of first place. The stress proved too much for Patterson, who suffered a heart attack between games and had to be rushed to Uniontown Hospital. He was done for the season.[26]

The Phillies wasted no time in sending Lou Krause, their minor league pitching coach, to take over as Vandergrift's "temporary" manager. The Pioneers lacked major league prospects, but they fielded the best hitting club in the league, batting .303 as a team. League leaders abounded: first baseman Bob Hall led in total bases; second baseman George Gasdaska coaxed 104 walks; third baseman Joe "Ricky" Tedesco collected 178 hits and 40 doubles; catcher Earl Lettenberger smacked 26 balls over the fence. In addition to the hitting, George Heller (20–4, 2.75) was the league's only 20-game winner and its best pitcher. By August 1, the Pioneers moved back into a tie for the lead. Then they pulled away in August to take the pennant. The highlight of their charge was a 30–4 trouncing of Oil City on August 17. That was the most runs scored in an MAL game. Tedesco batted in a record nine runs in the game.

Erie came back in the playoffs to take the championship. The Sailors had finished second in the regular season, with Uniontown and Johnstown rounding out the first division. Butler just missed making the playoffs, but Oil City, New Castle and Youngstown lagged far behind; indeed, Youngstown finished a staggering 50 games out of first place. The Tars, as sportswriters liked to call the Sailors, enjoyed great support from their fans. Erie again drew over 105,000 customers to Ainsworth Field. The club had no player who made it to the major leagues, but they had a solid crew of minor league veterans and hungry youngsters who did not know they were not prospects. Outfielder Bill Henry led the club with a .333 average and was selected the team's most valuable player.

The playoffs demonstrated the old adage about good pitching beating good hitting. Walt Cox (18–5, 2.71) and 19-year-old Hugh Oser (14–4, 2.86) helped Erie to a three-games-to-one victory over Johnstown in the first round of the playoffs. In the other first round series, Tedesco and outfielders Charley Hood (.312), Herman Kiel (.309) and Frank Merola (.308) led Vandergrift to a three-games-to-one win over Uniontown. In the finals, Erie prevailed, winning four games to one. Cox was the winning pitcher in games one and five. For leading the Sailors to the championship, sportswriters selected Don Ramsey, a 12-year minor league veteran, as manager of the year.

Despite the exciting pennant race and playoffs, Daily and the owners could not miss the danger signs. Both the major league and the minors set attendance records in 1948, but not the Mid-Atlantic. Only Johnstown and Uniontown showed increases at the gate. Johnstown's move from last place to fourth and Uniontown's improvement from seventh place to third accounted for the increases at those two cities. Johnstown, again, drew over 100,000 (102,365). Everywhere else around the league, attendance was down. Despite the exciting race and Vandergrift's second consecutive pennant, attendance at Davis Field dropped 40 percent to 51,367. New Castle's attendance of 42,297 was less than Niagara Falls had drawn in 1947. At Youngstown attendance fell 19 percent to the league low of 41,123. Butler went from pulling in 56,000 in 1947 to 41,500 in 1948. Oil City was off by 10,000 fans. Although Erie drew a league-high 105,562 fans, that was 2,000 fewer than in the previous year. The MAL's claim to be the best Class C league rang hollow when its total attendance ranked only ninth among fifteen leagues in that classification. The reality was that only Erie and Johnstown operated at the level of the pre-war MAL.

At the league's postseason meeting in November 1948, Butler and Youngstown appeared uncertain for 1949. Butler felt the effect of losing Jack Dunlevy, its long-time leader. It had just experienced its only losing season since it entered professional baseball in 1935. To make matters worse, after Dunlevy's death the Yankees dropped Butler as a farm club, breaking a connection that dated back to 1936. Fortunately, Ray Kennedy, the new farm director of the Detroit Tigers, recognized the need to rebuild the Tigers farm system. He willingly purchased the Butler club. In Youngstown, Bill Koval and minority owner Nick Andolina, who had controlled the club since 1946, were the only franchise owners to operate without a major league affiliation, and that had not worked out well for them. After two losing seasons, attendance at the league's most populous city had slipped to the league's lowest. Despite the financial difficulties, Koval and Andolina decided they could absorb the losses and continue for another season.[27]

League owners understood they needed to do something to revive fan interest in the coming season. For unknown reasons, their focus became the playoff system. They jettisoned the Shaughnessy playoffs and reverted to a split-season format. The Shaughnessy playoff system, which had replaced the split-season format throughout the minor leagues in the 1930s, put four teams instead of two into the postseason playoffs. Under that system, the third, fourth, fifth, sixth, and, maybe even the seventh-place team stood a chance of making the playoffs deep into the season. The logic, of course, was that with a chance of their team making the playoffs, fans continued supporting the team through the dog days of August. Because of the general decline in attendance, the owners concluded that the system had not worked well. Their answer was to revert to the split-season format, even though the MAL would be the only minor league with that system. The first half would run from

April 29 to July 1, and the second half from July 2 to September 5. The winners of the two halves would meet in a seven-game playoff. The owners also reintroduced an all-star game, which had not been played since 1938. The winner of the first half would host a team of all-stars selected by league managers.[28]

The major leagues, as well as the minors, feared a decline in the popularity of baseball in 1949. There certainly were reasons for anxiety. The euphoria that came from winning the war had dissipated, replaced by a pervasive dread. The Cold War had broken out, and the Soviet Union continued its blockade of Berlin. Scarier still, the U.S. lost its monopoly on the atomic bomb when the Russians exploded their own bomb. Communist forces drove the Chinese nationalists off the mainland and established control over the largest and most populous country in the world. The House Un-American Activities Committee convinced many Americans that Communists lurked under every bush. None of this was reason to suspect that Americans would stop attending baseball games, but reason did not always matter in 1949.[29]

At Johnstown, George Cooper had other fears, the effect that broadcasts of Pittsburgh Pirates games by a local station would have on attendance at Point Stadium. Cooper had the right to stop Pirates' broadcasts in Johnstown. Back in December 1946 the major leagues had adopted "rule 1(d)" which required major league clubs to obtain the consent of minor league teams before broadcasting games in the minor league home territory. The rule only applied only to cities outside a 50-mile radius from the major league ballpark. Cooper, nevertheless, felt pressure from fans, newspapers, and local radio who wanted unlimited broadcasts of Pirates games on Johnstown station WJSW. The station claimed that its survey of listeners found 831 favored hearing all Pirates games, while only nine opposed. The Pirates planned to broadcast all games, home and away, on a radio network of 20 stations. Cooper managed to negotiate an arrangement with the local station whereby the station would not carry Pirates games during Johnstown's 19 home night games. Only Pittsburgh and Erie had television stations, so that was not yet a concern, and, besides, the Pirates announced they would not televise any games in 1949. Attendance at Johnstown did dip slightly in 1949, but remained over 100,000. Cooper, however, understood the problem would not go away.[30]

Daily wanted to be proactive in making the MAL games more attractive. He saw the twenty-fifth anniversary of the league as an opportunity for celebration. Owners had agreed in November to an insignia for all players to wear on their left sleeves. The patch bore simply stated "M-A 25." To orchestrate the celebration, Daily hired Vandergrift business manager Charles Kramer as the league's first and only promotion director. Despite the title, Kramer's duties were limited to serving as the public relations director for the MAL. He went to work on a history of the league's 25 years of operation. Before the season, Kramer issued press releases focusing on various aspects of the league's past.[31]

Kramer's efforts generated favorable publicity for Daily and the MAL. Hugh Fullerton, Jr., in his nationally syndicated column, identifying Daily as "a country boy who owns a hotel," wrote glowingly of Daily's success with the MAL. Fullerton quoted Daily approvingly as saying, "I think maybe I've done something for American youth where I am." *The Sporting News* devoted a full page to the league and its leader. Although its description of Daily as "a personal favorite of the late Commissioner," rang hollow, Daily could find little fault with the overall tone of the article.[32]

Despite the troubling decline in attendance in 1948, the Middle Atlantic opened the 1949 season with the same eight teams that started and finished the previous year. However, once the campaign opened trouble spots quickly appeared. Butler got off to a terrible start on the field and at the box office. At the end of May with the club in last place, Detroit sent Walter "Boom-Boom" Beck to replace Charlie Engle as manager. Beck found ways to turn things around enough to get the club to fifth place by the conclusion of the first half. Uniontown also started poorly, but then got worse, finishing seventh in the first half and dead last in the second half. Speedway Park, four miles out of town, suddenly seemed a long trek. Unrest, wildcat strikes, and the reduced workweek in the bituminous coal mines took money for leisure time away from Uniontowners. By June rumors surfaced that the franchise would be transferred to Wheeling or Altoona. Vandergrift's problem was its close proximity to Pittsburgh. Fans had unlimited access to radiocasts of Pirates games. Attendance at Davis Field dropped 20 percent for the season; the Pioneers' losing record did not help at the box office, but league officials were convinced the Pirates' broadcasts were the greater culprit.[33]

Daily took up the issue of the broadcasts. In early June, he made an appointment with Commissioner Albert B. "Happy" Chandler to discuss the problem of broadcasts in minor league territory. As a minimum, Daily wanted to limit broadcasts to a 50-mile radius of the major league ballpark. Daily took Cooper and Andolina with him to Chandler's office in Cincinnati. Andoline's Youngstown club faced competition from broadcasts of Cleveland games. Chandler was polite, but would not give an inch. Daily could only say, "We couldn't change the rule."[34]

On the playing field, Erie and Johnstown exchanged the league lead the entire season. At one point the lead changed five times in a two-week span. Johnstown captured the first half and earned the right to host the all-star game. Helped by a home run by Youngstown shortstop Charles "Spider" Wilhelm and three hits from Butler's Ray Cabanaw, the all-stars held a seemingly commanding 10–3 lead going into the bottom of the ninth inning. With the crowd of 6,125 behind them, the Johnnies scored seven runs in the ninth to tie the game. The tying run scored on second baseman Bill Palumbo's single. Leo Baldino's game-ending hit in the eleventh inning gave Johnstown the win 11–10.[35]

Erie came back to capture the second-half crown. The Sailors lacked power, but they were better than any other team at hitting for average (.286), stealing bases, and fielding. They had no batter among the league leaders and only catcher Nick Testa made it to the majors. First baseman Ed Kestler (.335) was the sole all-star selection, although in Bob Spresser (20–6) they did have one of the best pitchers in the league.

Johnstown and Erie were nip-and-tuck throughout the season. In the playoffs, the rivalry continued. All-stars Palumbo, outfielder Joe Beran, and pitcher Murray Richardson led the Johnnies. Palumbo, the second baseman, seemed to always be on base. He coaxed a league-record 152 walks during

Ainsworth Field, which opened in 1939, served as home for the Erie Sailors. In the postwar years the Sailors regularly drew over 100,000 fans to the 3,000-seat park (courtesy BallparkReviews.com).

the season. Beran clubbed a league-best 36 homers, the most in the MAL since 1931, but he also established the all-time record by striking out 153 times. Richardson (14–4) was the best left-handed pitcher in the league. Over the regular season, Erie prevailed by one game over Johnstown, and the Sailors did the same in the playoffs. After Erie took game one of the playoffs, Johnstown's Harry Hintz (14–4) shut out the Sailors in the second game. The two teams traded victories until Erie prevailed 5–1 in the seventh game to capture its second straight playoff championship. Long-time Erie president Jocko Munch and business manager Fred Nash had plenty to crow about, having won the title and having had the MAL best 105,776 fans pass through the turnstiles of Ainsworth Field.

The split-season format deprived Youngstown of the opportunity to compete for the title. That was too bad because Youngstown, on paper, had the best team. Their outfielder Bob Betz was the league's top hitter. He batted an MAL-high .345, led in RBIs with 135, and tied for most hits. Wihelm tied Betz for most hits with 181 while leading in runs scored with 145. First baseman-manager Eddie Morgan, who had a taste of major league food in the mid–'30s, hit .339. Betz, Wilhelm, third baseman Bob Gardner and outfielder Charley Harig (.332) were all-star selections. Pitcher Johnny Kucab, who would get a chance to pitch for the Philadelphia A's the next three years, compiled a 21–7 record and pitched a league-record 25 complete games.

All the other teams finished the season with losing records. Oil City, Butler and Vandergrift were at least competitive. Uniontown and New Castle struggled all season to stay out of the cellar, reflecting the strengths of their parent clubs, Pittsburgh and Washington. Senators scout Joe Cambria delivered a half-dozen Cubans to New Castle's spring training. They did nothing to save the Nats. Only two managed to stick with the club, and the best of those hit a mere .205. The Nats did have veteran minor league pitcher Franklin Wagner who led the MAL in ERA, strikeouts, and innings pitched, and managed to win 18 games, which was one-third of the Nats' victories.

Following the season *The Sporting News* ran a headline proclaiming "Banner Season Reported by Most Minor Leagues." Indeed, 1949 was the high-water mark for the minors. The Mid-Atlantic, however, reported a far different story. Johnstown, Youngstown, and Oil City did enjoy an increase in attendance. The other five clubs declined. Johnstown led in attendance with 105,776 customers, followed by Erie with 101,038, Youngstown 62,667, Oil City 55,316, Vandergrift 40,523, Butler 40,221, Uniontown 38,037, and lowly New Castle, last in the standings and in attendance, at just 28,233. The attendance numbers virtually mirrored the final league standings.[36]

Despite New Castle's abysmal attendance, president and general manager

Mike Cannavino could report that the club finished debt free. New Castle "is a good baseball town," he said. The same could not be said for Uniontown. Club president Harry C. Isabel blamed his problems on Speedway Field. First, the club had invested heavily to improve the facility. Second, the field, as he said, was "in the middle of no man's land—in a town called Hopwood." No public transportation serviced the park. Others blamed the Pittsburgh Pirates for failing to stock the Coal Barons with decent players. Perhaps more importantly, the on-going disputes between coal miners and mine operators led to wildcat strikes and a three-day workweek that continued to take money from the pockets of fans.[37]

Daily cited two reasons for the overall decline. First, "economic conditions in our territory are hurting us." King Coal, which, along with steel primed the economic pump of western Pennsylvania, was on the decline as Americans turned to oil and natural gas, cleaner and more reliable fuels than coal. Second, Daily cited "the broadcasts of the Pirates and Cleveland games" into league territory. He lamented, "The major leagues haven't helped the minors with so much broadcasting." Daily concluded, "I sort of think our fans are getting too much baseball."[38]

The issue of radio and television of major league games quickly became a more problematic issue for the minor leagues. The Justice Department of the United States took exception to all efforts at limiting broadcasts of major league games. On October 27, 1949, Attorney General Howard McGrath issued a press release stating, in effect, that restrictions on broadcasts, such as rule 1(d), were illegal restraints. McGrath believed "the fans who desire to hear or see baseball broadcasts and telecasts, and the businessmen engaged directly or indirectly in bringing these broadcasts and telecasts to the public are entitled to freedom from unreasonable restraints." If McGrath's opinion held sway, minor league teams and leagues would possess no power to stop the broadcasting of major league games into their territories. The major leagues and the commissioner, fearful that baseball might lose its exemption from antitrust laws, complied with McGrath's wishes.[39]

The doors flew open for broadcasts of major league games without regard for local minor league teams. There was no shortage of broadcasters; the airwaves became inundated with voices of play-by-play announcers. In February 1950, the Mutual Radio Network announced it would air "the game of the day" over 350 radio stations across the country. In March, the newly created Liberty Network issued a release touting its own "game of the day" to be heard on 250 different stations. To spice up their broadcasts, Liberty promoted their announcers, Gordon McLendon and Dizzy Dean.[40]

Then the closest major league teams to MAL cities, Pittsburgh and

Cleveland, announced their broadcast plans. The Pirates put together a radio network that would beam games directly into MAL cities. All of the Pirates games would be carried on WBUT in Butler, WARD and WCRO in Johnstown, WKST in New Castle, and WKRZ in Oil City. Youngstown's WBBW signed on to carry all Cleveland Indians games. The Pirates still did not televise games, but the Indians did and they telecast their games into Youngstown.[41]

While baseball men worried about the impact of radio broadcasts of major league games into minor league territory and the growing telecasts of games, the greater danger may well have been television itself. Television was exploding on the American scene so rapidly it was hard for analysts to understand its impact. Attendance at movie theaters dropped sharply in cities with television stations, beginning in 1950. The era of "going out" was being replaced by a culture that focused on the family, children, home and television. It required people to stay home; people could be entertained without leaving their living room. The league's three largest cities, Johnstown, Erie and Youngstown, had their own television stations. With rooftop antennas, Pittsburgh TV stations could be picked up across most of the MAL territory.[42]

Neither radio nor television killed the first MAL casualty of 1950. After Uniontown struggled through the 1949 season, team president Harry Isabel threw in the towel. Charles "Pete" Yezbak then took over as president and began a fund-raising campaign. His efforts came to an end by February when John L. Lewis called the United Mine Workers of America out on strike. Yezbak had no choice but to turn the franchise back to the league. Sports editor Bob Wood of the *Uniontown Morning Herald* blamed the Pirates for sending weak talent to Uniontown, but he understood "there hasn't been enough business in Uniontown to operate a horseshoe tournament."[43]

With baseball dead in Uniontown, Daily dashed off to Niagara Falls. The previous franchise had left the city after the 1947 season, but Daily believed that poor management, not lack of community interest, was to blame. He found Judge Francis Giles ready to invest his own money in baseball, and to serve as team president. With Niagara Falls back, the league returned to eight teams. Daily, momentarily giddy with his quick success, exuded that "the league has never been in better financial condition." That, of course, hardly recognized the harsh economic reality for minor league baseball in general and the MAL in particular.[44]

In reality, as the *Oil City Derrick* reported, it looked like "tough sledding financially" for the MAL going into the 1950 season. In Youngstown, Koval threatened to transfer his franchise to Meadville, Pennsylvania, in order to escape broadcasts of Cleveland games, but most people recognized this as an idle threat. Jocko Munch, Erie president, claimed that Erie lost $20,000 despite having drawn over 100,000 fans, but it was difficult to understand Munch's accounting. He did not foresee disaster in the Lake City. In a more significant development, the Brooklyn Dodgers ended a nine-year affiliation with Johnstown, claiming they needed to scale back their farm system, which had risen to 25 teams. Using the same justification, the Chicago White Sox pulled out of Oil City. The franchises in Johnstown and Oil City were solvent, but neither had success in finding major league partners for 1950. Niagara Falls got a new business manager in Joe Brehany, but he had no luck in nailing down a major league affiliation. The situation looked so rocky in Vandergrift that George "Chick" Cooper of Johnstown predicted the Pioneers would be the first team to collapse. The failure of major league teams to seek working agreements with the three MAL teams spoke volumes about how the big leagues saw the Middle Atlantic circuit. New Castle posted good news for a change. A group of seven local businessmen purchased the team from the absentee owners for $18,000. They organized the New Castle Citizens Baseball, Inc., elected Alphouse "Al" Scarazzo team president, and appointed Frank Moreliti as business manager. To help beleaguered owners, the league reduced the salary cap from $3,400 to $3,000 per month.[45]

The 1950 season did prove to be disastrous. As Cooper had predicted, Vandergrift became the first club to fold during the season since before World War II. The club had finished 1949 in the red, but a fund-raising campaign had wiped out the debt. At the end of June, club president Joseph E. Bucci reported losing $5,000 a month in May and June. The club lacked the wherewithal to cover the losses, and local baseball supporters had been tapped out by the offseason fundraising campaign. Bucci blamed "lack of interest," but failed to identify the source of the decline in interest. The team the Phillies sent to town fell into last place, but it was not terrible. In fact, the team batted .305. The Pioneers' attendance average of 375 per game attested to the truth of Bucci's summation. He notified Daily that Vandergrift would withdraw after their July 19 game. When the Pioneers closed the gates, they had attracted a mere 13,493 fans. Daily said he would try to find a replacement within the "next 24 hours." The only town Daily checked out was Altoona, but just as in the past his efforts to generate interest in the Curve City fell flat.[46]

Attendance declined across the board, except at Niagara Falls where the Citizens drew more fans than Uniontown had ever done. The largest cities experienced the most drastic losses. Erie's attendance remained the league's highest, but it dropped by nearly 50 percent, from 105,000 down to 54,850.

Johnstown fell by almost 60 percent, down to 43,387. At Youngstown, Bill Koval's worst fears came true. The bottom dropped out of his operation, as attendance plummeted 78 percent to 14,003 for the season. Butler's fan base dipped to 31,816, a 20 percent decline. Oil City's attendance was off by 29 percent, down to 39,267, even though the Refiners had the best won-loss record in the league. Few teams could sustain such economic losses.[47]

Play on the field took second place to attendance woes in 1950. Oil City, an independent team with a roster of retreads that new general manager Charles Kramer put together, somehow managed to capture the regular-season flag. Outfielder Bob Huddleston, a 26-year-old holdover from 1949, posted the top batting average of .364. Fellow outfielder Larry Rush (.285), who had played at Vandergrift in 1949, also won all-star status. Manager Jim Davis, understandably, got the writers' vote as manager of the year for coaxing 70 wins out of the Refiners.

The Butler Tigers, who finished second in the regular season, then captured the playoff crown. The league had reverted to the Shaughnessy playoff system after the 1949 season. In the first round, the Tigers had a difficult time with fourth-place New Castle. The Nats featured outfielder Gene Bilo, who drew a league-high 132 walks and stole a record 72 bases. Butler prevailed in the series, three games to two, thanks to the shutout pitching of Nelson Reeves (10–6) in the deciding fifth game. Oil City had an easy time with Erie, winning its series three games to none. In the playoff final, Oil City went up three games to two. In game five Oil City seemingly destroyed the Tigers' chances by winning, 22–4. Butler then caught a break when the Refiners lost Rush and catcher Hal Meek, both of whom had to return to college. Butler then nosed out Oil City by taking the final two games of their series to capture the championship. In game six, Butler first baseman Tom Falk, who led the MAL in hits and doubles, stroked four hits and drove in four runs to lead the Tigers to a 13–7 win. Then Butler's pitching ace, Paul Foytack, pitched a three-hit shutout in the final game.[48]

Butler took understandable pride in having the league's best pitcher in Foytack, a teenager from Scranton. With a blazing fastball, he led the MAL in wins (18), ERA (2.78), strikeouts (219), innings pitched (217), and winning percentage (.750). A durable performer in both the MAL and the majors, he won two playoff games in the New Castle series and three against Oil City, including that three-hit shutout in the deciding game. He went on to complete a 11-year major league career, ten with Detroit.

Changes came quickly in the offseason. Even after winning the regular season, Oil City finished deeply in debt. Team president Raymond H. "Ray" Anderson, who owned Pennland Tankers and C. M. Marshall Truckers, had laid out $12,000 to pay off the Refiners' debts. In addition, during the 1949 season, he paid the salary of general manager Kramer. With his team in debt and the Korean War underway, Anderson urged the league to discontinue operations for the duration of the police action in Korea. At the league meeting in January, his motion failed for lack of a second. Anderson then announced that Oil City was closing down its operations. In making the official announcement two weeks later back home in Oil City, Anderson said the baseball team could not compete with "other entertainment mediums such as radio, movie theaters, both indoor and outdoor, and now television." He estimated that the club had lost $30,000 in the postwar years.[49]

Bill Koval at Youngstown knew disaster awaited if the league went into 1951 without changes. Koval had always operated as a hands-on owner. He sold tickets, cooked hot dogs, dusted seats, raked the infield, and cut the grass. He loved the life, but financial losses were mounting beyond his ability to absorb them. His partner Nick Andolina wanted off what he considered a sinking ship; so Koval bought him out. Koval talked of moving the team, and then attempted to get a franchise in the Class B Central League. Failing that, he tried unsuccessfully to push the MAL to move up to Class B. He did not attend the March MAL meeting, citing "illness," adding, "I'm also broke and couldn't put up the money for the franchise." Finally, he sold the Youngstown franchise to Orin Sterling of Mifflinburg, Pennsylvania. As part of the deal, Koval stayed on as general manager.[50]

Other changes came rapidly in the offseason. Chick Cooper gave up the helm of Johnstown, but he remained vice president of the league. John W. Trimble took over as the president of the Johnstown club. The Johnnies had fared poorly in 1950. Without a major league affiliate they fell to the bottom of the standings. The new operators quickly came to understand the difficulty of the situation. In February they issued a statement that because "public demand for minor league baseball has ceased to exist" in Johnstown, the club was notifying Daily that the Johnnies were dropping out of the league. That decision had to be a blow to Daily. The Johnnies' attendance was the third highest despite the decline from1949. Johnstown had been in the league for more years than any other city, and was only a few miles from Daily's home.[51]

Without Vandergrift, Oil City and Johnstown, the league needed another franchise just to make a six-team league. Bill Burns, Jr., a Rochester meat wholesaler, who had run the Niagara Falls franchise into the ground in 1947, had approached league owners in December 1950 about getting a franchise. He had run a team in Lockport, New York, in the Class D PONY League in 1950 and wanted to move up to the Mid-Atlantic. Daily put Burns off as long as possible, but by February he gave Burns the franchise for Lockport. A city of about 25,000, the seat of Niagara County, it had the advantage of proximity to Niagara Falls and Erie.[52]

Other changes around the league were less important. At Butler, Lee Handley, a former major league player, now an automobile dealer in Pittsburgh, replaced Hutchinson as president in April. Nick Andolina, former co-owner of Youngstown, became vice president. They managed to get a working agreement with the Pirates. Citing financial losses, the Washington Senators dropped its working agreement with New Castle and the New York Giants decided not to continue its agreement with Erie. Since 1944 the Giants had provided Erie with talented players and $4,000 to $5,000 in cash each season. Jocko Munch, long-time president of the Sailors, stepped down. Mike Cannavino, an Erie resident who had operated New Castle in 1950, took over as head of the Erie Citizens Baseball Club. He did manage to pick up a working agreement with Washington, but the Senators were known for operating on the cheap. New Castle president Al Scarazzo thought he had an agreement with Cleveland and changed the team name from Nats to Indians, but the deal fell through. Cleveland did provide New Castle with a handful of players. At Niagara Falls, Helen Hale became the first female business manager in the MAL. The league faced so many problems in 1950 that no one had time to comment much, on a woman running a club.[53]

At the MAL meeting in late February, Daily faced a rebellion. Daily had consistently opposed moving the MAL to a higher classification, even when the population of the league's cities more than justified such a move. Koval, especially, favored the upward move, believing a more prestigious classification would draw more fans. The new leadership at Butler and Lockport went along. Cannavino, however, believed that higher salaries necessitated by the higher classification would spell disaster. His threat that Erie would drop out of the league if the move up was approved led to a reversal of the initial vote. Daily reportedly became choked with emotion several times during the deliberations.[54]

The league made some adjustments to help with the player shortage due to the Korean War. The roster limit went from 16 to 17, but the monthly salary maximum stayed at $3,000. The limit of veteran players, those with three or more years of experience, was raised from six to ten. This was especially helpful for the independent teams who, typically, needed to hire older players outside the major league development pipeline. In 1951 only Erie and Butler were not independents.[55]

An influx of African-American players went largely unnoticed by newspapers around the league. Josh Gibson's son signed but failed to stick with Youngstown. Cleveland sent outfielders Ted Toles and Rudy Johnston to New

Castle. Johnson struggled, but Toles batted .308. Washington signed two players to Erie contracts. Willie Grace, a 34-year-old from the Cleveland Buckeyes, and young first baseman Maurice Peatros, off the Homestead Grays roster, contributed to the regular-season champs; Peatros batted .299 and Grace .293.[56]

Koval's preseason fears materialized even before the end of May. In an effort to find a drawing card, Youngstown hired former major league star Rudy York to manage and play first base for the Athletics. York brought power. In 13 major league seasons he had clubbed 277 homers and six times drove in over 100 runs. He could still hit, leading the MAL with 34 dingers while driving in 107 runs. Youngstown fans, however, took little notice of York's exploits. In the first three weeks of the season the A's averaged just 200 fans, as the team floundered deep in last place. Koval floated the possibility of moving the team to St. Catherine's, Ontario, but that idea went nowhere. He then tried, unsuccessfully, to interest Ray Anderson and J.J. "Joe" Connors, who had run the Oil City club in 1950, in purchasing the Youngstown team. Instead of buying, the Oil City men convinced Koval to take over the team and move the Youngstown franchise to their city. The move took place on May 25, 1951. Oil City greeted Koval's team with a turnout of 1,400 in their first game. Unfortunately, after that game attendance plummeted. Koval managed to convince investors Bror Anderson, Ben Gault and Gerald Barber to take the club off his hands. Connors, a local school teacher, would operate the club as general manager.[57]

Koval returned to his home in Braddock, Pennsylvania, but his troubles did not end. His Youngstown/Oil City corporation chartered in Ohio went into receivership. In an effort to retrieve some money to pay off debts that Koval had left in Ohio, Joseph Stewart, the court appointed receiver, appealed to George Trautman, president of the National Association. After hearing arguments, Trautman ordered the MAL to turn over the $1,700 franchise fee to the receiver. He also assessed each MAL team $200 to pay back salaries of the Oil City players.[58]

The Oil City club continued to flounder. The new owners changed the team name from Athletics to Refiners, and tried to put energy into the operation. For Independence Day they offered fireworks and the American Legion band at the park. They brought in a virtual train load of new players, dumped higher paid players, and brought in comedian Al Schach to add spark. Unfortunately, nothing changed on the field. After finishing with a 15–43 record in the first half, the Refiners followed that dismal record with only nine wins in their next 41 games. In a last-ditch effort to attract fans, Connors held a "free admission night" on August 3. Only 200 people came through the turnstile.

That was the last straw. On August 4, Connors announced the club was disbanding. In their final game at Oil City, the Refiners lost to Erie, 15–1. The *Derrick* lamented, "The departure of the Refiners leaves little if any grief with local fans."[59]

While Youngstown was getting off to such a terrible start, Erie raced out to an 11-game lead by the end of June, threatening to make a shambles of the pennant race. In hopes of increasing fan interest, Erie proposed creating a split-season. The other clubs jumped at the suggestion. So, the first half ended on July 1, with Erie well ahead of Niagara Falls. Lockport and New Castle filled in the middle, with Butler and Oil City well out of the running.[60]

Despite their mediocre 65–63 record, the Lockport Locks were noteworthy by becoming a socialist team. By midseason, Bill Burns experienced deep financial trouble. In mid-July he fired non-playing manager Bill Mongiello as a means of reducing salaries. In an unprecedented move, Burns allowed the players to select their own manager. They voted in Glenn Gardner, a 35-year-old pitcher, as their new skipper. Gardner was the Locks' pitching ace with 16 wins for the year. The Locks' number two pitcher, Pat McCullough (15–9), pitched the league's only no-hitter against Oil City on July 6. Late in the season, with the Locks short of pitchers, he pitched both ends of a doubleheader against New Castle. With the Locks averaging only 451 fans, Burns on August 24 turned the team over to the players. With just a week remaining in the season, Daily had little choice but to allow Burns' move to stand. The players elected another pitcher, Howard "Red" Kaiser (4–2), as business manager. The club managed to finish the season without incident.[61]

The second half saw a race, as Niagara Falls slipped past Erie to win by two games, although Erie compiled the best overall record, eight games better than Niagara Falls. In the playoff series, the Niagara Falls Citizens beat Erie in six games to take the league's last title. The club had the best pitcher in the league in Ken Yount, who led the league in wins (20–3), earned-run average (2.84), and innings pitched (212). In addition, they had two other solid pitchers in Zeke Zeisz (14–9, 3.09) and Dick Friel (15–12, 4.33). Erie countered with six pitchers who racked up double-digit wins. These included Keith Nicolls, who won 13 games while losing only two, a league-best .867 winning percentage. Nicholls' 2.49 ERA was also the league best. Sportswriters picked Dean Stone (8–3) as the best left-handed pitcher and the league's best prospect. Indeed, Stone went up to the Washington Senators in 1952 and stayed in the majors for eight years. In the final game of the championship series, Yount outdueled Stone to claim the championship for Niagara Falls.

At the conclusion of the 1951 season, only Erie and Niagara Falls were able to consider playing in 1952. The Youngstown/Oil City franchise had failed to complete the season. In January, when the Oil City Athletic Club offered to give the franchise away, no one expressed interest. The Lockport Locks averaged fewer than 400 fans per game in 1951, and clearly could not regroup. New Castle president Al Scarazzo lamented, "There doesn't seem to be any genuine interest in organized baseball in this city." He sold off the club's assets. Nick Andolina, who took over the Butler franchise near the end of the 1951 season, declared in January that "the town just won't support a minor league team." He stated flatly, "Butler is out!" Daily toyed with the idea of adding two Canadian cities, but the prospects across the border seemed too slim. He waited until February, but Daily finally announced that the league would not operate in 1952. In closing up shop he cited the inroads of radio and television into the minor league cities as the main culprit. Still, Daily held out the hope of resuming operation in 1953, but few believed that would happen. The door had closed on a glorious era in baseball history.[62]

Daily and others in the baseball establishment blamed the public's loss of interest on the broadcast of major league games into minor league territory, first via radio and then on television. There was no shortage of intrusion in minor league territory through the airwaves, but they might have just blamed television. In understanding what happened to baseball, it is illustrative to look at what happened to attendance at movie theaters during the same period. Movies had reached their peak of popularity in 1930 when 80 million people, 65 percent of the country's population, attended movies weekly. No doubt, in the trough of the Great Depression, people wanted to find escape, happy endings, or just to forget their troubles. Movie attendance declined gradually during the late-'30s and the early-'40s, but began to rebound toward the end of the war, experiencing a second peak between 1944 and 1947 when 60 percent of the population went to the picture show each week. Then attendance plummeted down to 50 percent in 1948, and 25 percent of Americans by 1954. Most students of the movies blame television for the decline. Since commercial TV began in 1947, and the number of stations exploded in 1951, the connection is easy to make.[63]

Some scholars, however, suggest other factors may have been involved. The baby boom was underway, making it difficult for young parents to get out to movies or ball games. The sudden popularity of drive-in movie theaters was a product of the new culture. It allowed whole families to go to the movies without having to find a baby-sitter. The move from cities to suburbs, directly linked to the baby boom, was also underway after World War II. Babies required a great deal of their parents' time, and in the suburbs, baby-sitters were not just around the corner in grandma's house. The configuration of the suburbs made it impossible for people to walk to motion picture shows, or to baseball games for that matter. A growing fear that downtowns were unsafe places further kept people away from the sidewalks of the cities. This was certainly true in cities as large as Youngstown, Erie and Johnstown, but it also influenced the habits of people in Oil City, Butler, and New Castle. The suburban move and the new tract houses and their large lots required an enormous amount of work, allowing less and less time to going out. By 1951 Little League baseball had become the favorite game for suburban parents. Mothers and fathers took pleasure in watching their sons play near home, in a clean, safe environment. Nowhere was this dichotomy more clear than in Oil City, where, in the same week, only 300 turned out for a free professional game, while 2,000 showed up for a Little League playoff game.[64]

This perfect storm of cultural shifts—the baby boom, the move to suburbia, and the emergence of television—was creating a very different postwar America. Weariness from economic depression and the dangers and hardships of war led people to seek safety and comfort. Postwar Americans believed security could be found in the hearth and home, in cultural conformity and in political conservatism. Joy in community, civic pride, boosterism, and pleasure in being part of the crowd were all part of a cluster of cultural values that had prevailed in the previous generation, but were lost by the 1950s. Minor league baseball, at least in the lower minors, was so much collateral damage. The minors were not dead, but it would take another generation to revive them. By then, the Middle Atlantic League would be long forgotten.

Chapter Notes

Chapter 1

1. *Cumberland Evening Times,* March 3, 1925, and April 9, 1925.
2. Robert Obojski, *Bush League: A History of Minor League Baseball* (New York: Macmillan, 1975), pp. 270–271.
3. *The Sporting News,* January 8, 1925, and February 19, 1925.
4. *Cumberland Evening Times,* February 9, 1925, and March 18, 1925.
5. *Johnstown Tribune,* April 22, 1925; George Ramsey, "A Brief History of Baseball in Fairmont," unpublished manuscript, Clarksburg (WV) Public Library; Russell Hockenbury, *A Short History of the Middle Atlantic League, 1925–1947* (Scottdale, PA: Middle Atlantic League, 1947).
6. *Cumberland Evening Times,* March 23, 1925.
7. Charles F. Kramer, *The Middle Atlantic League, 25th Anniversary, 1925–49* (Johnstown, PA: Middle Atlantic League, 1949), p. 148.
8. *Cumberland Evening Times,* March 18, 1925.
9. Rodney Sturtz and M. A. Mogue, "Play Ball! The Scottdale Young Cardinals," *Westmoreland History* 7 (December 2002): 38–40; *Cumberland Evening Times,* April 9, 1925, and April 14, 1925.
10. Al Hirshberg, *From Sandlots to League President: The Story of Joe Cronin* (New York: Julian Messner, 1962), p. 35; Randy G. Whittle, *Johnstown, Pennsylvania: A History, Part One, 1895–1936* (Charleston, SC: History Press, 2007), pp. 109–110.
11. Kramer, *Middle Atlantic League,* p. 149; *Clarksburg Telegram,* April 4, 1925, and May 21, 1925.
12. *Cumberland Evening Times,* January 23, 1925.
13. Gus A. Bolden, *West Virginia: The State Beautiful* (Charleston, WV: Tourist, 1929), p. 62.
14. *Cumberland Evening Times,* May, 19, 1925.
15. Ramsey, "History of Baseball in Fairmont," p. 6; *Cumberland Evening Times,* September 17, 1925.
16. Matt Miller, *Milltown Yank* (Scottdale, PA: Pinetree Enterprises, 2002), pp. 3–4.
17. Matt Miller, *Scottdale Young Cardinals, 1925–1931* (Scottdale, PA: Pinetree Enterprises, 1998), pp. 2, 3, 7.
18. Mark Armour, *Joe Cronin: A Life in Baseball* (Lincoln: University of Nebraska Press, 2010), pp. 19–21.
19. Ibid., pp. 28–31.
20. *Cumberland Evening Times,* June 23, 1925.
21. Rob L. Ruck, Maggie Jones Patterson, and Michael P. Weber, *Rooney: A Sporting Life* (Lincoln: University of Nebraska Press, 2010), pp. 30, 40–41, 50–53.
22. Ibid., pp. 76–77.
23. Ibid., pp. 52–53, 66–67, 76–77.
24. *Cumberland Evening Times,* September 19, 1925; *Uniontown Morning Herald,* January 1, 23, 1926.
25. *The Sporting News,* September 24, 1925; *Pittsburgh Press,* May 13, 1949; *Cumberland Evening Times,* September 18, 1925.
26. *Cumberland Evening Times,* February 19, 1926; *Uniontown Morning Herald,* March 20, 1926.
27. *Spalding's Official Baseball Guide* (New York: American Sports, 1940), pp. 298–99; *Oil City Blizzard,* July 16, 1952.

28. American Guide Series, *Pennsylvania: The Keystone State* (New York: Oxford University Press, 1941), p. 453.
29. *Uniontown Morning Herald*, February 4 and 6, 1926; *Cumberland Evening Times*, February 9, 1926.
30. *Indiana (PA) Evening News*, March 19, 1926; *Cumberland Evening News*, March 20, 1926; *The Sporting News*, March 11, 22, 1926.
31. Robert Peterson, *Cages to Jump Shots: Pro Basketball's Early Years* (New York: Oxford University Press, 1990), pp. 85–86.
32. Whittle, *Johnstown, Pennsylvania*, pp. 109–110; *Indiana Evening Gazette*, February 11, 1926; *Cumberland Evening Times*, July 26, 1926.
33. *Uniontown Morning Herald*, May 12 and 25, 1926, and July 1, 24 and 28, 1926.
34. *Cumberland Evening Times*, June 6 and 30, 1926.
35. *Cumberland Evening Times*, December 15, 1926.
36. *Uniontown Morning Herald*, January 1, 1927.
37. *Charleroi Mail*, January 10 and 12, 1927.
38. *Uniontown Morning Herald*, January 14, 1927; *The Sporting News*, January 20, 1927.
39. William M. Mowbray, *The Eastern Shore Baseball League* (Centerville, MD: Tidewater, 1989), pp. 20, 127.
40. Society for American Baseball Research, *Minor League Stars* (Cooperstown: SABR, 1978), pp. 15, 122.
41. *Cumberland Evening Times*, April 19, 1953.
42. *Indiana (PA) Evening Gazette*, December 28, 1926; *Uniontown Morning Herald*, June 23, 1927.
43. Tom Swift, *Chief Bender's Burden: The Silent Struggle of a Baseball Star* (Lincoln: University of Nebraska Press, 2008), pp. 259–260; *Charleroi Mail*, July 19, 1927.
44. *Cumberland Evening Times*, April 19, 1953.
45. William E. Akin, *West Virginia Baseball: A History, 1865–2000* (Jefferson, NC: McFarland, 2006), p. 125; Kramer, *Middle Atlantic League*, p. 149.
46. *Charleroi Mail*, February 6, 1928; *Cumberland Evening Times*, February 15, 1928.
47. (Fairmont) *West Virginian*, September 6–13, 1928; *Monessen Daily Independent*, August 8, 1928.
48. *Cumberland Evening Times*, July 26, 1928; (Fairmont) *West Virginian*, September 4, 1928; *Charleroi Mail*, August 6, 1928; *Monessen Daily Independent*, August 18, 1928.
49. *Altoona Mirror*, March 16, 1928; *Monessen Daily Independent*, April 20, 1928; *Uniontown Morning Herald*, July 9, 1929; *Huntingdon Daily News*, February 27, 1928; *Lebanon Daily News*, July 20, 1928.
50. *Charleroi Mail*, October 3, 1928, and December 6, 1928.
51. *Connellsville Daily Courier*, November 21 and 27, 1928, and February 22 and 28, 1929; *Uniontown Morning Herald*, November 21, 1928, and February 11, 1929; *Cumberland Evening Times*, February 15, 1929.
52. *Cumberland Evening Times*, March 6, 7, 11 and 14, 1929; *The Sporting News*, March 21, 1929.
53. *Cumberland Evening Times*, January 19, 1929.
54. *The Sporting News*, February 21, 1929.
55. *Cumberland Evening Times*, April 19, 1930.

Chapter 2

1. *Charleroi Mail*, December 30, 1929.
2. *Charleroi Mail*, December 2, 1929, and February 8, 1930; *Monessen Daily Independent*, April 7, 1930.
3. *Cumberland Evening Times*, May 11, 19 and 26, 1930.
4. *Cumberland Evening Times*, March 8, 1930, and May 6, 1930; *Monessen Daily Independent*, May 2, 1930.
5. *Bradford Era*, June 13, 1930; *Charleroi Mail*, June 23, 1930.
6. *The Sporting News*, January 9, 1930; *Cumberland Evening Times*, August 14, 1930.
7. John Heidenry, *The Gashouse Gang* (New York: Public Affairs, 2007), p. 85; Miller, *Scottdale Young Cardinals*, p. iii.
8. *Connellsville Daily Courier*, September 9, 1930.
9. *Cumberland Evening Times*, September 2, 1930; *Bradford Era*, August 22, 1930; *Connellsville Daily Courier*, August 30, 1930.
10. Whittle, *Johnstown, Pennsylvania*, pp. 202–210.

11. *Cumberland Evening Times*, August 22, 1930; David Pietrusza, *Lights On! The Wild Century-Long Saga of Night Baseball* (Lanham, MD: Scarecrow Press, 1997), pp. 56–57; Charles C. Alexander, *Breaking the Slump: Baseball in the Depression Era* (New York: Columbia University Press, 2001), p. 25.
12. *Charleroi Mail*, May 26, 1930; July 3, 14 and 15, 1930; December 16, 1930.
13. *Cumberland Evening Times*, July 22, 1930.
14. Pietrusza, *Lights On!*, p. 74; *Charleroi Mail*, July 4, 5 and 14, 1930.
15. *Charleroi Mail*, July 26, August 1 and 15, 1930.
16. *Cumberland Evening Times*, December 16, 1930.
17. *Cumberland Evening Times*, November 5, 1930, and February 16, 1930; *The Sporting News*, January 1, 1931.
18. *The Sporting News*, January 1, 1930; *Cumberland Evening Times*, December 16, 1930.
19. *Charleroi Mail*, January 16 and 17, 1931.
20. *Charleston Daily Mail*, February 8, 1931; *Charleroi Mail*, February 13, 1931.
21. Brian McKenna, "Joe Cambria," *SABR Baseball Biography Project*, Web; *Frederick News-Post*, February 4, 1931; *Hagerstown Daily Mail*, February 2, 7 and 10, 1931; Mark Zeigler, "History," *Class D Blue Ridge League, 1915–1918, 1920–1930*, Web.
22. *Hagerstown Daily Mail*, February 10 and 12, 1931; *Frederick News-Post*, February 4, 1931; *Charleston Daily Mail*, March 5, 1931.
23. *Charleroi Mail*, February 2, 1931; *Charleston Gazette*, February 15, 1931; *The Sporting News*, February 12, 1931.
24. *The Sporting News*, March 19, 1931; *Cumberland Evening Times*, March 2, 1931; *Charleston Daily Mail*, February 8 and 15, 1931; *Hagerstown Daily Mail*, February 16, 1931; *Charleroi Mail*, February 13, 1931.
25. *The Sporting News*, February 19 and 26, 1931; *Charleston Daily Mail*, July 16, 1931.
26. *The Sporting News*, February 26, 1931; (Beckley) *Raleigh Register*, May 8, 1931.
27. *The Sporting News*, March 19, 1931, and April 16, 1931; *Cumberland Evening Times*, January 1 and 25, 1931, and March 20, 1931.
28. *The Sporting News*, March 1, 1931, and April 15, 1931.
29. *Pittsburgh Press*, May 16, 1931; *Charleroi Mail*, May 18, 1931; *Cumberland Evening Times*, May 16, 1931.
30. *Altoona Mirror*, May 22 and 23, 1931.
31. *The Sporting News*, May 21, 1931; *Charleroi Mail*, May 25 and 28, 1931.
32. *Altoona Mirror*, June 16, 1931; *Monessen Daily Independent*, June 12, 1931.
33. *Hagerstown Morning Herald*, June 26, 1931.
34. *Parkersburg Daily Sentinel*, June 19, 23 and 29, 1931, and July 1 and 11, 1931.
35. *Charleroi Mail*, July 10–20, 1931; *Monessen Daily Independent*, July 11, 1931.
36. *Frederick News-Post*, July 10 and 11, 1931; *Charleston Daily News*, July 13, 26, 1931; *Cumberland Evening Times*, July 10, 1931.
37. *Frederick News-Post*, July 21, 1931; *Charleston Gazette*, July 13, 1931; *Charleston Daily Mail*, July 26, 1931.
38. *Monessen Daily Independent*, July 21, 1931; *Charleroi Mail*, July 16–18, 1931.
39. *The Sporting News*, September 10, 1931; *Hagerstown Morning Herald*, July 17, 1931; *Charleston Daily Mail*, July 17, 1931.
40. *The Sporting News*, April 16, 1931; *Pittsburgh Press*, July 31, 1931; (Fairmont) *West Virginian*, August 18, 1931; *Fairmont Times*, September 13, 1931.
41. *Pittsburgh Press*, September 20, 1931; *Pittsburgh Post-Gazette*, September 22, 1931; *Charleston Gazette*, September 17, 18, 19 and 24, 1931; *The Sporting News*, February 8, 1969.
42. Jerry Bruce Thomas, *An Appalachian New Deal: West Virginia in the Great Depression* (Lexington: University Press of Kentucky, 1998), pp. 24, 25, 90; *Charleston Daily Mail*, September 16 and 20, 1931.
43. (Fairmont) *West Virginian*, August 18, 1931; *The Sporting News*, May 12, 1932.
44. *Cumberland Evening Times*, September 24, 1931.
45. Whittle, *Johnstown, Pennsylvania*, pp. 210–213.
46. *Pittsburgh Press*, August 23, 1931; *The Sporting News*, August 27, 1931.
47. *Cumberland Evening Times*, January 18, 1932.
48. *Cumberland Evening Times*, March 1, 1932.
49. *Beckley Post-Herald*, February 22, 1932; *Cumberland Evening Times*, February 22, 1932.

50. *Wheeling Daily Intelligencer*, April 12, 1932; *Cumberland Evening Times*, March 1, 1932; *Charleston Gazette*, March 23, 1932.
51. *Wheeling Daily Intelligencer*, April 4–22, 1932.
52. *Zanesville Times Recorder*, March 25, 1932, April 6 and 20, 1932; *Charleston Gazette*, March 23, 1932.
53. *Cumberland Evening Times*, May 5, 1932.
54. Richard C. Crepeau, *Baseball: America's Diamond Mind, 1919–1941* (Orlando: University of Central Florida Press, 1980), p. 16; *Cumberland Evening Times*, June 26, 1932.
55. *Charleston Daily Times*, April 21, 1932.
56. *Charleston Daily Mail*, April 10, 15 and 24, 1932; *Cumberland Evening Times*, July 22, 1932.
57. Ken Brooks, *Last Rebel Yell* (Lynn Haven, FL: Seneca Park Publishing, 1986), p. 118.
58. Richard Scott, *Legends of Alabama Football* (Champaign, IL: Sports Publishing, 2004), pp. 38–43.
59. Neil J. Sullivan, *The Minors* (New York: St. Martin's Press, 1990), pp. 212–213.
60. *Pittsburgh Press*, February 20, 1932; *Altoona Mirror*, February 24, 1932.
61. *Cumberland Evening Times*, March 26, 1933.
62. *Clarksburg Telegram*, January 31, 1933; *Cumberland Evening Times*, February 12, 1933; *Charleroi Mail*, January 25, 1933.
63. *Charleston Daily Mail*, February 20, 1933; *Pittsburgh Press*, August 31, 1932; *The Sporting News*, March 2, 1933.
64. *Zanesville Times Recorder*, February 27, 1933, and March 21, 1933.
65. *Clarksburg Telegram*, February 15, 22 and 24, 1933; *Cumberland Evening Times*, February 27, 1933.
66. *Cumberland Evening Times*, April 2, 1933.
67. *Zanesville Times Recorder*, April 3, 1933.
68. *Clarksburg Telegram*, February 24, 1933, and April 23, 1933; *Charleston Daily Mail*, April 5, 1933; *Cumberland Evening Times*, February 27, 1933.
69. *Zanesville Times Recorder*, April 3 and 7, 1933.
70. *Lima News*, April 3, 1933; *Zanesville Times Recorder*, April 3, 1933; *Charleston Daily Mail*, April 5, 1933.
71. *Zanesville Times Recorder*, April 7 and 25, 1933.
72. *Zanesville Times Recorder*, May 7, 1933; *Charleston Gazette*, April 22, 1933.
73. James W. Johnson, *Double No-Hit: Johnny Vander Meer's Historic Night Under the Lights* (Lincoln: University of Nebraska Press, 2012), pp. 51–53.
74. Donald Honig, *Baseball Between the Lines* (New York: Coward, McCann & Geoghegan, 1976), p. 126; *Pittsburgh Post*, August 24, 1933.
75. *Zanesville Times Recorder*, November 7, 1933.

Chapter 3

1. *Charleroi Mail*, January 20, 1934, and February 7, 1934.
2. *Charleroi Mail*, February 7, 1934.
3. *Charleroi Mail*, February 28, 1934, and April 7, 1934.
4. *Charleroi Mail*, April 5, 1934; *Monessen Daily Independent*, April 19, 27, 1934.
5. *Monessen Daily Independent*, April 4 and 28, 1934.
6. *Monessen Daily Independent*, April 7, 19 and 28, 1934, and May 4, 1934.
7. Charlie Bevis, *Sunday Baseball* (Jefferson, NC: McFarland, 2003), pp. 255–259.
8. *Charleroi Mail*, February 28, 1934, and March 21, 1934.
9. Paul Rogers, "Mike McCormick," *SABR Baseball Biography Project*, Web.
10. *Charleroi Mail*, March 23, 1935; Philip J. Lowry, *Green Cathedrals* (Cooperstown: SABR, 1986), p. 45.
11. *Monessen Daily Independent*, September 6–12, 1935.
12. *Monessen Daily Independent*, January 23, 1936.
13. *Charleroi Mail*, January 21, 1936.
14. *Greenburg Record-Argus*, April 28, 1936.
15. *Monessen Daily Independent*, March 16, 17 and 24, 1936.
16. *Charleroi Mail*, April 24 and 27, 1936; David Pietrusza, *Minor Miracles: The Legend and Lure of Minor League Baseball* (South Bend: Diamond Communications, 1995), pp. 91–97.

17. Danny Litwhiler, *Living the Baseball Dream* (Philadelphia: Temple University Press, 2006), pp. 24–26; Jim Sargent, "Danny Litwhiler," *Baseball Almanac*, Web.
18. *Monessen Daily Independent*, March 16, 1937; *Charleroi Mail*, March 17, 1937.
19. *Titusville Herald*, January 14, 1937; *Charleroi Mail*, April 23, 1937; *Monessen Daily Independent*, May 10, 1937.
20. *Charleroi Mail*, April 23 and 30, 1937; *Monessen Daily Independent*, May 10, 12 and 13, 1937.
21. George Stone, *Muscle: A Minor League Legend* (Haverford, PA: Infinity, 2003), pp. 34–35.
22. Ibid., pp. 35–37.
23. *Uniontown News Standard*, June 11, 1937; *Monessen Daily Independent*, June 11, 1937.
24. *Monessen Independent*, May 15, 1937, and July 30 and 31, 1937.
25. Gene Schoor, *The Stan Musial Story* (New York: Messner, 1955), pp. 27–39; George Vecsey, *Stan Musial: An American Life* (New York: Ballantine, 2012), pp. 60–63.
26. *The Sporting News*, September 9, 1937.
27. Stone, *Muscle: A Minor League Legend*, p. 37.
28. *Charleroi Mail*, January 25, 1938, February 19, 1938, and March 1, 1938; *Titusville Herald*, February 24, 1938.
29. *Charleroi Mail*, April 18, 1938.
30. *Charleroi Mail*, April 5, 1938.
31. *Uniontown News Standard*, June 11, 1939; *Monessen Daily Independent*, June 11, 1939.
32. *The Sporting News*, April 6, 1939.
33. *Greensburg Record Argus*, January 5, 1939.
34. Robert L. Finch, et al., *The Story of Minor League Baseball* (Columbus, OH: Stoneman Press, 1952), pp. 39–41.
35. *The Sporting News*, January 21, 1940, and April 4 and 11, 1940; *New Castle News*, April 1, 1939.
36. *Altoona Mirror*, June 16, 1940;
37. *Pittsburgh Post-Gazette*, February 2, 1941; *Beaver Falls Daily Times*, February 6, 1941; *Pittsburgh Press*, February 6, 1941; *The Sporting News*, February 13, 1941.
38. William E. Akin, "Joe Page," in David L. Porter, *Biographical Dictionary of American Sports: Baseball* (Westport, CT: Greenwood Press, 2000), pp. 1162–1163.
39. Corey Seeman, "The Pennsylvania State Association, 1934–1942," in Paul Adomites and Dennis Dealaria, *Baseball in Pittsburgh* (Cleveland: SABR, 1995), p. 47.
40. *Oil City Derrick*, January 23, 1942.
41. Bill Kirkland, *Eddie Neville of the Durham Bulls* (Jefferson, NC: McFarland, 1993), pp. 9–10.
42. *Cumberland Evening Times*, December 9, 1942; *New Castle News*, January 16, 1943; *Huntingdon Daily News*, January 1, 1943, and February 18, 1943.
43. *Cumberland Evening Times*, December 9, 1942, and February 22, 1943; *Titusville Herald*, February 15, 1943; *New Castle News*, March 1, 1943.

Chapter 4

1. Obojski, *Bush League*, pp. 20–21; Sullivan, *The Minors*, p. 136; Pietrusza, *Minor Miracles*, pp. 42–44.
2. *Zanesville Times-Recorder*, January 4, 1934; *Charleston Gazette*, March 19, 1934.
3. Charlie Bevis, *Doubleheaders: A Major League History* (Jefferson, NC: McFarland, 2011), pp. 128–129.
4. *Wheeling Daily Intelligencer*, November 7, 1933, and May 15, 1934.
5. *Charleston Daily Mail*, December 17, 1933; *Charleston Gazette*, December 19, 1933; *Portsmouth Times*, September 16, 1934.
6. Donald Honig, *Baseball When the Grass was Real* (New York: Coward, McCann & Geoghegan, 1975), pp. 240–241.
7. *Charleston Daily Mail*, November 12, 1933; *Charleston Gazette*, May 15, 1934; *The Sporting News*, November 29, 1934.
8. Bill James, *The New Bill James Historical Baseball Abstract* (New York: Free Press, 2001), p. 452.
9. Honig, *Baseball When*, p. 242.
10. *Charleston Gazette*, June 15, 1934; (Beckley) *Raleigh Register*, September 7, 1934.
11. *Zanesville Times Recorder*, August 7, 1934.
12. *Zanesville Times Recorder*, September 11–19, 1934.
13. *Wheeling Daily Intelligencer*, November 7 and 12, 1934.
14. *Wheeling Daily Intelligencer*, November 12, 1934; *Zanesville Signal*, September 31, 1934.

15. *Portsmouth Times,* November 9, 1934, and December 17 and 19, 1934.

16. *Portsmouth Times,* December 2, 1934, and January 17, 1935; *Zanesville Times Reporter,* November 12, 1934.

17. *Zanesville Signal,* January 18, 1935.

18. Richard L. McBane, *Glory Days: The Akron Yankees of the Middle Atlantic League, 1935–1941* (Akron: Summit County Historical Press, 1994), pp. 4–10.

19. Richard L. McBane, *A Fine Looking Lot of Ball-Tossers: The Remarkable Akrons of 1881* (Jefferson, NC: McFarland, 2005), pp. 135–136.

20. McBane, *Ball-Tossers,* p. 137.

21. *Wheeling Daily Intelligencer,* February 2, 1935, March 18, 1935, and April 15, 1935.

22. (Beckley) *Raleigh Register,* February 15, 1935.

23. *The Sporting News,* April 25, 1935.

24. Lowry, *Green Cathedrals,* p. 1; McBane, *Glory Days,* pp. 8–9.

25. McBane, *Glory Days,* pp. 15, 19.

26. McBane, *Ball-Tossers,* pp. 47–48; *Zanesville Times Recorder,* September 9, 1935.

27. Peterson, *Cages to Jump Shots,* pp. 87–88.

28. *Zanesville Signal,* September 10–17, 1935.

29. *Charleston Daily Mail,* September 2, 14, and 20, 1935.

30. *Charleston Gazette,* July 10, 1935; (Beckley) *Raleigh Register,* September 9, 1935.

31. *Beckley Post-Herald,* July 6, 1935, and December 20 and 26, 1935; *Charleston Gazette,* January 7, 1936.

32. *Charleston Gazette,* October 15, 1935, and January 7, 1936; *Portsmouth Times,* March 13, 1936, and April 20, 1936.

33. James B. Holl, *The Canton Terriers: The Middle Atlantic Years, 1936–1942* (Canton, OH: Daring Books, 1990), p. 15; *Beckley Post-Herald,* April 19, 1936.

34. Holl, *Canton Terriers,* pp. 53–54.

35. Holl, *Canton Terriers,* p. 12; *Zanesville Signal,* April 12, 1936.

36. Holl, *Canton Terriers,* p. 14.

37. Holl, *Canton Terriers,* pp. 40–41.

38. *Portsmouth Times,* January 7, 1936, March 15, 1936, and April 9 and 15, 1936.

39. *Zanesville Times Recorder,* November 4, 1936.

40. *Zanesville Signal,* September 1, 1936, November 9, 1936, and December 2, 1936; *Charleston Gazette,* April 15, 1937.

41. *Zanesville Signal,* December 18, 19 and 24, 1936; *Zanesville Times Recorder,* January 14, 1937.

42. *Zanesville Signal,* December 5, 1936; *Portsmouth Times,* January 14, 1937.

43. *Portsmouth Times,* December 1 and 10, 1936, January 1, 1937, and February 18 and 27, 1937.

44. *Charleston Gazette,* February 13, 1937; *Zanesville Signal,* February 17, 1937.

45. *Zanesville Signal,* February 1 and 19, 1937.

46. Holl, *Canton Terriers,* p. 15; McBane, *Glory Days,* pp. 30–31.

47. *Zanesville Times Recorder,* March 3, 1937.

48. *The Sporting News,* March 4, 1937.

49. *Spalding Official Baseball Guide* (New York: American Sports, 1938), p. 246.

50. *Zanesville Times Recorder,* June 9, 1937; *Portsmouth Times,* July 23, 1937; *Hamilton Daily News,* August 14, 1937; *Massillon Evening Independent,* August 11, 1937.

51. *Massillon Evening Independent,* November 8, 1937; *Charleston Daily Mail,* November 7, 1937.

52. *Zanesville Signal,* November 6, 8 and 13, 1937, December 4, 1937, January 29, 1938, February 4, 1938, and March 22, 25 and 31, 1938; *Hamilton Daily News Journal,* March 24, 1938.

53. Pietrusza, *Minor Miracles,* p. 71.

54. *Massillon Evening Independent,* February 1–2, 1938; *Portsmouth Times,* March 29, 1938.

55. McBane, *Glory Days,* pp. 41–42.

56. Holl, *Canton Terriers,* p. 78.

57. *Portsmouth Times,* July 22 and 28, 1938, and August 5, 1938.

58. McBane, *Glory Days,* pp. 51–52.

59. *The Sporting News,* January 3 and 12, 1939, March 9, 1939, April 20, 1939, and December 19, 1939.

60. McBane, *Glory Days,* pp. 34, 45–49.

61. *Zanesville Signal,* January 4, 1939; *Charleston Daily Mail,* January 9, 1939; *Coshocton Tribune,* March 2, 1939; *The Sporting News,* March 23, 1939, and December 21, 1939.

62. *Charleston Daily Mail,* January 9, 1939; *Massillon Evening Independent,* April 27, 1939.

63. *Zanesville Times Recorder*, March 7 and 10, 1939; *Uniontown Morning Herald*, March 10, 1939; *Portsmouth Times*, September 9, 1938.

64. *The Sporting News*, March 16 and 23, 1939; *Lima News*, March 30, 1939.

65. *The Sporting News*, May 25, 1939, and June 1 and 29, 1939; *Charleston Daily Mail*, August 8, 1939.

66. *The Sporting News*, September 28, 1939; Holl, *Canton Terriers*, pp. 81–84.

67. Whitey Ford and Phil Pepe, *Few and Chosen: Defining Yankee Greatness Across the Eras* (Chicago: Triumph, 2001), p. 146.

68. *The Sporting News*, July 20, 1939.

Chapter 5

1. McBane, *Glory Days*, pp. 51–55.

2. *Portsmouth Times*, December 6, 1939, *The Sporting News*, January 11, 1940.

3. *Coshocton Tribune*, December 8, 1939; *Charleston Daily Mail*, December 23, 1939.

4. *Charleston Daily Mail*, December 5, 6, 10 and 31, 1939; *Charleston Gazette*, February 16–17, 1940.

5. *The Sporting News*, January 8, 1940, February 1, 1940, and March 14, 1940; *Massillon Evening Independent*, February 15, 1940.

6. Alexander, *Slump*, p. 242; David Pietrusza, *Judge and Jury: The Life and Times of Judge Kenesaw Mountain Landis* (South Bend: Diamond Communications, 1998), pp. 367–69; *Detroit News*, January 16, 1940.

7. *New York Times*, January 17, 1940; Pietrusza, *Judge and Jury*, p. 368.

8. *The Sporting News*, January 25, 1940.

9. Pietrusza, *Judge and Jury*, pp. 368–369.

10. Pietrusza, *Judge and Jury*, pp. 368–369; *The Sporting News*, January 25, 1940.

11. *The Sporting News*, February 1, 1940; *Hamilton Daily News*, January 27, 1940; *Titusville Herald*, January 26, 1940; *Akron Beacon-Journal*, January 27, 1940.

12. *Zanesville Signal*, February 15–16, 1940; *Portsmouth Times*, March 27, 1940.

13. *Charleston Gazette*, May 14, 1940, July 28, 1940, August 9 and 25, 1940, and September 1, 1940.

14. *Portsmouth Times*, September 8, 1940.

15. *Portsmouth Times*, February 16 and 19, 1941.

16. *The Sporting News*, November 21, 1940, December 5, 1940, and February 27, 1941.

17. *Charleston Daily Mail*, February 26, 1941, and March 13, 1941.

18. *Charleston Daily Mail*, February 27, 1941; *Zanesville Signal*, March 16, 1941.

19. *Zanesville Signal*, November 27, 1940, December 2, 1940, February 27, 1941, and March 6, 18 and 21, 1941.

20. *Zanesville Signal*, March, 6, 7, 15, 21 and 26, 1941; *The Sporting News*, November 21, 1940, February 27, 1941, March 13 and 20, 1941, and April 3 and 17, 1941.

21. *The Sporting News*, December 5, 1940, and May 1, 1941; McBane, *Glory Days*, p. 68.

22. McBane, *Glory Days*, pp. 67, 69, 72; *The Sporting News*, May 29, 1941.

23. Richard McBane, "The Lights Go Out on Baseball in Akron," *Minor League History Journal* (1993), pp. 28–31.

24. Holl, *Canton Terriers*, p. 102.

25. *The Sporting News*, January 15, 1942.

26. McBane, "The Lights Go Out," p. 30.

27. *Zanesville Times-Recorder*, February 27, 1942.

28. *Charleston Daily Mail*, March 9, 1942; *The Sporting News*, March 12, 1942.

29. *Zanesville Time Recorder*, March 9, 1942, and May 7, 1942; *Zanesville Signal*, March 23 and 30, 1942, April 4, 1942, and May 2, 1942.

30. *Zanesville Signal*, March 30, 1942; *Charleston Daily Mail*, July 19, 1942.

31. *Charleston Daily Mail*, June 28, 1942, August 14, 1942, and September 5, 1942.

32. *Charleston Daily Mail*, June 20, 1942, and September 6, 1942; *Hamilton Daily News*, August 17, 1942; *Portsmouth Times*, August 24, 1942; *The Sporting News*, August 6 and 13, 1942.

33. *The Sporting News*, August 20, 1942, and September 17, 1942.

34. John Frey, "Betty Peebles Hits Home Run for Erie Baseball," *Lake Erie LifeStyle*, February 2012, pp. 35–37.

35. *Zanesville Times Recorder*, April 27, 1942.

36. Holl, *Canton Terriers*, p. 109; *Charleston Daily Mail*, July 29, 1942.

37. *The Sporting News*, November 26, 1942.

38. Richard R. Lingeman, *Don't You Know There's a War On? The American Home Front,*

1941–1945 (New York: G. P. Putnam's Sons, 1971), pp. 289–291.

39. *The Sporting News,* November 12, 1942; *Pittsburgh Press,* December 6 and 7, 1942; *Charleston Daily Mail,* February 7, 1943.

40. *The Sporting News,* November 12, 1942, and February 4, 1943; *Zanesville Times Recorder,* February 20, 1943.

41. *The Sporting News,* February 4 and 11, 1943; *Charleston Gazette,* February 13 and 19, 1943; *Zanesville Signal,* February 21, 1943; *Zanesville Times Recorder,* February 20, 1943.

42. *The Sporting News,* February 2, 1943; *Charleston Daily Mail,* February 17, 1943; *Pittsburgh Press,* February 2, 1943; Obojski, *Bush League,* p. 278.

43. *Zanesville Signal,* March 11, 1943.

44. *The Sporting News,* December 9, 1943; Finch, *Story of Minor League Baseball,* pp. 46–47; Hugh Fullerton, Jr., "Notes and Things on Ball Meeting," *Montreal Gazette,* December 4, 1943.

45. *Zanesville Signal,* January 3, 27 and 31, 1944, and February 2, 1944; *The Sporting News,* January 6, 20 and 27, 1944, and February 10, 1944.

46. *The Sporting News,* February 3, 1944.

Chapter 6

1. *Oil City Blizzard,* October 1, 4 and 27, 1945; *Zanesville Signal,* October 3, 1945.

2. *Zanesville Times Recorder,* October 28–29, 1945.

3. *Zanesville Times Recorder,* October 27–29, 1945.

4. *Charleston Daily Mail,* October 30, 1945.

5. *The Sporting News,* November 11, 1945; *Oil City Blizzard,* November 10, 1945, and February 11, 1946.

6. *Charleston Daily Mail,* September 20, 1945; *Zanesville Times-Recorder,* December 7, 1945.

7. *Zanesville Times Recorder,* December 7, 1945.

8. *Charleston Daily Mail,* December 11, 1945.

9. *Oil City Blizzard,* October 29, 1945, and November 5, 1945; *The Sporting News,* November 5, 1945.

10. Finch, *Story of Minor League Baseball,* p. 49.

11. *Oil City Blizzard,* December 11, 1945, and January 21, 1946.

12. *Oil City Blizzard,* February 7, 1946; Kramer, *Middle Atlantic League,* p. 67; *Coshochton News,* February 8, 1946.

13. Kramer, *Middle Atlantic League,* p. 167; *Oil City Blizzard,* April 27, 1946; *The Sporting News,* June 5, 1946.

14. *The Sporting News,* June 5, 1946; *Oil City Blizzard,* June 7, 1946.

15. *Oil City Blizzard,* May 6 and 10, 1946; *The Sporting News,* June 5, 1946.

16. *The Sporting News,* September 25, 1946.

17. *The Sporting News,* November 13, 1946; *Charleston Gazette,* November 29, 1946.

18. *The Sporting News,* November 13, 1946; *Charleroi Mail,* November 23, 1946.

19. Kramer, *Middle Atlantic League,* pp. 177–78; *Titusville Herald,* November 4, 1946.

20. *Uniontown Morning Herald,* February 6–7, 1947, and April 16, 1947.

21. Kramer, *Middle Atlantic League,* pp. 179–181.

22. Ford and Pepe, *Few and Chosen,* pp. 157–159.

23. Whitey Ford and Phil Pepe, *Slick: My Life In and Around Baseball* (New York: William Morrow, 1987).

24. Kramer, *Middle Atlantic League,* p. 168; *New Castle News,* November 12, 1947; *Oil City Derrick,* May 3, 1948.

25. *Titusville Herald,* November 17, 1947; *Oil City Derrick,* May 3, 1947.

26. *The Sporting News,* July 21, 1948; *Oil City Blizzard,* July 16, 1948.

27. *The Sporting News,* November 24, 1948, and February 16, 1949.

28. *The Sporting News,* November 2 and 24, 1948.

29. *The Sporting News,* January 5, 1949, and February 16, 1949.

30. *Huntingdon Daily News,* April 2 and 4, 1949; *Altoona Mirror,* April 4, 1949.

31. *The Sporting News,* April 6, 1949.

32. Hugh Fullerton, Jr., "Sports Roundtable," *Reno Evening Gazette,* January 27, 1949; *The Sporting News,* April 6, 1949.

33. *The Sporting News,* June 8, 1949, and August 3, 1949.

34. *The Sporting News,* May 25, 1949, and June 22, 1949.

35. *Oil City Blizzard,* July 25, 1949; *Oil City Derrick,* August 2, 1949.

36. Lloyd Johnson and Miles Wolfe, eds., *Encyclopedia of Minor League Baseball* (Durham: Baseball America, 2007), p. 431.

37. *New Castle News*, January 5, 1950; *Uniontown Morning Herald*, August 5, 1949.

38. *Uniontown Morning Herald*, January 28, 1950; *New Castle News*, January 11, 1950.

39. Dean A. Sullivan, *Late Innings: A Documentary History of Baseball, 1945–1972* (Lincoln: University of Nebraska Press, 2001), pp. 44–45.

40. *The Sporting News*, February 15, 1950, and March 1, 1950.

41. *The Sporting News*, April 19, 1950.

42. David Nassan, *Going Out: The Rise and Fall of Public Amusements* New York: Basic Books, 1993), pp. 248–49; Erik Barnouw, *The Tube of Plenty: The Evolution of American Television* (New York: Oxford University Press, 1982), pp. 112–14.

43. *Uniontown Morning Herald*, August 5, 1949, January 11, 28, 30 and 31, 1950, and February 1 and 23, 1950; *The Sporting News*, February 8, 1950.

44. *New Castle News*, February 20, 1950; *The Sporting News*, February 15, 1950.

45. *Oil City Derrick*, September 20, 1949; *Oil City Blizzard*, October 20, 1949, and January 27, 1950; *Altoona Mirror*, September 22, 1949.

46. *Dunkirk Evening Observer*, July 20, 1950; *Oil City Blizzard*, May 20, 1950.

47. Johnson and Wolff, *Minor League Baseball*, p. 442.

48. *Oil City Blizzard*, September 7–18, 1950.

49. *Oil City Blizzard*, September 5, 1950, and January 5 and 21, 1951.

50. *Oil City Blizzard*, January 15, 1951; *Huntingdon Daily News*, January 31, 1951; *New Castle News*, March 12, 1951, and May 28, 1951.

51. *New Castle News*, February 24, 1951.

52. *New Castle News*, January 2 and 24, 1951; *The Sporting News*, December 6, 1950, and January 24, 1951.

53. *New Castle News*, January 29, 1951, February 27, 1951, and March 28, 1951; *The Sporting News*, March 7, 1951, and April 25, 1951.

54. *Oil City Blizzard*, January 15, 1951.

55. *Oil City Blizzard*, January 10 and 15, 1951.

56. *New Castle News*, March 28, 1951.

57. *Oil City Blizzard*, May 23 and 28, 1951, and June 1, 1951; *Oil City Derrick*, June 25, 1951, July 9, 1951, and August 4, 1951.

58. *The Sporting News*, July 18, 1951; *Oil City Derrick*, August 4, 1951.

59. *Oil City Blizzard*, July 7, 1951, and August 4, 1951; *Oil City Derrick*, August 4, 1951.

60. *Oil City Derrick*, June 30, 1951.

61. *The Sporting News*, July 18, 1951; *Oil City Derrick*, August 25, 1951; *Oil City Blizzard*, August 28, 1951.

62. *Oil City Blizzard*, September 13, 1951, and January 30, 1952; *New Castle News*, January 9, 1952, and February 4, 1952.

63. Thomas W. Bohn and Richard L. Stromgren, *Light and Shadow: A History of Motion Pictures* (Port Washington, NY: Alfred, 1975), pp. 236–237; Michelle Pautz, "The Decline in Average Weekly Cinema Attendance, 1930–2000," *Issues in Political Economy* 11 (July 2002), pp. 2–4.

64. Nasan, *Going Out*, pp. 248–250; *Oil City Derrick*, August 7, 1951.

Bibliography

Books and Articles

Addington, L.H. "Baseball Is Life to Daily." *Baseball Magazine* 62 (March 1939): 456.

Akin, William E. "Joe Page." In *Biographical Dictionary of American Sports: Baseball*, edited by David L. Porter. Westport, CT: Greenwood Press, 2000.

_____. *West Virginia Baseball: A History, 1865–2000*. Jefferson, NC: McFarland, 2006.

Alexander, Charles C. *Breaking the Slump: Baseball in the Depression Era*. New York: Columbia University Press, 2002.

American Guide Series. *Pennsylvania: A Guide to the Keystone State*. New York: Oxford University Press, 1940.

Armour, Mark. *Joe Cronin: A Life in Baseball*. Lincoln: University of Nebraska Press, 2010.

Aton, Rusty D. *Baseball in Springfield*. Charleston, SC: Arcadia, 2005.

Bevis, Charles. *Doubleheaders: A Major League History*. Jefferson, NC: McFarland, 2011.

_____. *Sunday Baseball: The Major Leagues' Struggle to Play Baseball on the Lord's Day, 1876–1934*. Jefferson, NC: McFarland, 2003.

Bolden, Gus A. *West Virginia: The State Beautiful*. Charleston, WV: Tourist, 1929.

Brooks, Ken. *Last Rebel Yell*. Lynn Haven, FL: Seneca Park, 1986.

Crepeau, Richard C. *Baseball: America's Diamond Mind, 1919–1941*. Orlando: University of Central Florida Press, 1980.

Finch, Robert L., et al. *The Story of Minor League Baseball*. Columbus, OH: Stoneman Press, 1952.

Ford, Whitey, and Phil Pepe. *Few and Chosen: Defining Yankee Greatness Across the Eras*. Chicago: Triumph, 2001.

_____. *Slick: My Life In and Around Baseball*. New York: William Morrow, 1987.

Frey, John. "Betty Peebles Hits Home Run for Erie Baseball." *Lake Erie LifeStyle*, February 2012.

Grosshandler, Stanley. "Heroes of the Middle Atlantic League." *Baseball Research Journal* 2 (1973): 56–57.

Heidenry, John. *The Gashouse Gang*. New York: Public Affairs, 2007.

Hirschberg, Al. *From Sandlots to League President: The Story of Joe Cronin*. New York: Julian Messner, 1962.

Hockenbury, Russell. *A Short History of the Middle Atlantic League, 1925–1947*. Scottdale, PA: Middle Atlantic League, 1947.

Holl, James B. *The Canton Terriers: The Middle Atlantic Years: 1936–1942*. Canton, OH: Daring Books, 1990.

Honig, Donald. *Baseball Between the Lines*. New York: Coward, McCann & Geoghegan, 1976.

_____. *Baseball When the Grass was Real*. (New York: Coward, McCann & Geohegan, 1975.

James, Bill. *The New Bill James Historical Baseball Abstract*. New York: Free Press, 2001.

Johnson, James W. *Double No-Hit: Johnny Vander Meer's Historic Night Under the Lights*. Lincoln: University of Nebraska Press, 2012.

Johnston, James P. *The Politics of Soft Coal*. Urban: University of Illinois Press, 1979.

Kirkland, Bill. *Eddie Neville of the Durham Bulls*. Jefferson, NC: McFarland, 1993.

Kramer, Charles F. *The Middle Atlantic League, 25th Anniversary, 1925–49*. Johnstown, PA: Middle Atlantic League, 1949.

Litwhiler, Danny. *Living the Baseball Dream*. Philadelphia: Temple University Press, 2006.

Lowenfish, Lee. *Branch Rickey: Baseball's Ferocious Gentleman*. Lincoln: University of Nebraska Press, 2007.

Lowry, Philip J. *Green Cathedrals*. Cooperstown: SABR, 1986.

Maroon, Thomas, et al. *Akron-Canton Baseball Heritage*. Charleston, SC: Arcadia, 2007.

McBane, Richard L. *A Fine Looking Lot of Ball-Tossers: The Remarkable Akrons of 1881*. Jefferson, NC: McFarland, 2005.

_____. *Glory Days: The Akron Yankees of the Middle Atlantic League, 1935–1941*. Akron: Summit County Historical Press, 1994.

_____. "The Lights Go Out on Baseball in Akron." *Minor League History Journal* (1993): 28–31.

McCrossen, Alexis. *Holy Day, Holiday: The American Sunday*. Ithaca: Cornell University Press, 2000.

McKenna, Brian. "Joe Cambria." *SABR Baseball Biography Project*. Web.

Metro, Charlie, with Tom Altherr. *Safe by a Mile*. Lincoln: University of Nebraska Press, 2002.

Miller, Matt. *Milltown Yank*. Scottdale, PA: Pinetree Enterprises, 2002.

_____. *Scottdale Young Cardinals, 1925–1931*. Scottdale, PA: Pinetree Enterprises, 1998.

Mowbray, William M. *The Eastern Shore Baseball League*. Centerville, MD: Tidewater, 1989.

Nagle, Herman R. *Altoona Scrapbook of Baseball Memory, circa 1900–1960*. Altoona: private printing, 2007.

Nasan, David. *Going Out: The Rise and Fall of Public Amusements*. New York: Basic Books, 1993.

Obojski, Robert. *Bush League: A History of Minor League Baseball*. New York: Macmillan, 1975.

Pietrusza, David. *Judge and Jury: The Life and Times of Judge Kenesaw Mountain Landis*. South Bend: Diamond Communications, 1998.

_____. *Lights On! The Wild Century-Long Saga of Night Baseball*. Lanham, MD: Scarecrow Press, 1997.

_____. *Minor Miracles: The Legend and Lure of Minor League Baseball*. South Bend: Diamond Communications, 1995.

Polner, Murry. *Branch Rickey: A Biography*. New York: Signet, 1982.

Porter, David L., ed. *Biographical Dictionary of American Sports: Baseball*. Westport, CT: Greenwood Press, 2000.

Pozar, Stephen M., and Jean B. Purvis. *Butler: A Pictorial History*. Virginia Beach: Donning, 1980.

Ramsey, George. "A Brief History of Baseball in Fairmont." Unpublished manuscript, Clarksburg (WV) Public Library.

Rogers, Paul. "Mike McCormick." *SABR Baseball Biography Project*. Web.

Ronald, Bruce W., and Virginia Ronald. *Dayton: The Gem City*. Tulsa: Continental Heritage Press, 1981.

Ruck, Rob L., Maggie Jones Patterson, and Michael P. Weber. *Rooney: A Sporting Life*. Lincoln: University of Nebraska Press, 2010.

Sargent, Jim. "Danny Litwhiler." *Baseball Almanac*. Web.

Scheeren, William. "The Best of the Bushes: The Middle Atlantic League." *Westmoreland History* 1 (Spring 1996): 20–27.

Schoor, Gene. *The Stan Musial Story*. New York: Messner, 1955.

Seeman, Corey. "The Pennsylvania State Association, 1934–1942." In *Baseball in Pittsburgh*, by Paul Adomites and Dennis Dealaria. Cleveland: SABR, 1995.

Sheridan, F. W. "Portsmouth, O., Dedication May 8." *The Sporting News*, April 25, 1935.

Society for American Baseball Research. *Minor League Stars*. Cooperstown: SABR, 1978.

Spalding Official Baseball Guide. New York: American Sports, 1926–1941.

Spink, J.G. Taylor. *Judge Landis: Twenty-*

Five Years of Baseball. New York: Thomas Y. Crowell, 1947.

Stone, George. *"Muscle": A Minor League Legend.* Haverford, PA: Infinity, 2003.

Sturtz, Rodney, and M.A. Mogus. "Play Ball! The Scottdale Young Cardinals." *Westmoreland History* 7 (December 2002): 38–40.

Sullivan, Dean A. *Late Innings: A Documentary History of Baseball, 1945–1972.* Lincoln: University of Nebraska Press, 2001.

Sullivan, Neil J. *The Minors.* New York: St. Martin's Press, 1990.

Swift, Tom. *Chief Bender's Burden: The Silent Struggle of a Baseball Star.* (Lincoln: University of Nebraska Press, 2008.

Vatavik, Mark K., and Richard E. Marshall. *Baseball in Erie.* Charleston, SC: Arcadia, 2005.

Vecsey, George. *Stan Musial: An American Life.* New York: Ballantine, 2012.

Whittle, Randy G. *Johnstown, Pennsylvania: A History, Part One, 1895–1936.* Charleston, SC: History Press, 2007.

Zeigler, Mark. "History." *Class D Blue Ridge League, 1915–1918, 1920–1930.* Web.

Newspapers

Altoona Mirror
Beaver Falls Daily Times
Beckley Post-Herald
(Beckley) *Raleigh Register*
Bradford Era
Charleroi Mail
Charleston Daily Mail
Charleston Daily News
Charleston Gazette
Clarksburg Telegram
Connellsville Daily Courier
Cumberland Evening News
Fairmont Times
(Fairmont) *West Virginian*
Frederick News-Post
Greenburg Record-Argus
Hagerstown Daily Mail
Hagerstown Morning Herald
Huntingdon Daily News
Indiana (PA) *Evening News*
Lima News
Massillon Evening Independent
Monessen Daily Independent
New Castle News
New York Times
Oil City Blizzard
Oil City Derrick
Parkersburg Daily Sentinel
Pittsburgh Post-Gazette
Pittsburgh Press
Portsmouth Times
The Sporting News
Titusville Herald
Uniontown Morning Herald
Uniontown News Standard
Wheeling Daily Intelligencer
Zanesville Signal
Zanesville Times Recorder

Index

Numbers in **_bold italics_** indicate pages with photographs.

Adams, Charles "Babe" 29–30
Adams, Walker 180
African-American players 70, 92, 196
Ainsworth Field (Erie) 136, 149, 178, 181, 185, **_189_**, 190
Akron, Ohio 1, 2, 8, 42, 95, 117
Akron Beacon-Journal 117, 207
Akron Times-Press 117
Akron Yankees 117, 121, 132, 138, 140, 145, 147–153, 157–159, 161, 162, 175, 177, 182, 183, 186
Albright, Dan 27
Alexander, Bob 105
Alston, Walter "Smokey" 127, 129, 137, 138, 143, 153, 159, **_163_**
Altoona, Pennsylvania 16, 20, 52, 55, 61, 62, 63, 69, 74, 75, 84, 101, 116, 117, 125, 188, 193
Altoona Engineers 8, 58–62, 65, 69, 74, 75, 84
Amberg, Richard 101
American Association 7, 57, 123, 135, 140, 149, 156, 169
American Bantam Car Co. 105
American Basketball Association 23, 123
Anderson, Bror 197
Anderson, Raymond H. "Ray" 175, 176, 195, 197
Andolina, Nick 186, 188, 195, 196, 199
Archer, George 162, 168, 170, 173
Archibald, Raymond 8–10, 19–21
Arkansas-Missouri League 154
Armstrong, Matt 99
Association for Colored Community Work 140
Athletic Field: Charleroi 40, 93; Erie 136, 149
attendance 2, 29, 37, 60, 79, 88, 89, 91, 95, 97, 106, 108, 112, 113, 115, 130, 139, 141, 143, 151–154, 157, 161, 178, 182, 184–188, 190, 192–195, 197, 199

Babe Ruth League 6
baby boom 3, 199, 200
Baker, Floyd 143
Baker, Orville 124
Baker, Willis "Bill" 158
Baldino, Leo 189
Ball, Bobby 105
Baltimore Orioles 179
Bamberger, George 179

Barber, Mayor Charles 156
Barber, Gerald 195
Barkey, Oscar 125, 126, 168, 170, 173
Barnes, Cal 165
Barnett, Harry 92
Barrett, Tracy "Dick" 25
Bartleson, Horatio 159, 165, 166
Baseball Hall of Fame 17, 28, 30, 46, 47, 50, 71, 72, 79, 98, 100, 129, 143–145, 153, 163, 182, 183
Baseball Magazine 166
Basketball Hall of Fame 123, 162
Batts, Matt 165
Bayliss, Don 164
Beacom, J. Pat 111
Bearinger, James I. 169
Beaver Falls, Pennsylvania 62, 67, 74, 91, 93
Beaver Falls Bees 93, 96, 97
Beaver Falls Browns 100,–104, 106, 136
Beck, Walter "Boom-Boom" 188
Beckley, West Virginia 35, 37
Beckley Black Knights 57, 61–68, 70–73, 79, 81, 87, 111–118
Beckley Miners 118–120, 122, 124, 125, 130
Belden, Paul B. 125
Bender, Charles Albert "Chief" 30–31, 36, 47, 182
Bengough, Benny 88
Beran, Joe 189, 190
Bernadino, Johnny 133
Bethany College 20
Betz, Bob 190
Bilbrey, Jim 160
Bilo, Gene 194
Binks, George "Bingo" 93, 133
Birk, J.P. 21
Black, Dave 29
Black Sox Scandal 7
Blackwell, Joe 123
Blatnik, John 160, 163–166
Bloomsburg State Teachers College 95, 133
Blue Ridge League 8, 13, 36, 40, 54, 60, 203, 212
Boggs, Joe 120
Bonham, Ernie "Tiny" 129
Border League 177
Borgmann, Benny 122–123, 137–138

213

Index

Bosciak, Ted 100
Boston Bees 93, 97, 127, 132, 135, 139
Boston Braves 41, 68, 80, 159
Boston Red Sox 17, 64, 126, 165
Boyle, Ralph "Buzz" 158
Bradfield, Gibson 26
Bradford, Dr. Warren G. 38, 174
Bramham, "Judge" William 74, 108, 145, 168–170, 174–175
Branch Rickey Park 119
Brandenberger, Ray 140, 147–148
Breadon, Sam 111, 154
Brehany, Joe 193
Bridges, Tommy 40
Brieter, John K. 180
Brookhauser, Betty 166
Brooklyn Dodgers 63, 68, 79, 90, 94, 99, 104, 111–113, 123, 140, 154, 168, 178, 179, 193
Brooklyn Royal Giants 153
Brophy, Joe 16
Brown, Norm 143
Brown, Russell 120
Browne, Jim 134
Bucci, Joseph E.
Buchoski, Mike 127
Buffalo Bisons 94–95
Bugher, James 58
Bugher, Lenn 102
Bumgardner, J. Lewis 119, 124
Burns, William J. 177
Burns, William J. "Bill," Jr. 177, 182, 184, 195, 198
Buskey, Joe 25
Butler, Pennsylvania 89, 90, 192
Butler Indians 90
Butler Tigers 190, 194, 196, 198–200
Butler Yankees 94–100, 102–107, 150, 168, 172, 175–186
Buzas, Al 157
Byard, Lafe "Red" 24, 30, 34, 36
Byrnes, John 17, 25, 29, 31, 33, 34

Cabanaw, Ray 189
Cain, T.B. 32
Cambria, Joe 54–56, 58, 60–62, 65, 66, 68, 69, 77, 78, 116, 130, 190
Canadian-American League 146
Canadian Baseball Hall of Fame 129
Cannavino, Mike 154, 184, 191, 196
Canonsburg, Pennsylvania 84–85, 101, 118
Canton, Ohio 2, 8, 69, 117, 125
Canton Amusement Company 125
Canton Bulldogs 125, 126
Canton Terriers 126, 132–134, 137, 138, 142, 143, 151, 152, 157–159, 164–167, 169, 170, 172, 173, 175, 177, 182
Cape Breton League 146
Carnegie Tech 8
Carolina League 1, 170
Carpenter, Bob 181
Carr, Joe 74, 85, 87, 100, 108, 122, 125, 126, 141, 145

Catholic Youth Organization 121, 140
Central League 8, 38, 52, 57, 62, 69, 77–79, 117, 118, 125, 140, 142, 156, 195
Chandler, Albert B. "Happy" 188
Charleroi Babes 27, 28, 30–32, 35–37
Charleroi Governers ("Guvs") 37, 39–41, 44, 45, 51–53, 55–62, 68, 74, 75
Charleroi Mail 37, 44, 60, 75, 92, 94
Charleroi Tigers 84, 87, 90, 92–94, 101, 106, 118
Charleston, West Virginia 33, 52–55
Charleston Daily-Mail 148, 153, 155, 164, 167, 174
Charleston Senators 57, 58, 61, 64–66, 68, 70–73, 79, 81, 87, 109, 111, 113, 117, 124, 125, 130, 137, 139–143, 148–153, 155, 157, 160–165, 167, 172–175, 177, 180
Charleston War Industrial League 170
Cherunko, Paul 164
Chesapeake and Ohio Canal Towing Co. 12
Chicago Cubs 36, 63, 96, 156, 166
Chicago White Sox 48, 132, 156, 181, 193
Cincinnati Reds 57, 64, 71, 80, 87, 90, 96, 113, 114, 118, 120, 126, 131, 140, 149, 154, 159, 178
Ciraldo, Al 132
Civilian Conservation Corps 75, 83, 98
Clark, Harless L. 37, 75, 77
Clarksburg, West Virginia 9, 11, 12, 118
Clarksburg Generals 10–14, 17, 19, 21, 22, 24, 25, 27, 30–33, 35–37, 41, 45, 47–50, 53, 55, 57, 58, 61, 66–68, 70, 72, 75–77, 109
Clastet, Gowel "Lefty" 34–35
Clawson, Alex 93
Clay, Darin 138
Cleveland Indians 76, 87, 89, 94, 101, 130, 133, 144, 152, 192
coal mine leagues 16, 33, 37, 42, 84, 103, 106, 188
Collins, Jimmy "Ripper" 16, 23, 129
Collins, Joe 100, 102, 157
Community Baseball, Inc. 39, 45
Comstock, Warren "Cowboy" 28
Conley, Ed 29, 34
Connatser, Clint 160
Connell, Bernie **65**
Conners, J.J. "Joe" 197, 198
Conti, Joe 29
Cook, Frank B. 9, 12, 29
Cooper, George E. "Chick" 99, 106, 168, 172, 174, 176, 184, 187–188, 193, 195
Cortazzo, Jesse "Shine" 17, 25, 29, 30, 36, 111, 113, 114, 122, 132, 133
Cosgrove, John C. 29
Cotelle, Cosmo 159, 165
Cotton States League 146
Cousins, Art 25, 35
Cox, Walt 185
Craft, Harry 90
Cramer, Harry E. 38
Crawford, C.D. 119, 124
Cronin, Joe 14, 16–17, 22, 47, 113
Crouch, Bob "Boots" 164
Cumberland, Maryland 8–10
Cumberland Colts 8–14, 16–20, 22, 25–27, 29–

Index

34, 36, 37, 39, 41, 44, 47, 51, 52, 54–58, 60, 61, 64–70, 73, 75–78, 84, 102
Cumberland Evening Times 19, 51, 52, 74, 75
Cummings, Jack 18, 26
Cunningham, John E. "Jack" 175
Cycler Park 85, 93, 94, 97
Cyran, Tony 24, 33, 63, 66

Daily, Elmer Michael efforts to depose 27, 34, 124, 125, 196; and farm system 68, 87, 89, 115, 116, 126, 132, 152, 156; and Hockenbury 68, 69, 75, 76, 109, 117, 122, 125, 130, 135, 172; Holmes 122, 124–126, 128, 134, 139, 156, 164, 174; and Judge Bramham 145, 169, 170; league expansion 54–56, 77, 78, 89–91, 111, 116, 125, 156; league meetings 20, 27, 39, 55, 61, 66, 67, 77, 78, 117, 123, 124, 125, 168, 170, 172, 173, 175, 176; locating owners and franchises 26, 39, 59, 91, 93–95, 97, 99, 101, 104, 125, 131, 156, 162, 172, 176, 192, 193; opposition to higher classification 57, 134, 136; and Penn State Association 2, 83–87, 91, 98, 104, 110, 162, 168, 173, 175; personal life 39, 65, 74, 91, 95, **98**, 169, 175; personal opinions 51, 52, 65, 74, 78, 88, 110, 141, 145, 160, 192; praise of 37, 65, 81, 83, 94, 188; rulings 26, 27, 45, 49, 79, 101, 102, 114, 122, 124, 128, 134, 139, 164; World War II 105, 107, 168, 170
Danaher, David 138
Daniels, Doff 55, 118, 119
Davis, Jim 85
Davis, Maurice J.K. 85
Davis, Woody 127
Davis Field (Vandergrift) 180, 186, 188, 194
Daviu, Augie "Gus" 47, **65**, 66
Dawson, Daniel Boone 173, 180
Dayton, Ohio 2, 8, 69, 77–79, 117
Dayton Ducks 79–82, 109, 111–114, 117, 119–124, 126, 128–130, 132, 134, 139–141, 154, 157, 159–163, 165–167, 169, 170, 172, 174, 175, 177, 180
Dayton Triangles 141
Dayton Wings 141, 142, 151–154
Dean, Dizzy 191
Dedeaux, Rod 122, 123
DeKoning, Bill 102
Delahanty, Frank **35**
DeManicor, Frank 127
Densmore, Jimmy 64, **65**
Detroit Tigers 38–41, 51, 57, 68, 69, 79, 87, 111, 126–129, 148–151, 186, 188, 194
Devine, Jimmy 23, 25, 31
Devine, Joe 16
DeWitt, William O. 132, 135, 141, 142, 161, 174, 176, 177
DiBlasi, Sam 165
DiCeasare, Joe 165
Dillinger, Bob 153
Dinges, Vance 165
Doljack, Frank "Dolle" 40, 51
Donald, Atley 112, 115
Donelly, Claire 170

Dorish, Harry, "Fritz" 158
Dorman, Fred 153
Dorringer, Fred L., "Joe" 9, 19–21, 27, 37, 54–56, 58, 63, 67, 68, 70
Doyle, Denny 158
Drews, Karl 99–100
Drugmond, Joe 26, 28, 36, 40, 41
Dubiel, Walt "Monk" 158, 159
Ducks Park (Dayton) 112, 122
Dudick, John 88, 93
Duke, Marvin 61, 64, **65**
Dunlevy, Jack 89, 95, 97, 103, 104, 106, 168, 175, 181, 184, 186
Dunn, James H. 26
Durocher, Leo 127
Dykes, Chuck 165

East Liberty Academy 8
East Texas League 146
Eastern League 30
Eastern Shore League 28, 40
Eisenstat, Harry 122, 123
Elks Park (Uniontown) 7, 26
Embree, Charles "Red"
Engle, Charlie 188
Engle, Joe 17
equipment shortages 178
Erie, Pennsylvania 8, 9
Erie Citizens Baseball Club 198
Erie Daily Times 166
Erie Dispatch-Herald 156, 166
Erie Sailors 106, 136, 139, 140, 148, 150, 166, 176–178, 189
Evans, Arnold 100
Evans, Billy 76, 126

Fairmont, West Virginia 9, 11, 12–14, 20, 118, 180
Fairmont Black Diamonds 22, 24, 25–27, 30–37, 41, 45, 48, 49, 54–58, 61, 63, 66–68, 7-, 74, 80, 108, 110
Fairmont Fairies 14, 16–19, 22
Falk, Tom 194
Falor, Edith 117, 147, 148
farm system 2, 21, 37, 38, 56, 63, 69, 75, 76, 78, 79, 88–90, 92, 107, 110, 111, 115, 121, 123, 126, 131, 132, 135, 148, 150, 162, 165, 170, 173, 178, 181, 186, 193
Farrell, Kirby 141, 143, 159, 165, 166
Fayetteville Angels 154
Federal Emergency Relief Agency (FERA) 75, 116
Feller, Bob 133, 154
Ferry, Cy 12
Fest, Justin 99
Feuker, Egon 184
Field of Dreams 5
fines 27, 124–126, 134, 139
Finley, Bob 138, 140
Firestone Stadium (Akron) 117, 118, 148
Flaharty, Irwin "Skeet" 30, 36
Flaherty, J. Preston 180, 184

Fleming, Brooks 9, 36, 63
Flood, Ray 25
Floyd, Ray 30
Flynn, I.F. 85
Ford, Edward Charles "Whitey" 145, 182–184, *183*
Ford, Dr. James K. 20, 21, 26, 39
Ford City 9, 91
Fort Wayne 8, 123, 147, 169
Foytack, Paul 184, 194
Fralik, Warren "Moose" 138
franchises
Franklin, Jack 164
French, Andy 95, 96, 165
Frest, Lenny 100
Friel, Dick 198
Friend, Danny *35*
Fuchs, Bill 93
Fullerton, Hugh, Jr. 169, 179, 188
Fulton Park (Wheeling: *aka*, Stogie Park) 13, 68, 76, 118

Gabri, John 177, 184
Gallupe, Peter 30, 33, 40
Gant Municipal Stadium (Zanesville) *155*, 157
Gardner, Bob 190
Gardner, Glenn 198
Garman, Ed 117
Garst, H.E. 168
Gasdaska, George 185
Gault, Ben 197
Gee, Howard 96, 99
Genovese, Frank "Chick" 138, 143
Gentile, Sam 165
Gibson, James E. 180
Gibson, Josh 71
Gilchrist, C.E. 10
Giles, Judge Francis 192
Giles, Warren 131
Gillenwater, Claude 31
Gionfriddo, Al 104, 105
Gleich, Frank 29
Gold, James 86, 94, 95
Goldstein, Isadore "Izzy" 35
Goliat, Mike 182
Gomez, Lefty 182
Good, Wilbur 8, 9, 48
Gorman, Herb 175
Grabowski, Alex 182
Grace, Willie 197
Graham, Jack 133, 134
Great Depression 81–84, 88, 106, 107, 108, 109, 117, 1290, 133, 199, ***200***
Greble, Steve 103
Greensburg, Pennsylvania 8, 27, 52, 84, 87
Greensburg Green Sox 94, 96–99, 101, 106, 107, 152
Greensburg Red Wings 90, 92, 94
Greensburg Trojans 85–89
Greenwalt, Ward 21
Griffith, Bob 132

Griffith, Clark 54, 55, 63, 78
Grilk, Jim 123
Grimes, Oscar 127, 128
Grimm, Bert 80, 86, 113, 114, 122, 132
Gugler, Don 127
Guy, Richard "Dick" 7–10, 18–21, 26, 27, 32, 118
Gwathmey, Bill "Kid" 35

Hagerstown Hubs 40, 54–58, 60, 61, 63, 67
Hale, Helen 196
Hall, Bob 185
Hall, Buddy 61, 64, *65*, 70
Hamilton, Jimmy 156
Hammock, Elbert 25
Handley, Lee 196
Hansen, Ed 122
Harig, Charles 90, 190
Harris, Eli 119
Harris, John H. 85, 86, 91
Harris, John P. 85
Hart, Bill 138
Hartman, Joe 23
Hartman, Larry 103
Hatfield, Fred 165
Hawke, Alex 104
Hayes, Dan 98
Haywood, Gene 132
Heath, Jeff 127–129
Hegan, Jim 145
Heintzelman, Ken 90, 92
Heller, George 185
Helmick, William "Chick" 25, 31, 33, 35, 36, 64, *65*, 66, 80, 122
Henrich, Ed 165
Henrich, Tommy 88, 89, 112, 121, 131
Henry, Bill 185
Hickey, Nat 16, 23, 32, 80, 113, 122, 132
Highland, Cecil 77
Highland, Virgil 32, 37, 77
Hinchman, Julius S. "Judy" 125, 126
Hintz, Harry 190
Hockenbury, Russell 9, 20, 21, 39, 42, 44, 58, 61, 62, 67–69, 75–77, 88, 97, 109, 110, 117, 122, 125, 130, 135, 141, 156, 162, 163, 172
Hockett, Oris 140
Hodkey, Al "Eli" 143
Holand, Orrel "Apples" 24
Holbrook, George 164
Holden, Bob 178
Holloway, Charles 26, 38, 39, 51, 52, 56, 61, 68, 76
Holmes, Howard "Ducky" 77- 80, 112–114, 120, 122–126, ***128***, 132, 134–141, 145, 154–157, 160–162, 164, 165, 167, 168, 170, 174, 175
Homestead Grays 45, 70, 92, 184, 197
Hood, Charley 185
Hooper, Clay 88
Hootey, Joe 155
Hope-Harvey's 19
Hopkins, John 25
Hopkins, Tom 68, 110, 115

Index

Hopwood Speedway Park 181, 191
House of David 45, 56, 71, 92
Howard, Bob 136
Howe, Charles 101
Hoyle, Roland "Tex" 105
Hubbell, Carl 170
Huddleston, Bob 194
Hudson, Dick 143, 155, 174, 175
Huffman, Carl 88, 89, 127
Hughson, Cecil "Tex" 138
Humbert, Lloyd 181
Huntington, West Virginia 52, 53, 180
Huntington Boosters 53–55
Huntington Red Birds 57, 59, 66–69, 72, 79, 80, 82, 87, 109, 111, 114, 116, 117, 121–124, 129, 131, 136
Hutton, Henry H. 111
Hyde Park (Niagara Falls) 178
Hyder, John 98

Ideal Park (Johnstown) 6, 9, 11, 12, 53, 58, 71
Idora Park (Youngstown) 142, 178
Ifft, Ralph 102
International League 7, 13, 30, 45, 94, 108, 113, 129, 169
Iott, Clarence "Hooks" 153
Ireland, Bob 148, 151, 154, 170, 173
Isabel, Harry C. 181, 182, 191, 192

James, Bill 112
Jamin, Charles 100
Jeannette, Pennsylvania 21
Jeannette Jays 21–22, 30, 32, 36, 41, 45, 47, 49, 51–55, 57–60, 62, 65, 74, 84–95, 106–109
Jeannette Reds 87, 88–95, 105, 107, 109
Jenkins, Ernest "Lefty" 96, 98
Jewish Community Center 121, 140
The Johnnies, Inc. 99
Johnson, Billy 96
Johnson, Judy **70**
Johnston, Rudy 196
Johnstown, Pennsylvania 8, 9, 11, **24**
Johnstown Johnnies 12–14, 16–19, 21–25, 29–34, 36, 41, 45, 47, 48, 50–55, 58, 61, 63, 64, 66–71, 75, 78–82, 99–107, 109, 114, 117, 122–125, 129, 132, 133, 135, 139, 141–143, 168, 172–178, 181, 184–190, 192–195, 200
Johnstown Tribune 99
Jones, Bob 160
Jones, Earl "Lefty" 100, 160
Judnick, Walt 120

Kain, Tom "Shakey" 103
Kaiser, Howard, "Red" 198
Kalin, Frank "Fats" 99
Kanawha Park (Charleston) 53, 65, 153, 154, 172
Karpel, Herb "Lefty" 98
Katz, Bob 133, 134, 165
Kelly, Clair N. 180
Kelly, Joe 138
Kennedy, Ray 186
Kerksieck, Wayman 133, 134

Kestler, Ed 189
Kiel, Herman 185
Kimble, Dick 160
King, Lee 17, 25
King, Mayor S. Quay 9, 10, 31, 38
Kirkman, Hugh 143
Kitchell, Paul 182
Kittanning-Ford City 9, 91
Klieman, Ed 160
Knight, Jack 164
Knothole Gangs 120, 121, 127, 140
Koewing, Wilson 100
Koon, Thomas 39
Korean War 195, 196
Kounts, Joseph L. 116
Koval, Bill 176, 177, 186, 192, 195–197
Kramer, Charles A. "Brute" 95, 177, 180–182, 187, 188, 194, 195, 201, 202, 208, 211
Kraus, Jack 127
Kraus, Lou 93
Krichell, Paul 57, 117
Kucab, John 179, 190
Kurowski, George "Whitey" 137
Kuzava, Bob 164, 165

LaFlamme, Howard "Red" 113
Lakeside Park (Canton) 125, 126, 134, 138, 168, 173
LaMaster, Wayne 73, 113
Landis, Judge Kenesaw Mountain 7, 78, 89, 90, 101, 102, 106, 121, 131, 149–151, 170
Langenbacker, Clarence 36, 37
LaPalme, Paul 166
Layh, Harry W. 95
Lazerson, Hyman 177, 184
Lazor, John 143
League Park (Akron) 117–120, 131, 130, 140, 147, 157, 158, 161
Leffingwell, Tom 101
Lembo, Steve 179
Lemon, Bob 143, **144**, 145
Leonard, Tom "Red" 114
Leslie, Del 165
Lettenberger, Earl 185
Lewis, Chester 148
Liberty Network 191
Liebhartz, Glenn
lights *see* night games
Lima, Ohio 69, 77, 78, 130, 147, 162
Little League 6, 200
Litwhiler, Danny 93, 113
Lockport, New York 195, 196
Lockport Locks 198, 199
Lombardi, Vic 104
Long Park (Huntington) 131
Lopat, Eddie 96–97
Lucas, Fred "Fritz" 27, 40, 41, 48
Lucier, Lou 158, 159
Luntz, Darwin 125
Lutz, Joe 157, 160
Lynch, Jack 123

Lynch, J.T. 124
Lynn, Jerry 88
Lytle, Blake "Spook" 10, 22

Mack, Connie 87
Mack, Harry A. 132
Mack, Joe 90
Mackey, Leo 64, **65**, 69, 73, 101, 134, 135
Mackie, Vern 113
Mallet, Ted 159
Marion, Marty 128
Marion County (WV) Baseball Association 9, 32
Mark Park (Zanesville) 76, 114, 127
Martin, Eugene "Gene" 92, 110, 116, 120, 124, 131, 135
Martin, Fred 138
Martynik, Mike 122, 123
Masi, Phil 133
Maxwell, Clarence "Moose" 31
Mayo, Eddie 80
Mayo, Jackie 182
Mazer, Al 143
McCabe, Ralph 104
McCallister, Jack 125
McCann, Gene 98
McCloy, Merritt "Jake" 61, 64, **65**, 66
McConnell, Mickey 141
McCormick, Frank 111–113
McCormick, Mike 89, 90
McCosky, Barney 127, 128
McCullough, Clyde 129
McCullough, Dr. J.H. 124
McCullough, Pat 198
McDermott, Frank "Red" 114
McGrath, Howard (Attorney General) 191
McGuire James F. "Jimmy" 8–10, 19–22, 26–30, 32, 34, 36, 37, 39
McIlvaine, John "Scissors" 27, 28, 31, 32, 93
McIntyre, Milt 121
McKeesport, Pennsylvania 27, 84, 85–87
McKeesport Braves 90, 91, 93–95, 97–99, 101, 103, 106
McKeesport Tubers 87, 90
McLendon, Gordon 191
McNally, George **35**
McNichol, D.E. "Dan" 32
McPhail, Larry 57, 111, 112, 141, 150
McWilliams, Bill 160
Medwick, Joe "Ducky" **46**–48, 127
Meehan, Harry J. 29
Meek, Hal 194
Meinert, Maurice 26–27
Mele, Al, "Dutch" 88
Melton, Reuben Franklin "Rube" 92
Memphis Chicks 57, 111
Merola, Frank 185
Merrills, William O. 32
Michigan State League 93, 169
Mid-City Baseball Association (Cumberland) 32, 39

Mid-City Park (Cumberland) 12, 19
Mifflinburg, Pa. 195
Miller, Eddie 112
Miller, Leo Thomas 140, 149, 150
Millicent, Irving "Babe" 9, 10, 19, 26, 39
Milliken, W.E. 102
Mills, Doyle 100
Milner, Holt "Cat" 63, 72, 73, 81, 111, 114
Milosevich, Mike 95
Milton, Huston 128
Milwaukee Brewers 179
Mize, John 129
Mizerak, Steve 178
Mohr, Lee 158
Monessen, Pennsylvania 28, 58, 84, 86, 87, 177
Monessen Cardinals 94–97, 106
Monessen Independent 95
Monessen Indians 87–91, 93, 121
Mongiello, Bill 159, 165, 198
Monongahela Valley Association 84
Montague, Ed 14, 16, 22
Moore, Lloyd "Dinty" 96
Moorehead, Tom V., (Mayor) 155
Moreliti, Frank 193
Morgan, Bill "Cy" 29
Morgan, Ed 88, 190
Morrison, Joe "Jo-Jo" 41
Moscowitz, Emil **85**
Mountain State League 93, 96, 131, 161, 180
movies 5, 85, 91, 199
Munch, Julius "Jocko" 140, 156, 159, 170, 175, 176, 190, 193, 196
Municipal Stadium (Zanesville) 130, 155, 157
Murdeski, Howard 103, 104
Murray, Joe 105
Murray, Tom 176, 189
Musial, Stan "The Man" 96
Mutual Radio Network 151
Myers, Lynn 88

Nanty Glo, Pennsylvania 16, 59
Nash, Fred 190
National Agreement 3
National Association of Professional Baseball Leagues 7, 66, 74, 108
National Basketball League 23, 123
National Recovery Administration (NRA) 83
The Natural 5
Neale, Earl "Greasy" 31, 45, 48–50
Neun, Johnny 120
Neville, Eddie 105
New Castle, Pennsylvania 8, 62, 93, 147, 180, 184
New Castle Chiefs 184, 185, 190–194, 196, 198–200
New York Mets 179
New York–Pennsylvania League 17, 55, 91, 92
New York Yankees 57, 61, 69, 75, 76, 84, 87, 89, 110, 120, 121, 140, 145, 161, 175, 177, 182
Niagara Falls Citizens 192, 193, 195, 196, 198
Niagara Falls Frontiers 177–179, 181, 184, 186, 192

Index

Niarhos, Gus 158
Nicolls, Keith 198
Nieman, Elmer "Butch" 158, 159
night games 51–53, 55, 57, 65, 70, 88, 94, 95, 97, 98, 101, 118, 136, 149, 177, 178, 180
Noonan, Mickey 50, 80, 132
North Carolina State League 135, 170
Norwood Park (Clarksburg) 12, 13

O'Brien, Bill 94
O'Brisky, Myron 170
Oceak, Frank "Fez" 102, 105, 122
Ochs, Henry 132
Ohio State League 53, 162, 170, 171, 173, 174, 180
Oil City, Pennsylvania 93, 101
Oil City Athletic Association 93, 101, 175, 199
Oil City Blizzard 101
Oil City Derrick 192
Oil City Oilers 101–106, 168, 172, 175–178, 181
Oil City Refiners 181, 185, 186, 190, 192–195, 197–200
O'Keefe Dennis **35**
Olivares, Jose 16, 22
Orange, Nick 102
Osborne, Ed 114
Oser, Hugh 185
Osley, William L. 142
Ostermuller, Fritz 31
Ostrowski, Joe 158, 159
Outlaw, Jimmy 88, 112
Owens, Jesse 153

Pacific Coast League 1, 7, 53, 169
Page, Joe 102, 103
Paiement, Don 61, **65**, 128
Palagyi, Mike 93
Palasy, Mike 127
Palumbo, Bill 189
Parker, Dave "Red" 139
Parker, Loren "Riley" 122
Parkersburg (West Virginia) Parkers 8, 60, 61, 74
Parnell, Mel 165, 166
Partenheimer, Stan 165
Passeau, Claude 112
Patterson, Floyd "Pat" 123, 126, 134, 143, 165, 182, 184, 185
Patterson Legionaires 123
Paul, Lewis 97
Peatros, Maurice 197
Peebles, Ray 156, 166, 170
Pellagrini, Eddie 143
Penn State Association *see* Daily, Elmer
Pennsylvania-Ontario-New York (PONY) League 170, 171, 176–178, 195
Pennsylvania-West Virginia League 20
Perry, Norman A., Jr. 140
Perry, Norman A., Sr. 140
Perry, Paul 132
Peterson, Robert 123
Petko, Joe 181

Petonic, Michael J. 38
Philadelphia Athletics 80, 87, 129, 181, 197, 199
Philadelphia Phillies 25, 26, 28, 79, 92, 93, 99, 100, 133, 181, 182
Phillips, Bill "Lefty" 15
Phillips, George 26, 38
Phillips, Joe "Hooker" 22, 26, 44, 45, 61, 62
Phillips, Lew 40
Phipps, Carl J. 131
Pietrusza, David 1, 136
Pioneer League 116
Pisula, Alex 77, 78, 116, 117, 125–127, 129, 130, 131
Pitts, Alabama 92
Pittsburgh Collegians 8, 10, 18, 32
Pittsburgh Crawfords 92, 153
Pittsburgh Gazette Times 8
Pittsburgh Industrial League 20
Pittsburgh Pirates 14, 16, 17, 19, 29, 49, 59, 81, 87, 90–93, 97, 104, 116, 126, 127, 129, 130, 133, 175, 178, 181, 187, 188, 191, 192, 196
P.J. Flaherty Field (New Castle) 180, 184
Point Stadium (Johnstown) 9, 23, **24**, 29, 31, 50, 52, 102, 178, 187
Poland, Hugh 122, 123
Politano, Sam 131
POM (PA, OH, MD) League 8
Portsmouth, Ohio 75, 92, 94
Portsmouth Pirates 116, 117, 119, 120, 125–127, 129, 130, 131
Portsmouth Red Wings 131, 133–135, 137, 139, 140, 147, 148, 151, 153–154, 156, 177, 180
Posey, Cumberland 92
Posnack, Max **65**
Potter, Dykes 112
Powell, Jake 79, 81
Powell, Watt 52–55, 65–67, 81, 131, 139, 148, 149, 167–170, 172, 173, 180
Prichard, Bill 33, 35, 48, 50, 63, 64, 80
Proctor, Dick "Red" 48–50, 133
Pullman Park (Butler) 89, 94, 177
Purcey, Walt 90

Queen, Mel 95, 152, 153
Quinn, Bob 132
Quinn, John 132

Rackley, Marv 164
radio stations 11, 132, 192
Ragan, Pat 25
Ragon, Bill **35**
Raleigh Coal Company 124
Raleigh Manufacturing Institute (RMI) Park 55, 113, 123, 124
Ramage-Hasson Field (New Castle, PA) 101, 178
Ramazotti, Bob 102
Rambo, Warren "Pete" 25, 29, 31
Ramsey, Don 185
Rase, Irving "Stub" 29, 41
rationing 105, 106, 167, 168

Reeder, Earl 132
Reeves, Nelson 194
Reichert, Arnold 164
Reilly, Bob 126
Reilly, Emmett "Turk" 76, 125, 126, 127, 129
Reis, Tommy 89, 127
Reisser, Charles 124
reserve clause 150
Reynolds, Allie 145
Reynolds, James L. 31
Rice, Bob 40, 104
Rice, Grantland 72
Richardson, Murray 189, 190
Richardson, Sam 35
Rickey, Branch 38, 67, 69, 95, 100, 116, 117, 119, 122, 131, 148, 149, 154, 168
Rickey, Branch, Jr. 141, 154
Rinder, M.A. 162
Ripple, Jimmy 41
Robertson, Russ 31
Robinson, Aaron 145
Robinson, Red 35
Rodgers, Ira "Rat" 17
Rollings, Russell "Red" 137
Rooney, Art 18
Rooney, Dan 18–20
Roosevelt, Franklin D. 73, 139, 147, 151, 160, 167
Rosar, Warren "Buddy" 112, 115
Rosenberg, Ben 97
Rosenblum, Dr. Charles H. 84
Rosenthal, Si 114
Rossi, Mike 104
Rowland, E.G. 97, 99
Rubeling, Al 88, 90
Rush, Larry 194
Rushmock, Steve 179
Russell, Jim 98
Russian, John 96
Ryan, Ray 85, 89, 91, 93, 180
Ryba, Mike 41, 47

Sabbatarian law (*aka* Blue Laws) 2, 57, 58, 70, 87, 110
Sabine, George 170
Sackville, Ernest H. 84
Saint Bonaventure College 18
St. Louis Browns 97, 99, 103, 132, 133, 135, 141, 153, 161, 174, 176
St. Louis Cardinals 16, 38, 41, 47, 57, 67, 69, 78, 85, 87, 94, 97, 99, 100, 111, 116, 123, 128, 148, 149, 151, 168
salaries 21, 27, 44, 88, 94, 96, 110, 135, 137, 184, 193, 196
Sample, Bill 102
Sams, Tony 152
Sanders, Malone "Bones" 158
Sandlot 5
Sanford, Fred 152
Sauer, Ed 158, 160
Sauer, Hank 96–98, 197, 145
Savage, Don 98

Scala, Jerry 179
Scalzi, Frank "Skeeter" 127, 133
Scarazzo, Alphonse "Al" 193, 196, 199
Schacht, Al 157
Schapp, Charley 135
Scheffing, Bob 100
Schlemmer, Jim 117, 161
Schmidt, Charley 35
Schroy, Lee D., (Mayor) 148
Schulte, Len 143, 160
Scottdale, Pennsylvania 1, 9, 10
Scottdale Athletic Association 31, 32
Scottdale Cardinals 38–42, 45–47, 52–58, 61, 64, 66, 67, 109
Scottdale Scotties 14–17, 19–22, 25, 31, 36–38
Secrist, Paul 17
Shaughnessy, Frank 108, 169, 131
Shaughnessy playoff system 100, 108, 109, 129, 134, 186, 194
Shea, Pat 65, 66
Sheehan, Frank E. 116
Sheehan, Jack 80, 110
Sheely, Hollis "Bud"
Sherrill, Lee 134
Shilling, Jim 127
Shoals, Leo "Muscle" 94, 96, 97
Shriver, Harry "Pop" 17
Shriver, Ken 156
Shupe, Vince 102
Sickman, Dr. Albert S. "A.S." 32, 44
Siebert, Dick 81, 112
Silvanic, Frank 138
Simpson, William S. "Bill"
Sisler, Dick 100
Sisler, George 100
Slapnicka, Cy 130
Smith, George "Pappy" 184
Smith, Jack 15, 26
Smokeless Coal Athletic Association 119
Smolko, Joe 104
Snyder, John W. 34
Sobb, Eddie 40
Sodd, Bill 127
Solomone, Bill 65
Solters, Julian "Moose" 36, 41
Sommers, Bill 165
Souchock, Steve "Bud" 152
South Side Park (*aka* Traction Park; Fairmont) 12, 49, 60
Southern, Dennis 25
Southern Association 7, 72, 111, 121, 133
Spalding ball 40, 163
Sporting News 17, 150, 188, 190
Spresser, Bob 189
Springfield, Ohio 2, 8, 69, 77, 78, 109, 125
Springfield Cardinals 154, 159, 162, 166, 168, 170,-175
Springfield Indians 130, 131, 133, 134, 137, 138, 142–145, 147, 148, 151
Springfield Pirates 79, 81, 87, 113, 114, 116, 117
Stallcup, Virgil 165

Index

Stanceu, Charley 89
Stanky, Eddie "The Brat" 129
Star Spangled Banner 166
Starr, Dick 104, 105
Stathers, William E. 32
Steinecke, Bill 114
Steiner, Ben 159
Sterling, Orin 195
Stevens, Bill 165
Stewart, Joseph 197
Stock, Milt 90
Stogie Park (Wheeling) *see* Fulton Park
Stone, Dean 198
Stoops, R.J. 102
Storck, Carl 141
Strange, Howard 99
Stuart, John 53, 55, 111, 131
Suche, Charley 127
Suder, Pete 90, 129
Summit Beach Park 119, 140
Sunkel, Tom 88
Sweeney, Harry 99
Swift, Bob 129
Synott, Bob **65**

Tamalis, Vito 61, 64, **65**
team nicknames 24
Tedesco, Joe "Ricky" 185
television 3, 133, 187, 191, 192, 195, 199, 200
Testa, Nick 189
Texas League 7, 146
Thomas, Bill 28, 34, 35
Thomas, Clair 180
Thomas, Don 141
Thomas, Sam 32, 48, 50, 64, 80, 81, 113, 122, 132, 133
Thompson, Gus "Mike" 25, 29
Thompson, Harvey "Tommy" 50, 64, 80
Tighe, Ed 152
Tin Plate Park (Momessen) 86, 94, 97
Tipton, Joe 163
Toledo Crawfords 153
Toles, Ted 196, 197
Traction Park (Fairmont) *see* South Side Park
Trautman, George 135, 156, 197
Tredwell, George 103
Trimble, John W. 195
Tri-State League 23, 53, 55, 61, 72
Tri-Stste Series 40
Tunney, Gene 164

Uber, John 179
umpires 26, 27, 29, **35**, 44, 45, 101, 102, 109, 128, 135, 139, 158, 167, 174
uniforms 6, 7, 13, 33, 40, 92, 112, 152, 178
Uniontown, Pennsylvania 7-9, 19-21, 25-28, 32, 83, 91, 109, 180
Uniontown Coal Barons 180-182, 185, 188, 190-193
Uniontown Cokers 26-28, 32
Uniontown Elks Baseball Club 25, 32

Uniontown Morning Herald 192
United Mine Workers of America 37, 192

Vandergrift (Pennsylvania) Pioneers 180-182, 184, 185, 187, 190, 193-195
Vanek, Ollie 96
Vassey, Dick 30, 66
Verbeck, George 158
Verdi, Frank 158
Voiselle, Bill 143, 159
Voyles, Phil 41

Wagner, Frank 159
Wagner, Franklin 190
Waite, Ralph 143
Walingham, Bill 111
Walker, Gerald "Gee" 40
Wallace, Bill 66
Wallace, Bobby 111, 112
Waller, Dr. Homer B. 39
Walsh, Bob **65**
Walsh, Francis "Red" 158
War Fund games 162, 164
WARD 192
Warren, Dallas 105
Warren, Ohio 101, 103, 104, 106, 162
Wasdell, Jimmy 121
Washington, Pennsylvania 8, 20, 50, 52, 58, 85
Washington and Jefferson College 50, 84, 91, 99
Washington Generals 87-88, 90, 91, 97, 99, 100, 101
Washington Red Birds 103, 104-105
Washington Senators 17, 54, 63, 78, 79, 88, 99, 101, 184, 190, 196-198
Waters, Ray 166
Watson, James 9
WBUT 192
WCRO 192
Webb, Sam "Red" 179
Weber, Karl "Doc" 31
Weigel, Ralph "Wigs" 160, 163
Wernke, Sam 31
West Side Park (Dayton) *see* Ducks Park
West Virginia Wesleyan College 20, 55
Western Association 66, 146
Wetzel, Buzz 76, 113, 114, 130-132, 148, 154, 165, 173
Wetzel, Stan 165
Weyranch, Bob 103
Wheeling, West Virginia 8, 9, 11, 13, 17-19, 22, 53, 74, 76, 109-111, 125, 136, 154, 188
Wheeling Independent 39
Wheeling Intelligencer 57, 110, 115
Wheeling Stogies 10, 11, 17-19, 26, 30-35, 38-43, 45, 51-55, 57, 58, 61, 62, 67-69, 74-81, 84, 87, 92, 109-111
White, Ernie 138
White, Herb 138
White, Jerry 153
White, J.P. 124

Index

Whittle, Charles 138
Widmar, Al 165
Wiezorek, Chet 138
Wilhelm, Charles "Spider" 190
Wilkes-Barre, Pennsylvania 123
Williams, Woody 128
Williamson, West Virginia 96, 180
Wilson, George 165
Windon, Ross E. 154
WKRZ 192
WKST 192
Wolfe, Roger 112, 113
Wolgamot, Earl 89, 114, 121
Woodling, Gene 160
Woods, George "Pinky" 159
Woodward, Milt 159, 167
Woodward, Steve 32, 61, 93
working agreements 32, 71, 83, 94, 111, 149, 150, 193
Workman, Chuck 133
World War II 195, 107, 168–170
Worstall, Frank 173
Worth ball 40, 44, 51, 110, 113, 127, 129, 137, 141, 163
Wynn, Charles 162

Yankovich, Frank 163
Yarnell, Waldo "Rusty" 25

Yezbak, Charles "Pete" 192
YMCA 15, 121, 140
York, Rudy 197
Young, William H. 79, 112
Young Field (Dayton) 112
Youngstown, Ohio 8, 142, 173–175, 177
Youngstown Browns 130, 136, 141, 142, 151–153, 157–162, 167–169
Youngstown Colts 181, 183–188, 190, 192, 194–200
Youngstown Gremlins 176–181
Youngstown Tubers 61, 62, 66, 68, 69, 74, 77
Youngstown Vindicator 176
Yount, Ken 198

Zagami, Joe 96
Zanesville, Ohio 2, 68, 69, 75, 76, 106, 109, 130–132, 147, 154, 155
Zanesville Bees 132, 135, 136
Zanesville Cubs 156, 157, 160, 162, 166–168, 170–175
Zanesville Greys 79, 81, 83, 87, 89, 90, 111, 113–115, 117, 121, 122
Zanesville Signal 136, 155, 162
Zeisz, Zeke 198
Zeller, Jack 149
Zimmerman, Ray 123
Zuber, Ed 127

www.ingramcontent.com/pod-product-compliance
Ingram Content Group UK Ltd.
Pitfield, Milton Keynes, MK11 3LW, UK
UKHW041950140426
5217IPUK00014B/730